(i)

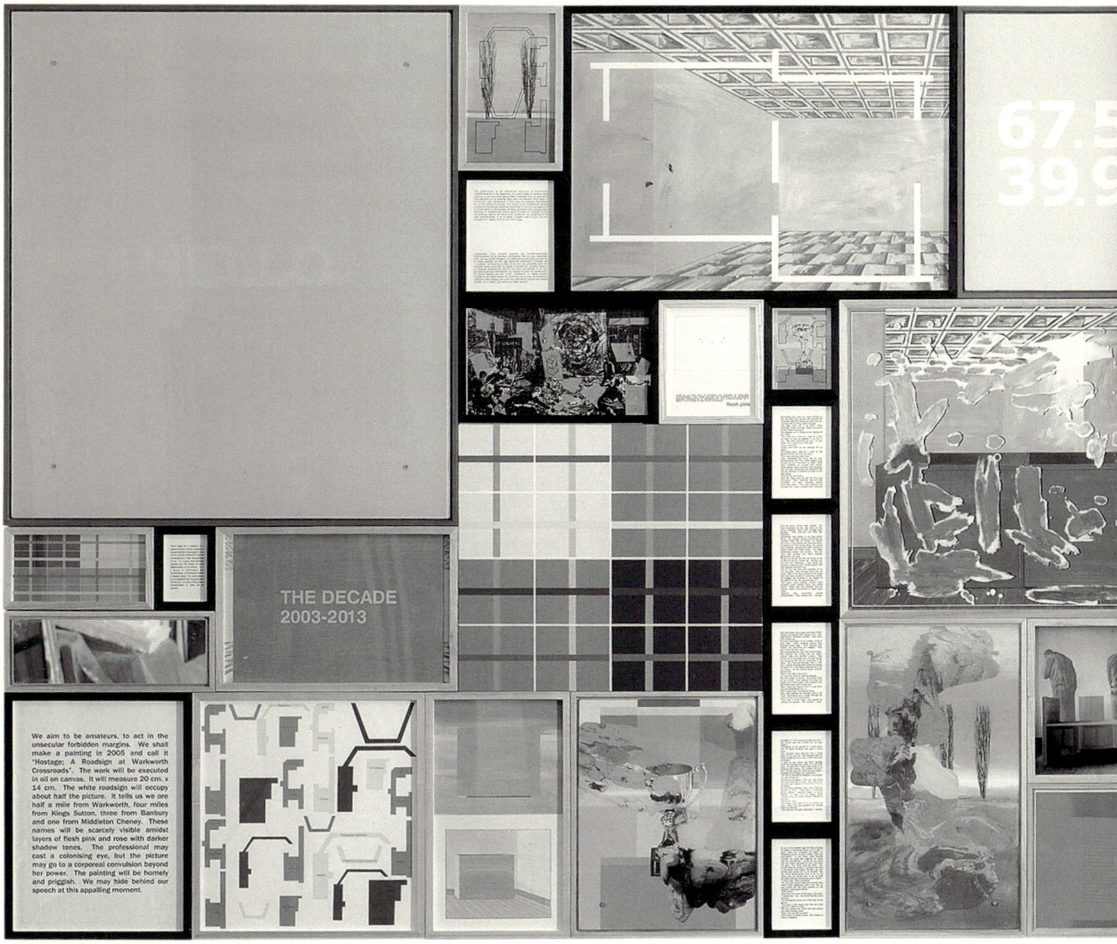
67.5
39.9
flesh pink
THE DECADE
2003-2013
We aim to be amateurs, to act in the unsecular forbidden margins. We shall make a painting in 2005 and call it "Hostage; A Roadsign at Warkworth Crossroads". The work will be executed in oil on canvas. It will measure 20 cm. x 14 cm. The white roadsign will occupy about half the picture. It tells us we are half a mile from Warkworth, four miles from Kings Sutton, three from Banbury and one from Middleton Cheney. These names will be scarcely visible amidst layers of flesh pink and rose with darker shadow tones. The professional may cast a colonising eye, but the picture may go to a corporeal convulsion beyond her power. The painting will be homely and priggish. We may hide behind our speech at this appalling moment.

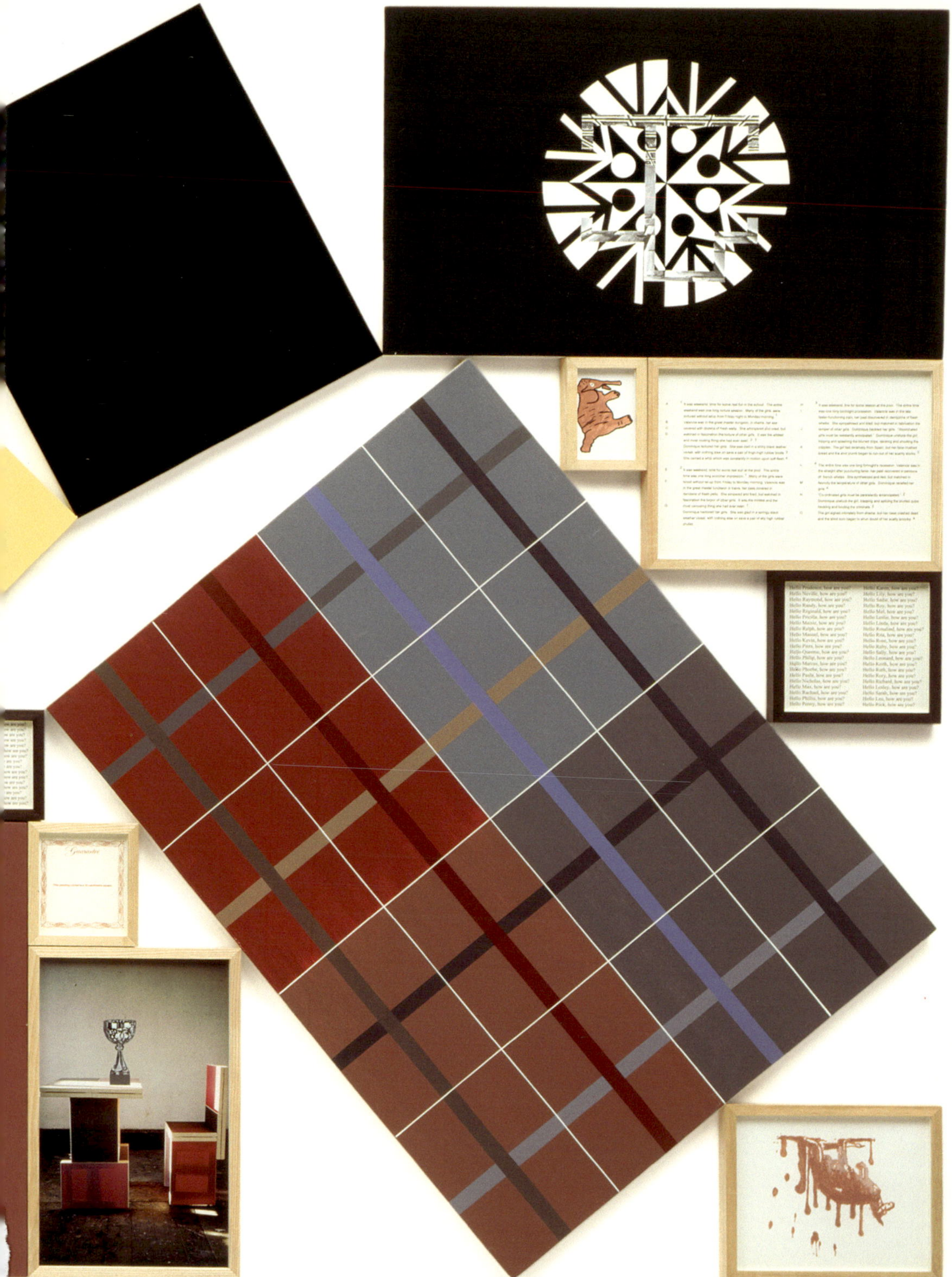

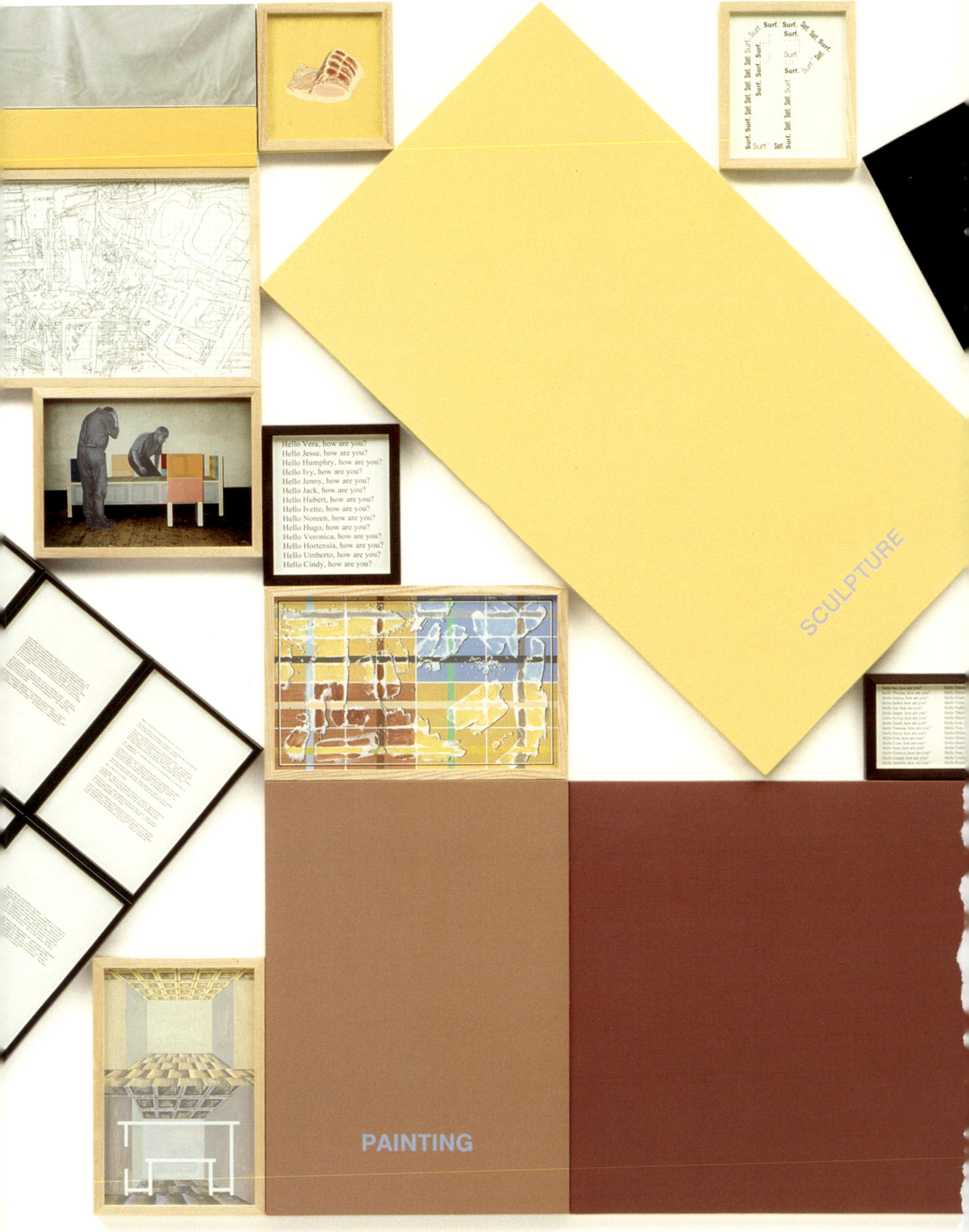
Hello Vera, how are you?
Hello Jesse, how are you?
Hello Humphry, how are you?
Hello Ivy, how are you?
Hello Jenny, how are you?
Hello Jack, how are you?
Hello Hubert, how are you?
Hello Ivette, how are you?
Hello Noreen, how are you?
Hello Hugo, how are you?
Hello Veronica, how are you?
Hello Hortensia, how are you?
Hello Umberto, how are you?
Hello Cindy, how are you?
SCULPTURE
PAINTING

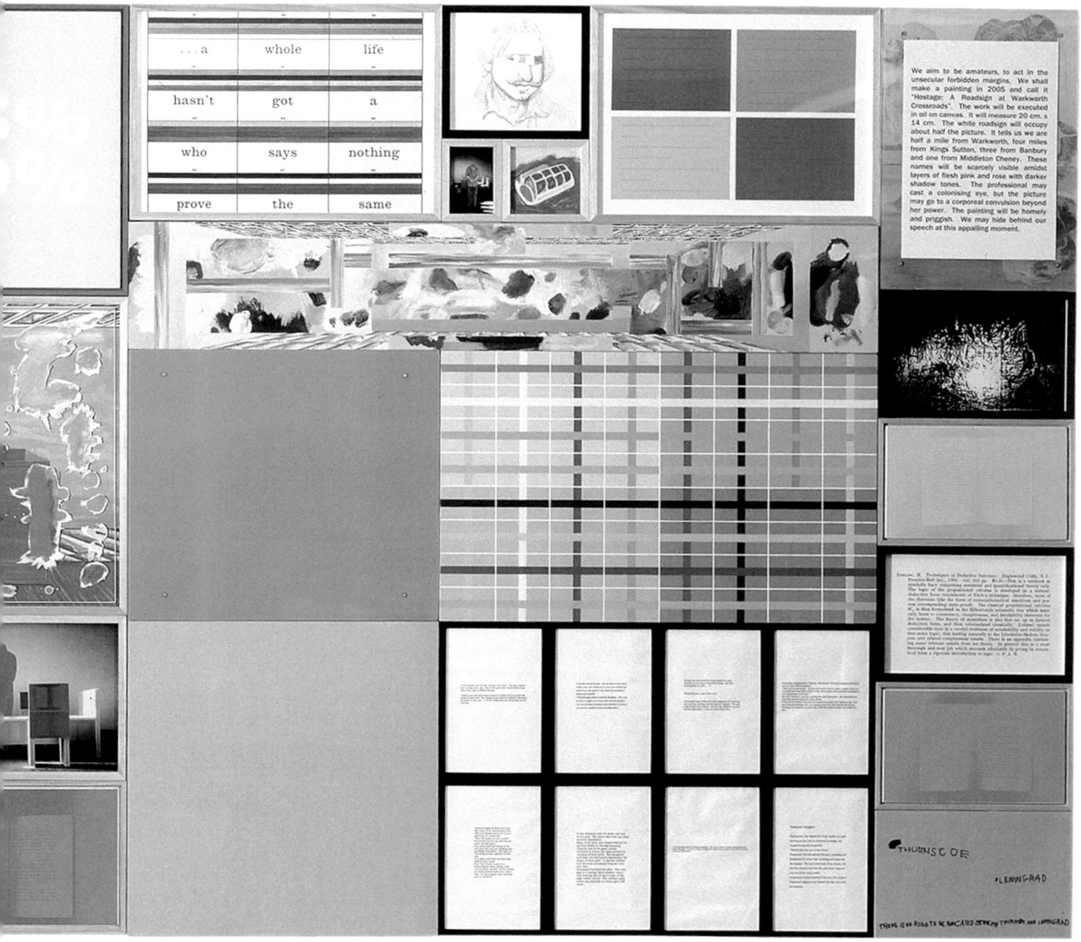

. . . a whole life
hasn't got a
who says nothing
prove the same
We aim to be amateurs, to act in the unsecular forbidden margins. We shall make a painting in 2005 and call it "Hostage: A Roadsign at Warkworth Crossroads". The work will be executed in oil on canvas. It will measure 20 cm. x 14 cm. The white roadsign will occupy about half the picture. It tells us we are half a mile from Warkworth, four miles from Kings Sutton, three from Banbury and one from Middleton Cheney. These names will be scarcely visible amidst layers of flesh pink and rose with darker shadow tones. The professional may cast a colonising eye, but the picture may go to a corporeal convulsion beyond her power. The painting will be homely and priggish. We may hide behind our speech at this appalling moment.
THURNSCOE
LENINGRAD

Art & Language

Homes from Homes II

by

Art & Language

–

Michael Baldwin, Charles Harrison
and Mel Ramsden

Preface

Homes from Homes II is a work by Art & Language now in the permanent collection of the migros museum für gegenwartskunst, Zurich. It was originally exhibited in the museum in November 2003 under circumstances which will be described below. It is composed of three distinct installations of three identical sets of works. The installations take the following form: (i) a billboard, where the set is seen hanging either on the perpendicular or at a variety of acute angles; (ii) an apparently conventional hanging where the set is ordered from left to right according to a pseudo-chronological principle; and (iii) a 'viral' distribution, where the set breaks up to seek the company of works by others. The billboard is usually set within one and-a-half metres of a facing wall, so as to limit the distance from which it can be viewed.

Homes from Homes II is a project of indexing and redescription. While it possesses a certain retrospective aspect, it is not bound by the narrative conceit of the retrospective exhibition. *Homes from Homes I* and *II* were described by one critic as 'forming a philosophical centre, a centre that explodes to form a self-contextualizing critique of institutional temporality'. What we would say is that both *Homes from Homes I* and *Homes from Homes II* essay a context as and for themselves, and in doing so they resist certain of the powers of the institution.

Background

In 1999, faced on two occasions with the need to organise old and new work into substantial displays, Art & Language conceived of entire walls as kinds of indexes upon which assemblies of disparate works could be composed, and across which they could be connected. In installations at the Fondació Antoni Tàpies in Barcelona [P.1] and at P.S.1 in New York, [P.2] pamphlets, prints, indexes, posters and paintings drawn from the production of over 30 years were butted up against one another so as entirely to cover the available surfaces. Texts containing illustrations adjoined paintings containing texts, so that it ceased to be consistently evident or relevant where significant technical distinctions were to be made. One could still tell the difference between text and picture on 'technical' grounds. What one could not do was determine just what was to be made of that distinction in 'cultural' terms. In fact what did become clear was that the most informative observations to be made were rarely those that rested on comparisons of medium or genre. (A certain sense of *déjà vu* attended upon this conclusion. Twenty-seven years earlier, when the first *Index* P.3 was shown at 'Documenta 5', the relations between those texts deemed incommensurable had in the end proved of more abiding interest than the more straightforward relations of compatibility or incompatibility.) If Art & Language's early Conceptual Art had a distinct presence in these installations, it was as a kind of mortar. On the one hand the ribbons of text served to fill the interstices between those components that were more pictorial or larger, and thus more readily individuated, binding them together into a whole. On the other they marked the points at which the entire ensemble might be unglued.

Homes from Homes I, the Billboard: a conversation of the displaced

The wall installations for Barcelona and New York provide the precedents for the two 'billboard' displays, each composed of some 40 more-or-less distinct elements. More properly, it should be said that what motivates these displays is what was learned in designing and installing the two previous exhibitions, and what was learned from them once they were installed. Like those former examples, the billboard installation of *Homes from Homes I* assembles diverse examples of Art & Language work, butted together without interval to make a large rectangle. Apart from a few unglazed canvases, each item is individually framed. No clear distinction is made between those works — or parts of works — that are wholly contained within a single frame and those sets of framed items that may actually compose one work. Some items are unglazed paintings, some glazed paintings or drawings, some glazed texts, some paintings that have sheets of glass fixed to their surfaces. A small version of a landscape, *Hostage*, has a text on paper affixed over its sheet of glass. At the opposite edge there is a small work in the form of a mirror. At the centre there is a work from the series *Incident, Foreground*, in which a picture including a represented sheet of glass is seen through the actual glass of its literal frame. In viewing the total configuration we assimilate marked differences in opacity and transparency, in readability and obscurity, in surface properties and reflective properties, in literal surfaces and illusionistic depths, and in various modalities between these. These contribute to the complexity of the whole, along with other marked differences in graphic and expressive character and in pictorial and textual content.

The works included in the two billboard installations are referred to here as examples, but they might more accurately be described as versions, based on 'originals' from the entire long span of Art & Language production. Some of these versions are complex hybrids that owe their genesis to more than one 'original' and more particularly to *Homes from Homes* itself. But each represents its source-work in some significantly altered form, whether through reduction in scale, through change of colour, through transformation of technique, or through modification of a component text. Some frames of text are included that are like extracts or extrapolations from more complex wholes. The versions exist as shadows and reflections, both dark and light; shadows drained of colour and reflections in which new colours emerge; texts draining others of a redundant or spurious significance, other texts importing a strange new significance to those that had their origins in the redundant and the spurious.

In the context of expectations generated by the idea of the retrospective, the versions have the status of memories purged of melancholy and sentimentality, their cherished significance re-examined, sometimes transformed by change of interest, sometimes dissipated in laughter. Recollection of this order is hard to manage in our personal or even our shared narratives. Perhaps it is especially hard to manage where narratives are held in common. We need the agency—the feedback—of work in process, of things that have to be made to work in production and *as* production, that have to be made generative of other things, and of other ways of looking at these and other things, other readings, other narratives. The work has to be made to keep talking, keep revising its *own* retrospect, otherwise it will be as though it ought never to have been begun.

The reflexive turn has a long history in the art of the modern period, though the necessities involved have been far from stable. We have continually to work for a feel of its realistic conditions. Approaching the zenith of abstract art in 1948, Barnett Newman asked how he and his American contemporaries could be making a sublime art without a faith that would sustain the building of cathedrals. His answer was, 'We are making it out of ourselves, out of our own feelings.' Among his resonant titles for the works that followed were *The Command*, *Abraham*, *Vir Heroicus Sublimis* and others of that ilk. Our problems may seem more mundane. The token of the faith we have lost is not the cathedral but the museum, and the 'selves' out of which we have to make our art will not bear the weight of heroic predicates. In the world we now occupy it is necessary that that which has attained the status—been accorded the authenticity and 'originality'—of art object be once again brought low and put back to (art) work. Nor are 'our own feelings' reliable as the first-order materials of a plausible art. The requirement of self-reference can be met only under conditions of quotation, repetition and travesty, by works that remember or half-remember each other, that forget their lines, misquote each other, and speak in damaged voices.

We might imagine both billboards as kinds of chattering asylums, places of transit in which the disenfranchised, the displaced and the dispossessed are brought together in an alien world to seek the new grounds of a common cause. Or perhaps we should rather conceive of the component items as the remnants of a once coherent community, now dispersed and fragmented, its various members cast out to find uncongenial employment among the speakers of another language. In 2001 Art & Language reviewed Niklas Luhmann's book *Art as a Social System*—a work addressed somewhat shakily to the autopoietic (self-referential, self-generating) character of modern art. Luhmann sees the Roma people, for all their exclusion from the 'spirit of Europe', as 'the most sophisticated in accounting for boundaries. They cross them, they "deconstruct" them.' The review was published under the title 'Roma Reason'—an apt metaphor, perhaps, for that conversation of the dispossessed for which the billboards provide a platform.

Homes from Homes II, the Billboard: the hazard of the spectator

The second billboard — *Homes from Homes II* about which this book is concerned — introduces a new complication to the scheme of the first. As with its predecessor, the overall configuration is rectangular. But the various works included are now composed according to a design requiring that some of them, whether composed of texts or of coloured chequers, should be set at an angle to the expected horizontal. In two separate works made in 2000/2001, *Down to the Stone* and *Over the Trees,* P.4 assemblages of 35 separately framed panels are set at angles that evoke the 'shaped canvases' explored in American painting of the late 1960s and early 1970s. Yet what the plastic panels contain, black on white in one case and brightly coloured in the other, is text, both 'raw' and mutated, rendered harder to read by its physical disorientation.

This canting of different surfaces places new demands upon the reading spectator. These may be related in kind to the exertions required by the landscape *Hostages,* whose reflecting surfaces of glass encouraged the spectator to remain alert and mobile in pursuit of an appropriate but always contingent position. Subsequently, during the mid-1990s, Art & Language adopted a self-conscious strategy of frustrating the normal viewing position and reading angle. Among the more extreme results were paintings slotted vertically into narrow steel boxes that rest on the ground. P.5 To act the part of responsive spectator of such a work is to find one's gaze drawn down into an actual darkness in which represented space and figurative details disappear. Though the kind of self-projecting exertion demanded of the spectator may be related to the works in the series *Index: Now They Are*, these paintings in boxes have no sensuous image to offer as enticement and reward. They are militantly uncongenial and difficult works.

Art & Language pursued the strategy of disorientation on less uningratiating terms through works produced for exhibition at 'Documenta X' in 1997. These were variously composed from coloured panels in the series *Sighs Trapped by Liars*, versions of which appear on the billboard. In *Sighs Trapped by Liars 1–192,* P.6 192 of these separate panels were laid flat in a broad square composed of 12 vitrines. A spectator standing at one edge of the square can easily read the text on the nearest row of panels, contrast and shadow permitting. The next row is harder to read, the third very difficult, and so on. As the detail of the work becomes gradually unrecoverable, the potential for frustration increases, until the spectator's regard reaches the work's further horizon, which appears as a line of brightly coloured checks. At this point frustration may perhaps give way to acceptance or even enjoyment of the decorative vividness of the whole, the ideal of a complete reading yielding to the intuition of a purely formal completeness.

In the second group of works initiated at Documenta X the various panels are composed into the simplified shapes of domestic furniture. This genre is represented by *Sighs Trapped by Liars, 373–391, 413–507*, P.7 and by others that are individuated numerically under the same generic title. When contained in the surfaces of 'tables' or 'beds' or on the seats and backs of 'chairs', the various passages of text may be comfortably examined. But where what is required is scrutiny of the more awkwardly oriented or more inaccessible panels, even the most assiduous or clerkish spectators may ask themselves whether the distant possibility of a 'complete' reading could really justify the discomfort and embarrassment entailed. Perhaps the 'content' of the texts need be considered of no more abiding relevance than the 'news' contained in a Cubist collage. There is an alternative, of course. Perhaps they are like Cubist collages differently conceived: works in which the strips of news *must* somehow be reassembled—assemblages that must be dismantled so as to be read, or be 'ruined' in being read.

In these and other works produced during the past few years, Art & Language has seemed both to lure and to contend with the spectator, at one moment as though uncertain that any responsive relationship between work and viewer could now plausibly be sustained, at another as though testing to the limit a relationship in danger of degenerating into a repressive habitude—a transaction reduced to the supply and demand of readable detail. This is not mere game-playing. Without some critical activity on the part of an interested public, there is no effecting the practical transformation of 'versions' into the constituents of significantly new displays, of 'old work' into 'new work'. What this transformation requires is a marked change of *use,* and this in turn requires a change in how the works in question are seen. They need not simply to be the familiar constituents of new ensembles, but objects that have been allowed to grow up and that are not possibly now what they could once have been. Some may perhaps have improved with age. Others will have lost their looks.

Accounting for boundaries

There is one last point to be considered. As we noted at the outset, each of the 'versions' represented on the billboard has been made in three 'copies'. The second, apparently conventional hanging scheme is ordered by the chronology of the earlier works by Art & Language that are the putative prototypes for the individual constituents of *Homes from Homes II.* For example, the mirror in the upper register of the billboard installation takes an *Untitled Painting* of 1965 as its prototype, so it appears at the beginning of the conventional installation, on the left side, while the photograph inscribed with the image of a silver cup finds its ancestry in *There Were Sighs Trapped by Liars* of 2000, so it appears among the 'later' works on the right. For the 'viral' distribution, the works are either hung singly or are assembled in groups so as to form resonant pairings with other works or combinations of works from the collection of the institution in which they find themselves. Prised loose from the contingent security of their framing rectangle, they serve both as subordinates and as irritants to the larger and more established bodies of work by Art & Language to which they relate. They may sometimes act to affirm the more considerable critical status accorded to their putative parents. Sometimes, however, they will insinuate a note of deflating adolescent scepticism, embarrassing to any uncritical appreciation and fatally compromising to any unself-conscious and aggrandising account.

Items from the third set of copies are distributed about the galleries so as to impinge upon—and in turn to be impinged upon by—the permanent collection of the institution in which *Homes from Homes I* or *II* may be installed. Like refugees clustering about a border, they may be thought of either as excluded from the proper population of *Homes from Homes*, or as threatening to extend its reach and resonance into the larger institution of modern art, in the process, however, opening a channel through which the combined forces of that larger institution might be allowed to flow back into *Homes from Homes* itself, testing the critical security of its organisation. Once subject to this actual or threatened diaspora, the versions may strive to preserve some defensible identity of their own, either, against heavy odds, by establishing the provisional autonomy and difference of the solitary exile, or by inviting some account of their presence among unexpected companions.

The circumstances of the work's exhibition at the migros museum für gegenwartskunst in 2003 were unprecedented. For the purposes of the third 'viral' installation, a large proportion of the Migros permanent collection was made available to the artists. The collection itself is unusual, having been compiled in accordance with changing aesthetic, cultural and social principles over four decades. From a canonically-minded perspective it is of uneven aesthetic value. In terms of the kinds of consideration that such a perspective tends to encourage, it is composed of works whose cost and presumed monetary value vary considerably. There are works by famous and fashionable international artists and by artists of solid provincial reputation, but also by virtual amateurs whose local eminence is now lost or greatly faded. The collection reflects, then, a growing cultural scope on the part of the successive directors of the Collection between the late 1950s and the early twenty-first century. The works chosen as 'hosts' for the 'viral' installation of *Homes from Homes II* reflect the unevenness proportionately, the majority being items that would not easily attract the attention of an accultured critic or a sophisticated consumer, the minority works of undoubted 'international' status. The 'viral' constituents of *Homes from Homes II* were thus able to consort with other works of great formal and semiological diversity from a collection that, while determined by a single material continuity, is nevertheless formed as a discontinuous curatorial line. The chronological aspect of the collection consists, in fact, of a set of non-convergent pathways that come together only in the historical contingency of the institution.

We might ask, however, why works by the little celebrated should cast down their eyes in the presence of so much that enjoys high status in the world of the contemporary art museum. It is with regard to this question that *Homes from Homes II* provides and was provided with a distinctive critical axiology. *Homes from Homes II* is composed of works that have overdone it in attempting to regain their looks, or that have misread their lines due to failing eyesight, or that have stumbled and literally fallen. They are works that, even as they represent and exemplify travesty and perversion, also go to the possible redescription of the conditions of their existence and to the possibility of a continued autopoietic life. It is possible that in this they have become virtual; not things that hold within them something virtual as their internal contents, but artefacts that are virtual in themselves.

Is it possible that the works that are highly valued within the contemporary art canon contain in the semiosis of their memories the forms and values of the provincial and overlooked, or that these latter anticipate an agency—a determining role—in the cultural prominence of the former? *Homes from Homes II* may thus inhabit a place that has been bedecked with contents whose narratives have been absolved of the need to maintain the world as it customarily seems. In other words, all of *Homes from Homes* and all of the works of the migros museum collection appear as the objects of a fiction, objects whose aetiology and relations to others are narrated outside the remit of specious historical truth.

The travesties and fictions that have escaped the billboard and regained their composure in a pseudo-chronology now form the symmetrical indices (symmetrical because they are indexing *and* indexed) of works and groups of works that like them, are not on speaking terms. What is on offer, then, is either silence and embarrassment or a conversation that is wounding to history.

What the viral elements and their companions compose is a virtual world in which a dominant axiology can be inflected by the rhetoric of its excluded others. We might say that the fiction makes travesties of all, and in doing so suggests that the imperatives of cultural history can at least be resisted—that the objects that still mediate the supposed truths of coercive cultural narratives are no more than favoured names and their descriptive shadows.

In testing and destabilising the relations of replication, parody, travesty, masking, camouflage and digression, *Homes from Homes I* and *Homes from Homes II* refer reflexively to Art & Language's past and to other pasts which do not belong to Art & Language. These reflexive relations and self-describings are the terms by which these works are also hetero-referential and talk about the world. These relations provide the circumstances in which *Homes from Homes* knows a little about the world, both artistic and non-artistic. This is not at all paradoxical: what is (almost) clear is that it is a condition of the realism (and certainly of the non-triviality) of any art that it begins its address to the world with a reflexive and internally complex dialogue. This internal reference will be inflected contingently by its external conditions. Self-contextuality has an institutional context to be sure, but a work that lays some real claim to the former can represent a negative transformation of the latter. It seems that such complex and only seemingly paradoxical structures will have to be built into any art if it is not finally to melt undifferentiated into the world and its secular institutions, or to seek 'rejuvenation' in such reactionary convulsions of the dialectic as a return to authenticist painting.

Each part of *Homes from Homes II* is possessed of some degree of internality that is under threat at its margins, either from within the potentially supervening internality of the billboard, or from the institutional decorum of the pseudo-chronology, or from the uncertainties of life as a stray. This is however, an internality that returns this threat with a menace of its own: the works on the billboard trespass and fight; those of the pseudo-chronology are as much a threat to the decorum of institutional temporality as it is to them; and strays attract the attention of the authorities.

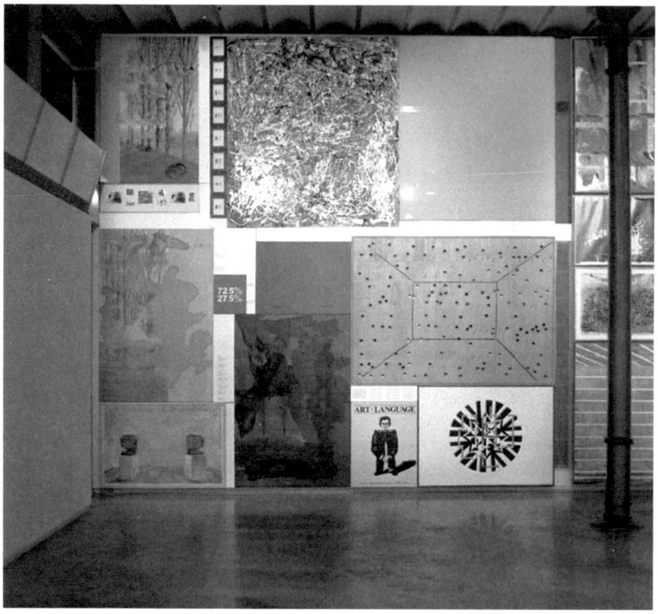

P.1

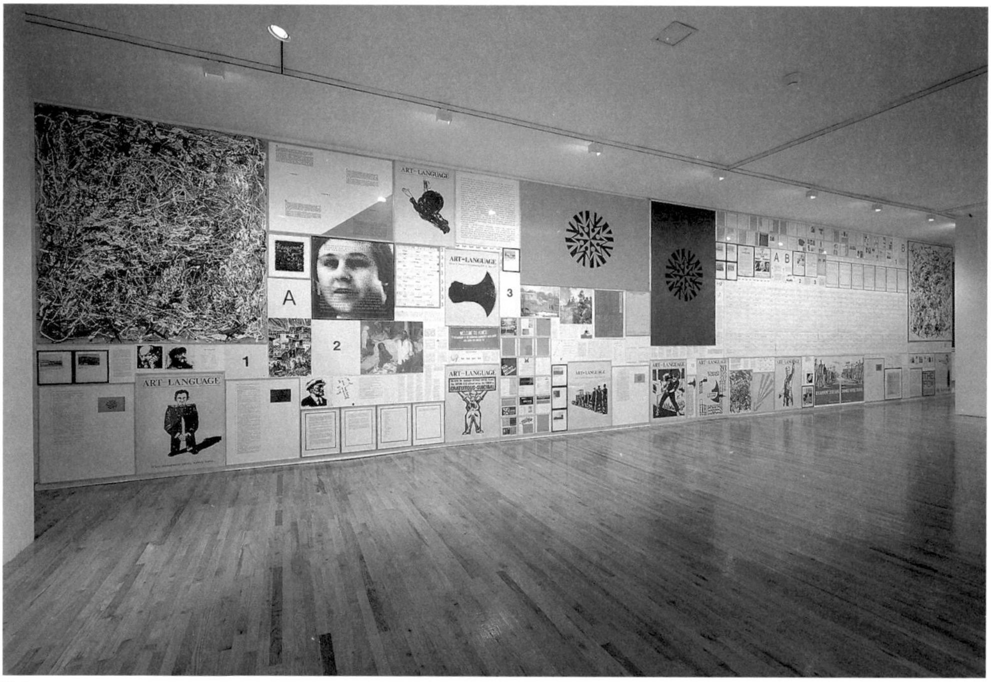

P.2

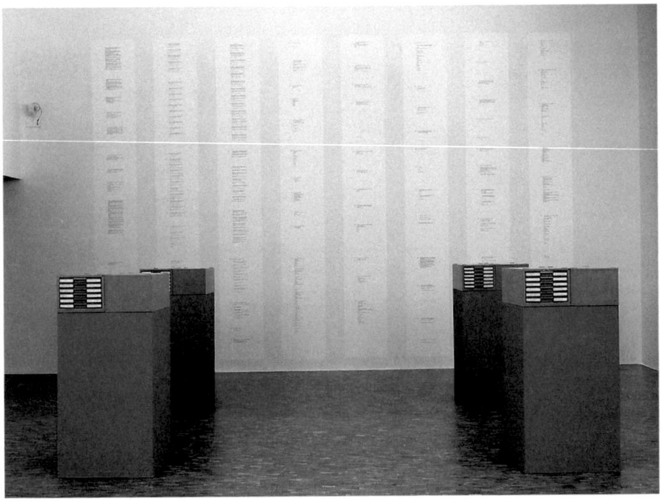

P.3

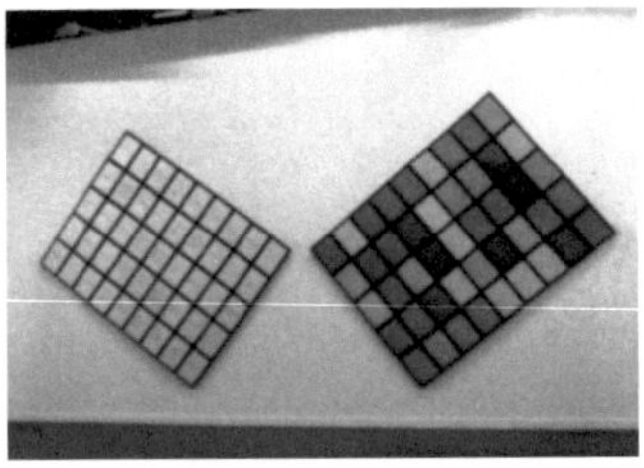

P.4

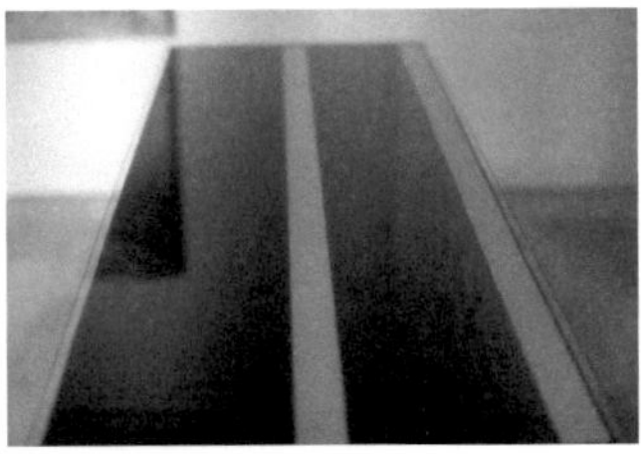

P.5

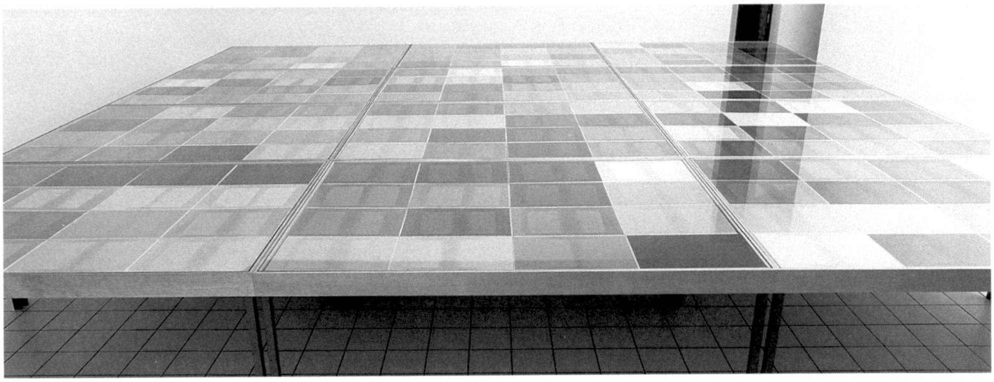

P.6

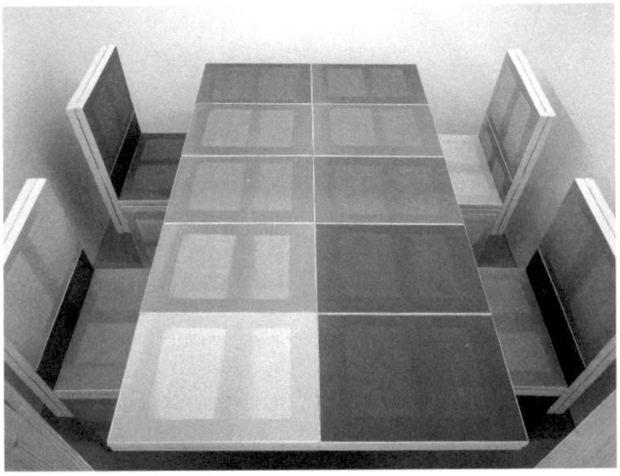

P.7

(ii)

6

7

(ii)

19–30

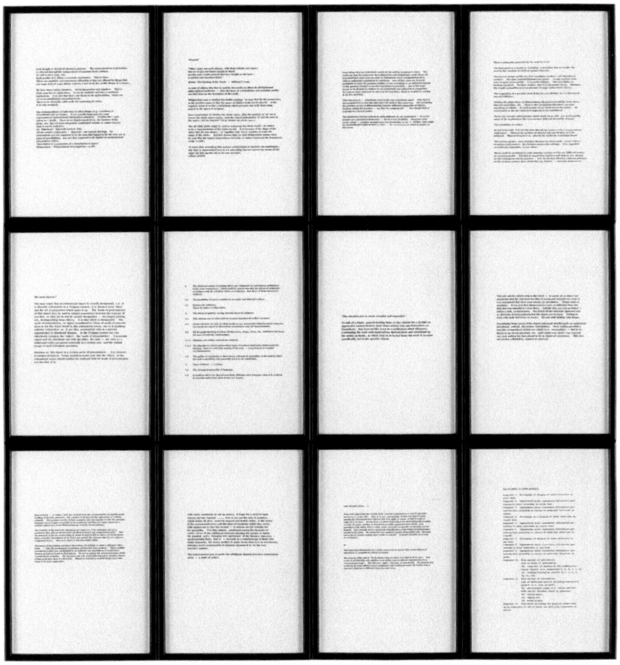

41

9

4

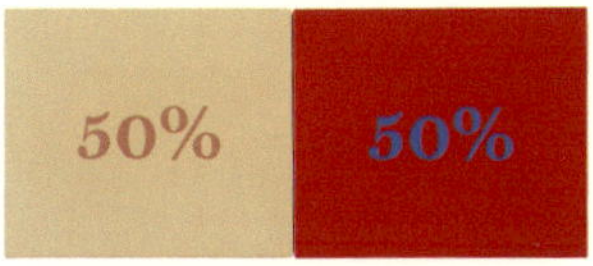

42

43

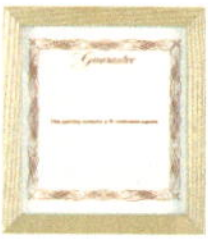

13

18

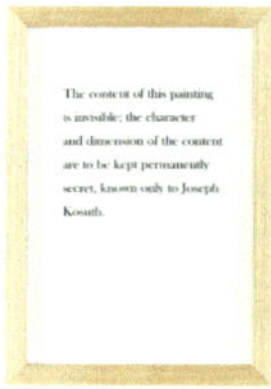
The content of this painting
is invisible; the character
and dimension of the content
are to be kept permanently
secret, known only to Joseph
Kosuth.

(ii)

10

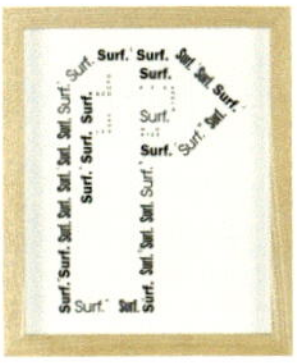

17

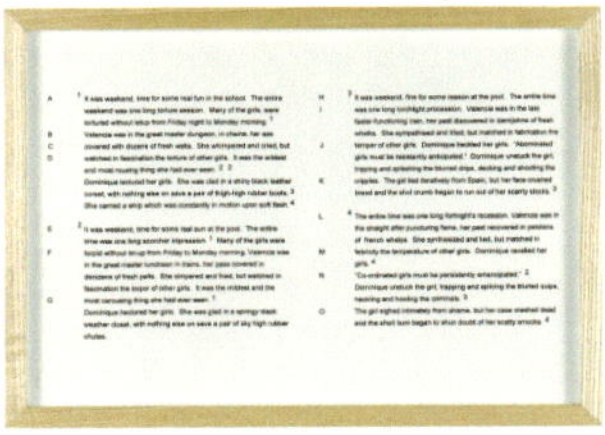

45

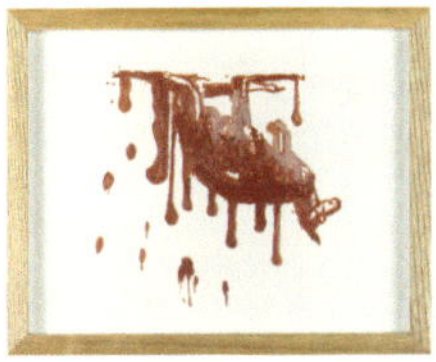

5

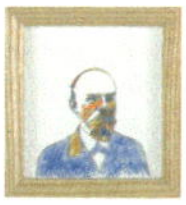

15

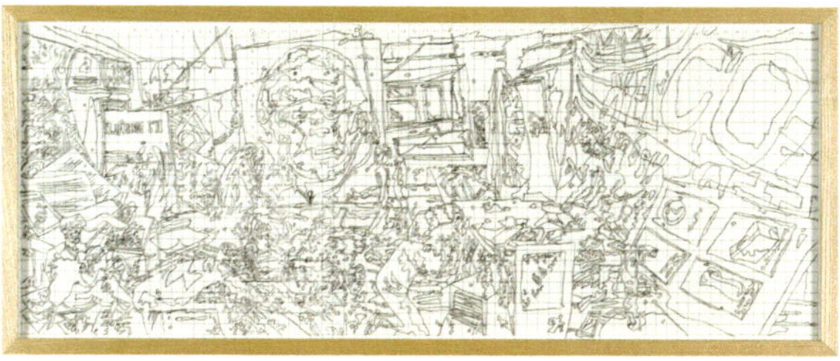

2

(ii)

40

38

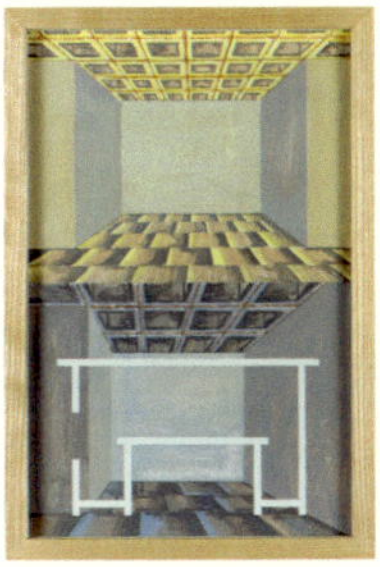

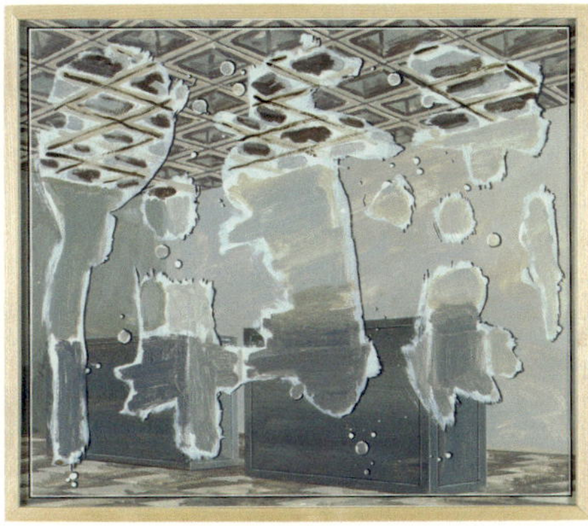

12

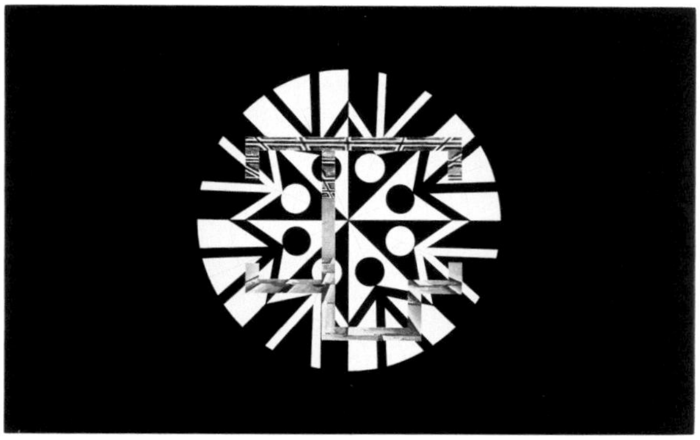

11

(ii)

35

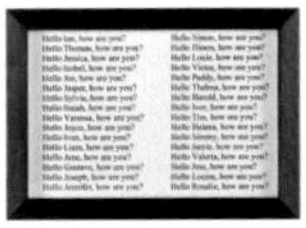

32

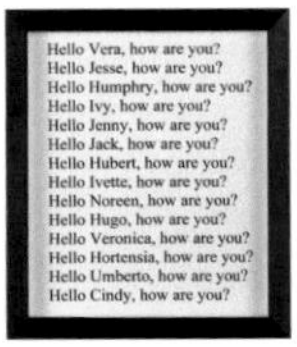
Hello Vera, how are you?
Hello Jesse, how are you?
Hello Humphry, how are you?
Hello Ivy, how are you?
Hello Jenny, how are you?
Hello Jack, how are you?
Hello Hubert, how are you?
Hello Ivette, how are you?
Hello Noreen, how are you?
Hello Hugo, how are you?
Hello Veronica, how are you?
Hello Hortensia, how are you?
Hello Umberto, how are you?
Hello Cindy, how are you?

1

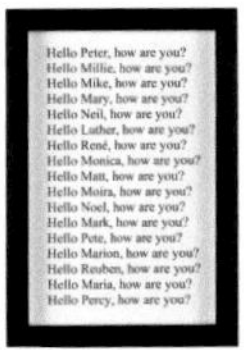
Hello Peter, how are you?
Hello Millie, how are you?
Hello Mike, how are you?
Hello Mary, how are you?
Hello Neil, how are you?
Hello Luther, how are you?
Hello René, how are you?
Hello Monica, how are you?
Hello Matt, how are you?
Hello Moira, how are you?
Hello Noel, how are you?
Hello Mark, how are you?
Hello Pete, how are you?
Hello Marion, how are you?
Hello Reuben, how are you?
Hello Maria, how are you?
Hello Percy, how are you?

33

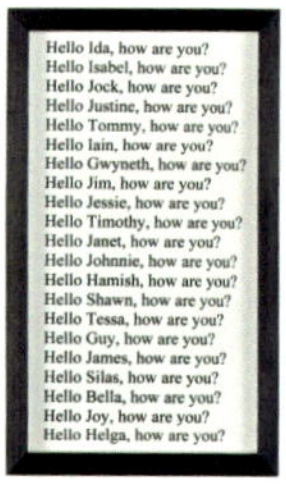
Hello Ida, how are you?
Hello Isabel, how are you?
Hello Jock, how are you?
Hello Justine, how are you?
Hello Tommy, how are you?
Hello Iain, how are you?
Hello Gwyneth, how are you?
Hello Jim, how are you?
Hello Jessie, how are you?
Hello Timothy, how are you?
Hello Janet, how are you?
Hello Johnnie, how are you?
Hello Hamish, how are you?
Hello Shawn, how are you?
Hello Tessa, how are you?
Hello Guy, how are you?
Hello James, how are you?
Hello Silas, how are you?
Hello Bella, how are you?
Hello Joy, how are you?
Hello Helga, how are you?

37

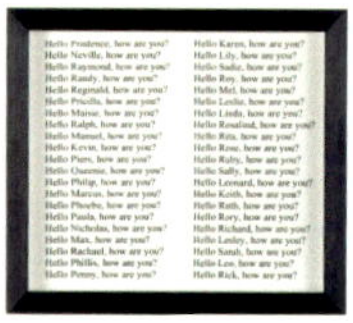
Hello Prudence, how are you?
Hello Neville, how are you?
Hello Raymond, how are you?
Hello Randy, how are you?
Hello Reginald, how are you?
Hello Maisie, how are you?
Hello Ralph, how are you?
Hello Manuel, how are you?
Hello Kevin, how are you?
Hello Piers, how are you?
Hello Philip, how are you?
Hello Marcus, how are you?
Hello Phoebe, how are you?
Hello Paula, how are you?
Hello Nicholas, how are you?
Hello Max, how are you?
Hello Rachael, how are you?
Hello Phillis, how are you?
Hello Penny, how are you?
Hello Karen, how are you?
Hello Lily, how are you?
Hello Sadie, how are you?
Hello Roy, how are you?
Hello Mel, how are you?
Hello Leslie, how are you?
Hello Linda, how are you?
Hello Rosalind, how are you?
Hello Rita, how are you?
Hello Rose, how are you?
Hello Ruby, how are you?
Hello Sally, how are you?
Hello Leonard, how are you?
Hello Keith, how are you?
Hello Ruth, how are you?
Hello Rory, how are you?
Hello Richard, how are you?
Hello Sarah, how are you?
Hello Lee, how are you?
Hello Rick, how are you?

8

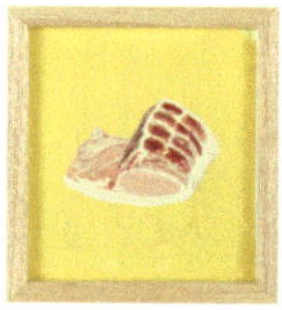

(ii)

3

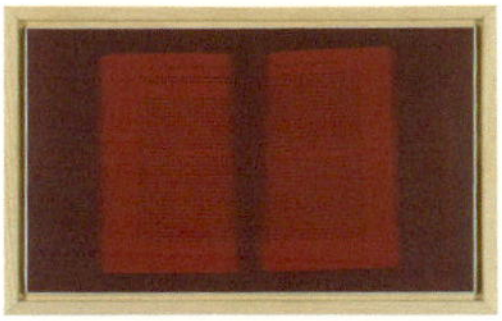

14

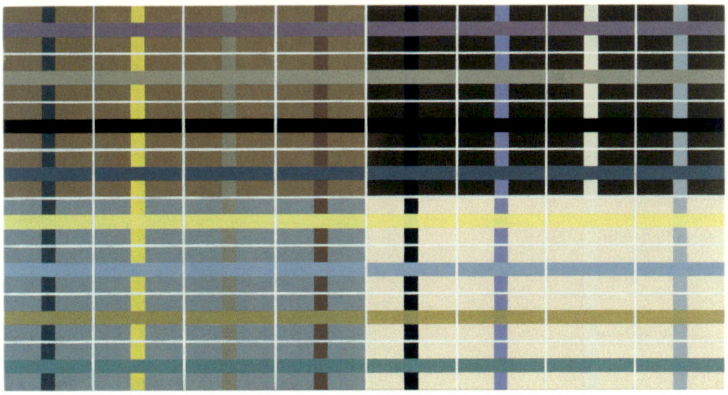

34

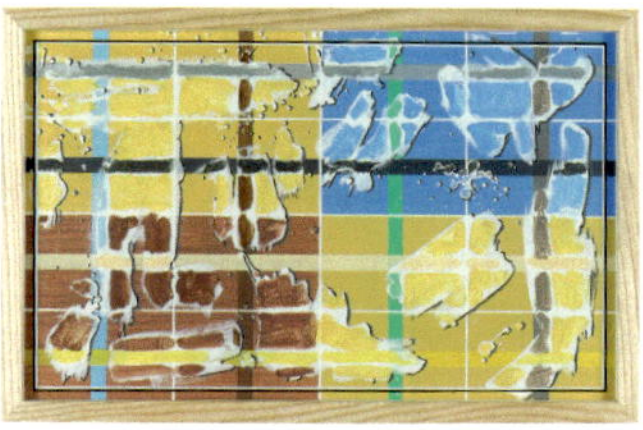

16

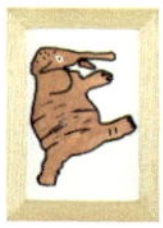

(ii)

36

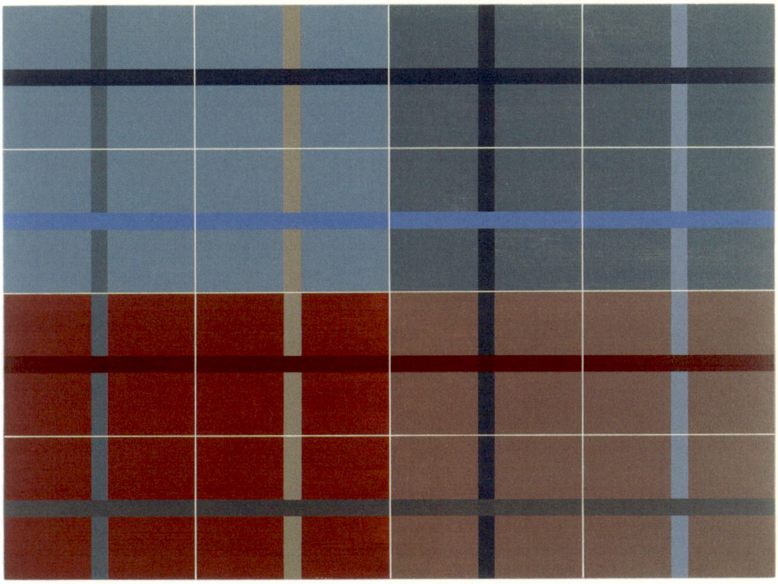

39

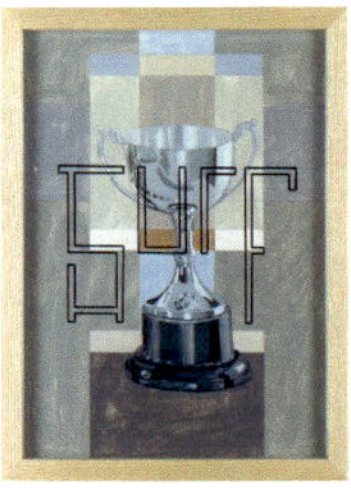

44

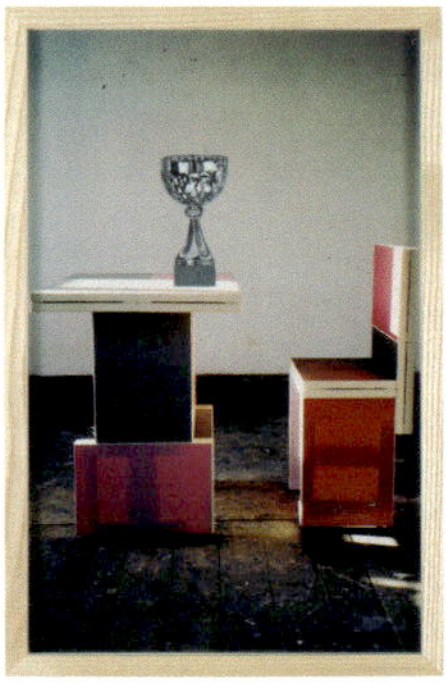

31

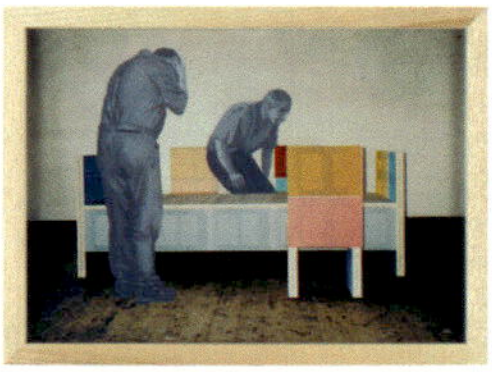

(iii)

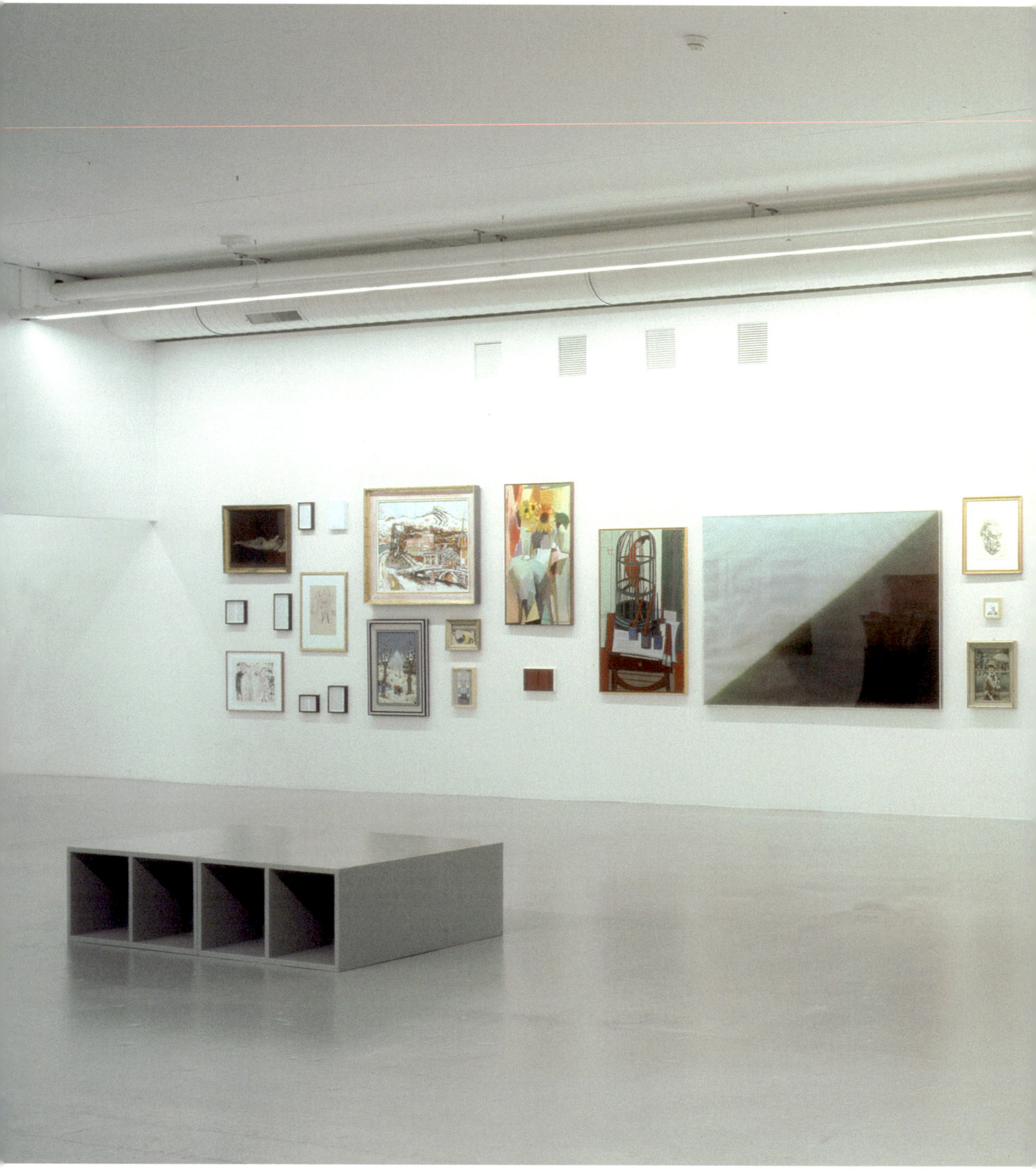

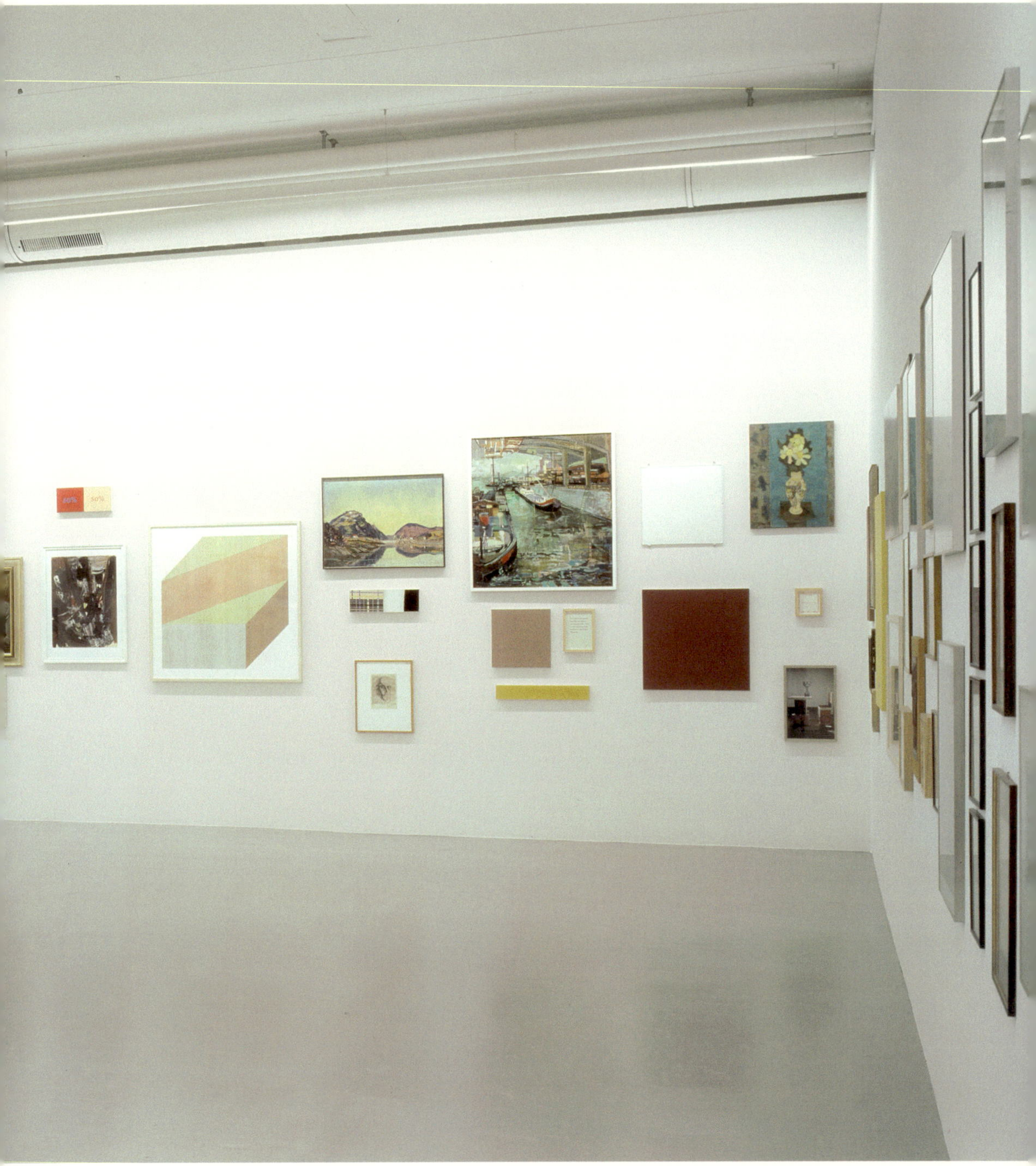

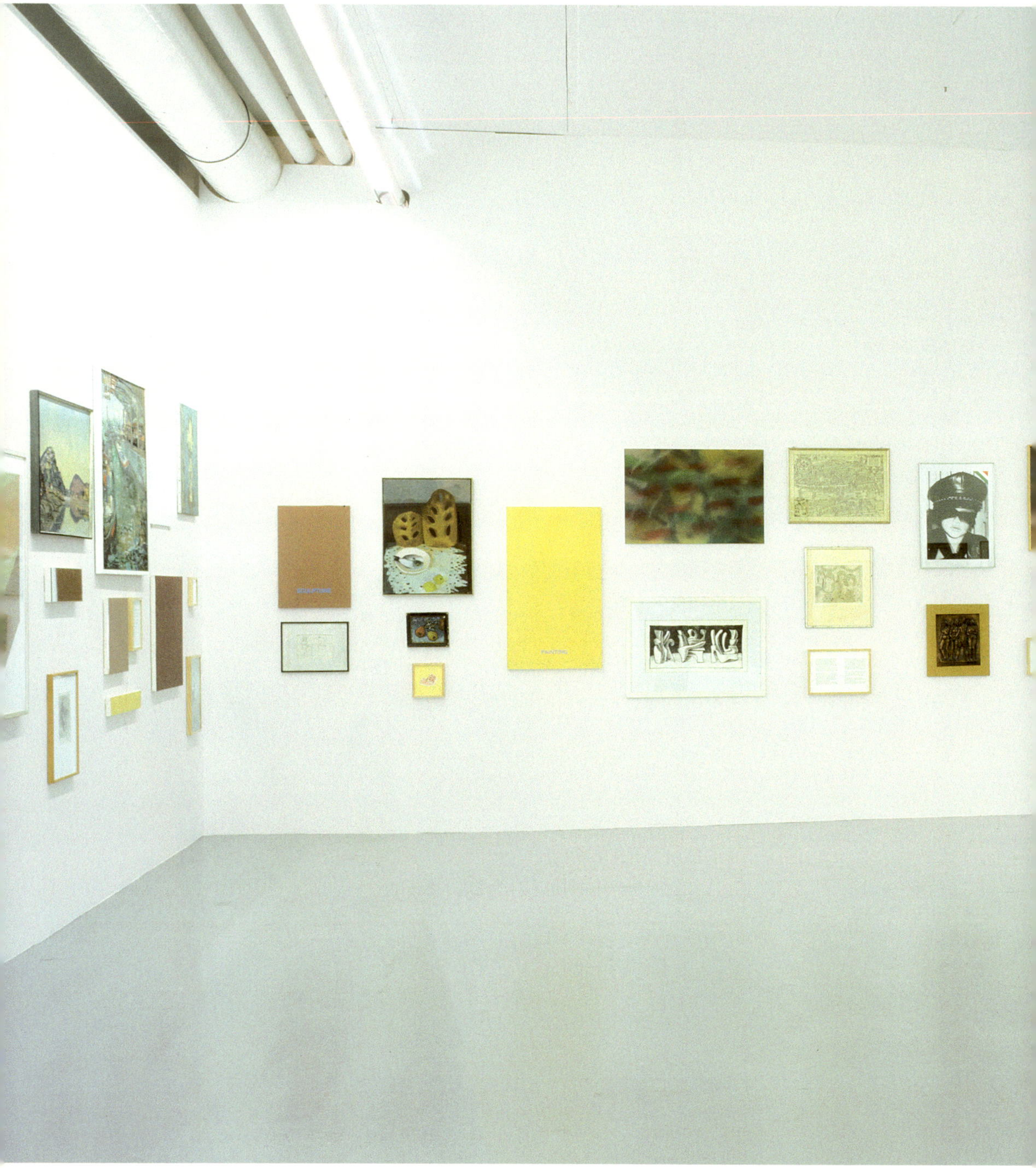

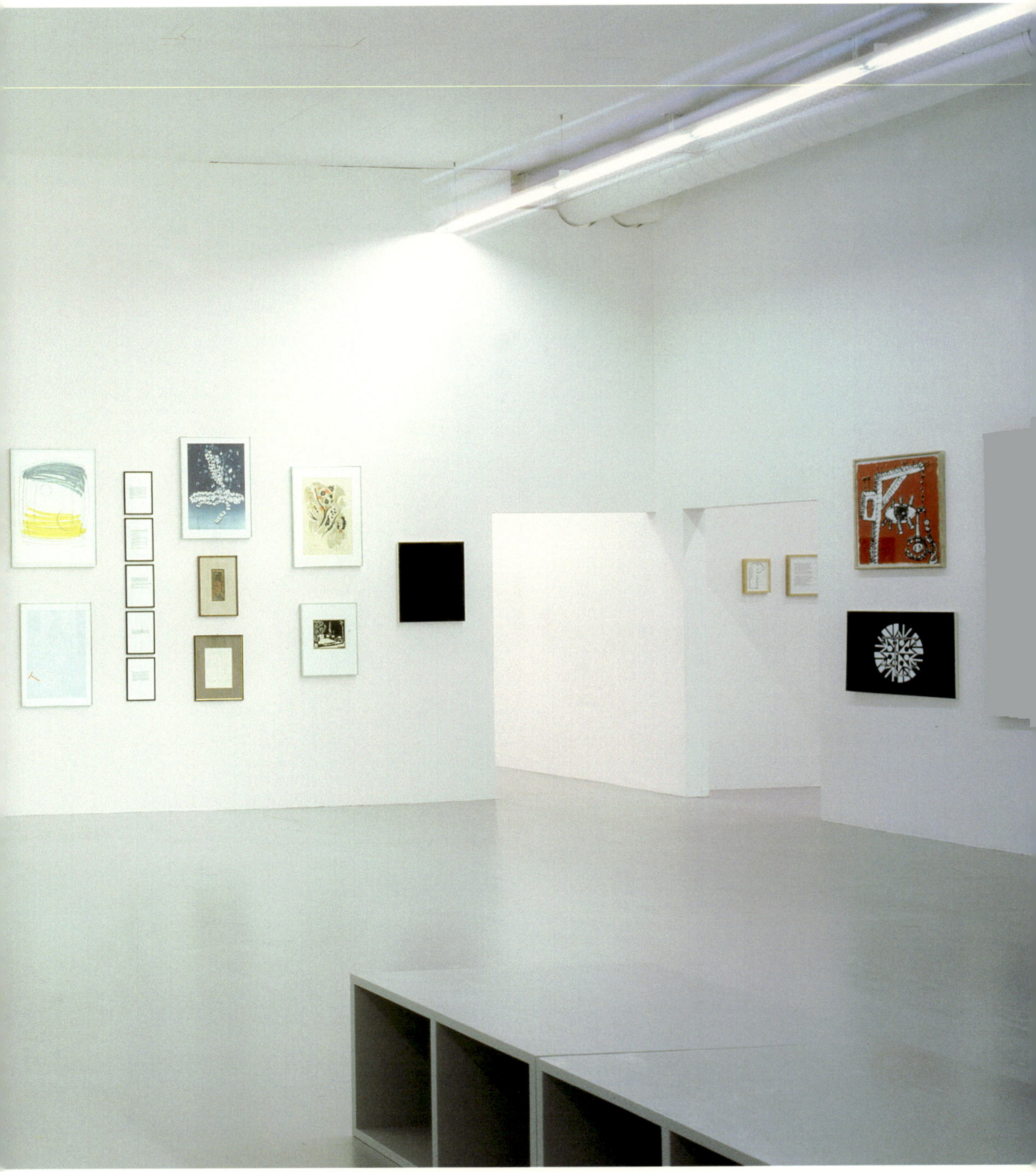

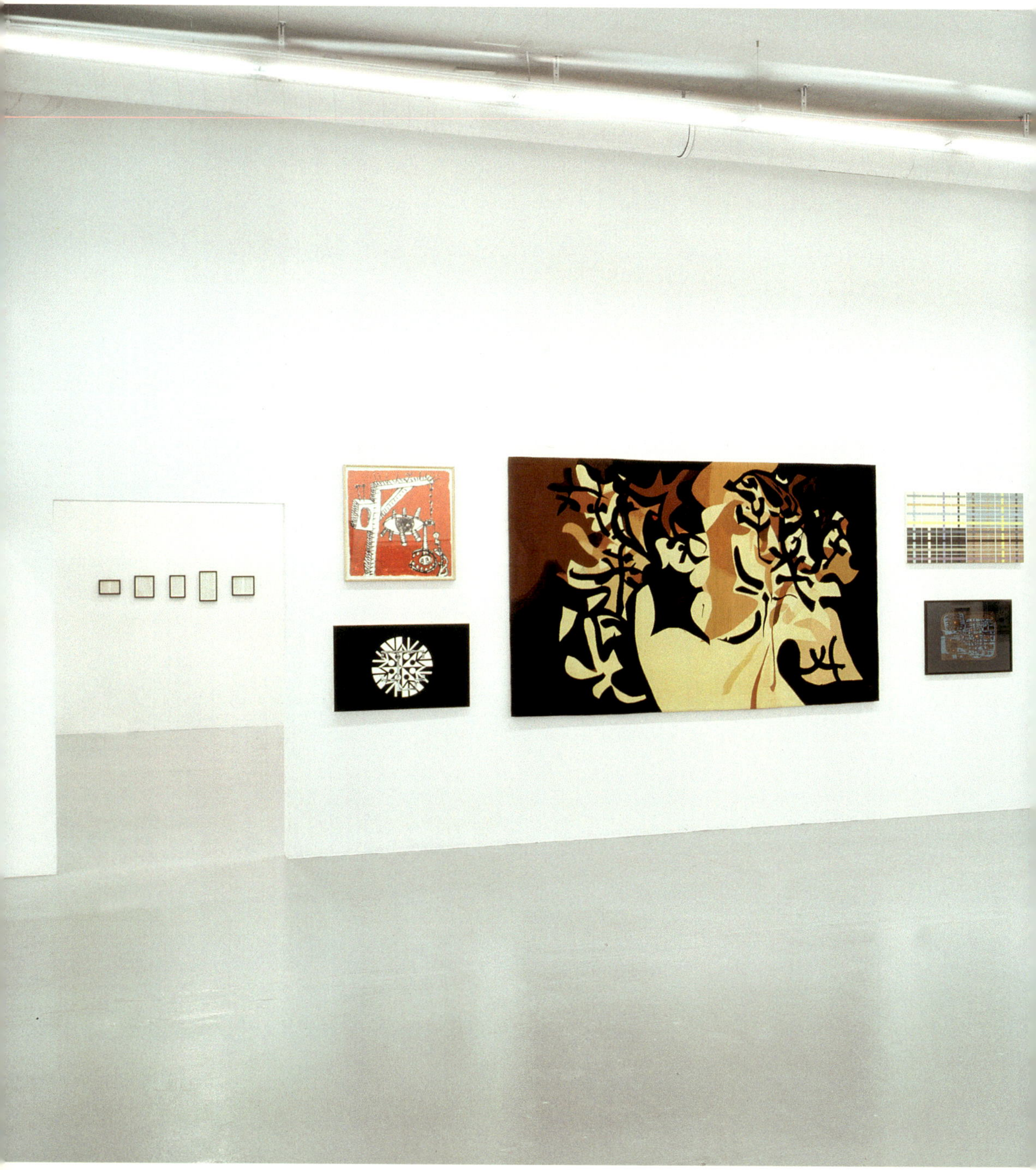

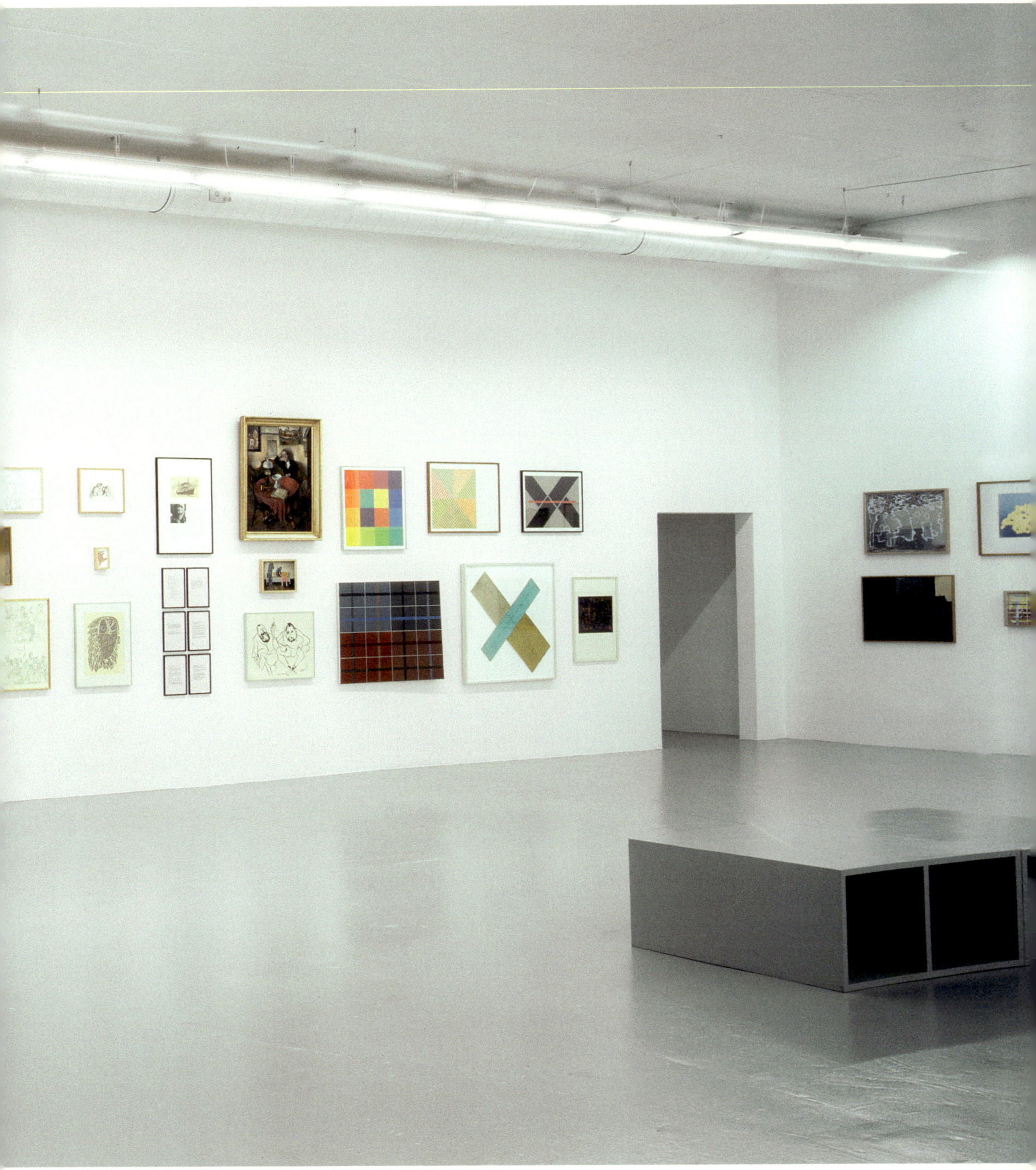

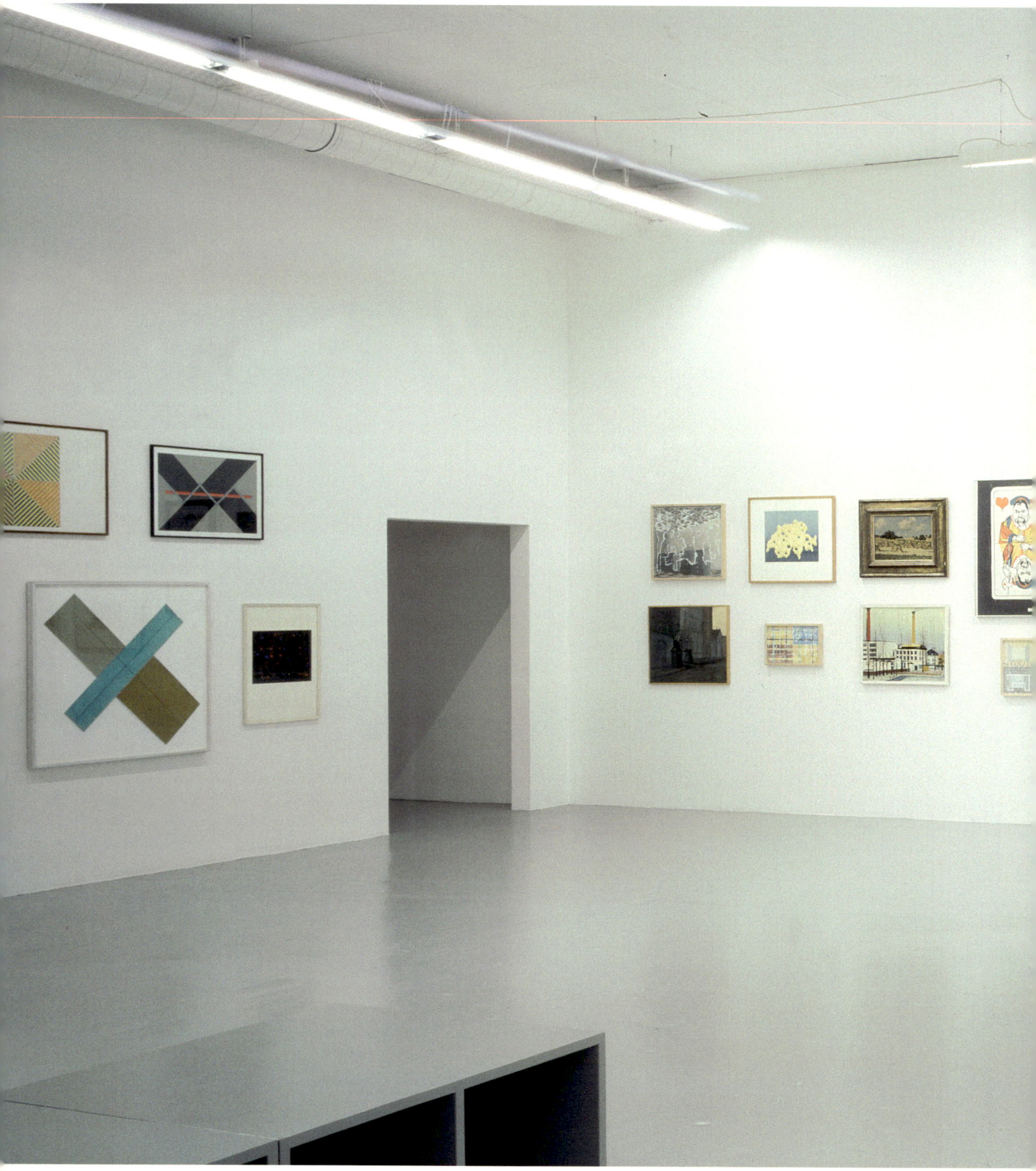

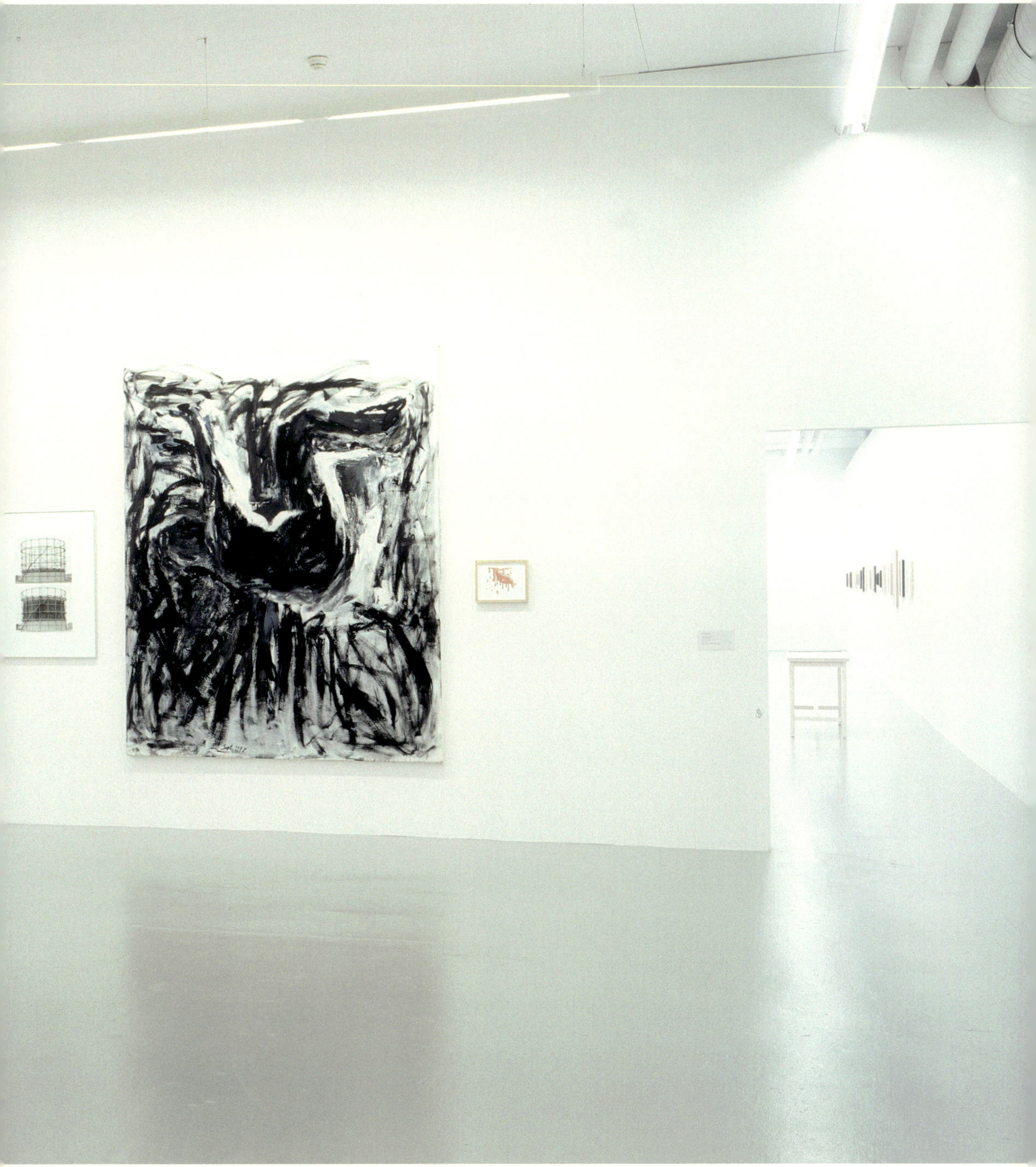

(iii) *Wall 1*

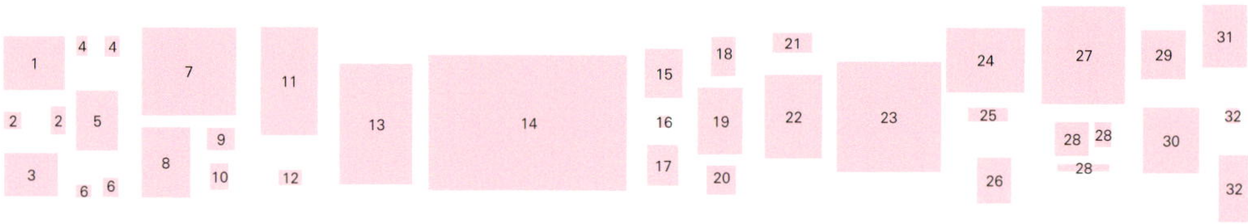

1 Heinz Müller, *Untitled (Liegender Akt)*, ca. 1955, oil on cardboard, 51 x 66 cm
2 Art & Language, *Homes from Homes II*, 2000–2001
3 Eugen Jordi, *Arbeiter — Bauern,* 1967, lithograph; edition 51/84, 43 x 55 cm
4 Art & Language, *Homes from Homes II*, 2000–2001
5 Alois Carigiet, *Rütlischwur 1939,* 1939–1940, indian ink on paper, 65 x 50 cm
6 Art & Language, *Homes from Homes II*, 2000–2001
7 Alois Carigiet, *Untitled (Winterlandschaft),* 1965, oil on canvas, 75.5 x 97.5 cm
8 Turiddu Forini, *Ritorno a casa,* ca. 1970, oil on canvas, 60 x 42 cm
9 Fritz Bitterli, *Stillleben mit Gefäss und Apfel,* 1966, oil on canvas, 20 x 29 cm
10 Art & Language, *Homes from Homes II*, 2000–2001
11 Max Hegetschweiler, *Untitled (Sonnenblumen)*, 1960, oil on canvas, 116 x 68 cm
12 Art & Language, *Homes from Homes II*, 2000–2001
13 Claude Loewer, *Untitled (Vogelkäfig)*, 1949, oil on canvas, 130 x 81 cm
14 Bernhard Lüthi, *Untitled*, 1973, watercolour on paper, 149 x 213 cm
15 Vogler, *Gottlieb Duttweiler*, charcoal on paper, 59 x 49.5 cm
16 Art & Language, *Homes from Homes II*, 2000–2001
17 A. Droit, *Untitled (Frau mit Sonnenschirm)*, oil on canvas, 37 x 27 cm
18 Karl Dick, *Untitled (Junger Mann mit Schnauz)*, ca. 1930, oil on canvas, 42 x 26 cm
19 Hahnel, *Portrait Gottfried Kleiner*, 1958, oil on canvas, 60 x 50 cm
20 Robert Mangold, *Distorted Circle within a Polygon*, 1973, silkscreen; edition 1/50, 37 x 37 cm
21 Art & Language, *Homes from Homes II*, 2000–2001
22 Carl Liner, *Abstrakte Komposition*, 1961, watercolour and gouache on paper, 69 x 50 cm
23 Sol LeWitt, *Form Derived From a Cube with Lines in Four Directions and Four Colors*, 1984, silkscreen; edition AP 7 from an edition of 50 + 10 AP, 106.5 x 106.5 cm
24 Wek, *Stausee Wägital*, 1961, oil on canvas, 60 x 80 cm
25 Art & Language, *Homes from Homes II*, 2000–2001
26 Leo Maillet, *Selbstporträt*, 1945, etching; edition 70/100, 46 x 36 cm
27 Arnold Gfeller, *Rheinhafen Basel*, ca. 1960, oil on canvas, 100 x 90 cm
28 Art & Language, *Homes from Homes II*, 2000–2001
29 Robert Ryman, *Painting with Steel and Line*, 1978, oil and silverpoint on paper, steel, 54.5 x 49.6 cm
30 Art & Language, *Homes from Homes II*, 2000–2001
31 Georges Girard, *Untitled (Blumenstillleben auf blauem Grund)*, 1963, oil on canvas, 65 x 50 cm
32 Art & Language, *Homes from Homes II*, 2000–2001

(iii) *Wall 2*

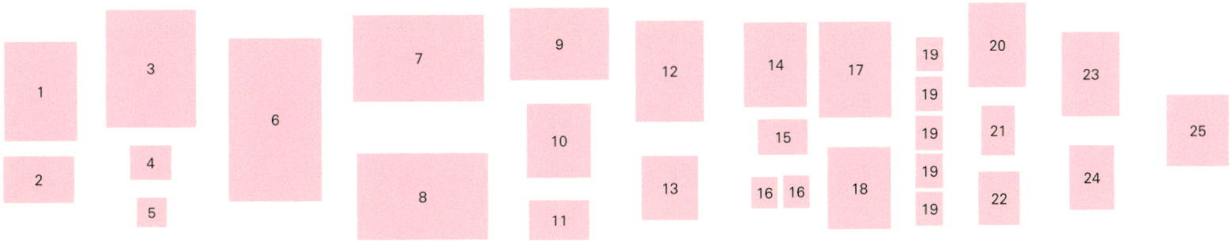

1 Art & Language, *Homes from Homes II*, 2000–2001
2 Joan Jonas, *Kniendes Mädchen*, indian ink on paper, 31.7 x 42 cm
3 Bruno Bischofberger, *Brote und Fische*, ca. 1967, oil on canvas, 71 x 52 cm
4 Hanna Lutz-Sander, *Birnen*, oil on canvas, 18 x 21 cm
5 Art & Language, *Homes from Homes II*, 2000–2001
6 Art & Language, *Homes from Homes II*, 2000–2001
7 Gerhard Richter, *Untitled (425–2)*, 1977, oil on wood, 62 x 91 cm
8 Max von Moos, *Untitled*, 1974, lithograph; edition 26/150, 53 x 72 cm
9 Josen Murer / Froshower Christoffel, *Plan der Stadt Zürich im Jahre MDLXXVI*, etching, 50 x 68.3 cm
10 Marlies Werder, *Jugendfest*, 1967, etching, 52 x 45 cm
11 Art & Language, *Homes from Homes II*, 2000–2001
12 Luciano Castelli, *Untitled*, 1978, silkscreen, 60 x 42 cm
13 Angelo Molinari, *Urteil des Paris*, 1965, copper engraving, 35 x 30 x 3 cm
14 Heinz Bühler, *Untitled*, 1980, b/w photograph, 70 x 50 cm
15 Joan Jonas, *Kleiner Hafen*, watercolour on paper, 15 x 22 cm
16 Paul Diethelm, *Traum*, 1978, silkscreen poster, 60 x 42 cm
17 Barbara Hepworth, *Untitled*, lithograph; edition 70/200, 75 x 56 cm
18 Art & Language, *Homes from Homes II*, 2000–2001
19 Art & Language, *Homes from Homes II*, 2000–2001
20 Bachmann / Davi / Marbach / Willimann, *Untitled*, 1978, silkscreen poster, 60 x 42 cm
21 Jonas, *Weiblicher Akt*, 1956, woodcut, 40 x 26 cm
22 Otto Bachmann, *Scène amoureuse*, 1946, indian ink on paper, 43 x 33 cm
23 Pierre Tal-Coat, *Untitled*, lithograph, 57 x 38 cm
24 Giovanni Giacometti, *La Notte*, ca. 1964, woodcut; edition 28/30, 43 x 29 cm
25 Art & Language, *Homes from Homes II*, 2000–2001

(iii) *Wall 3*

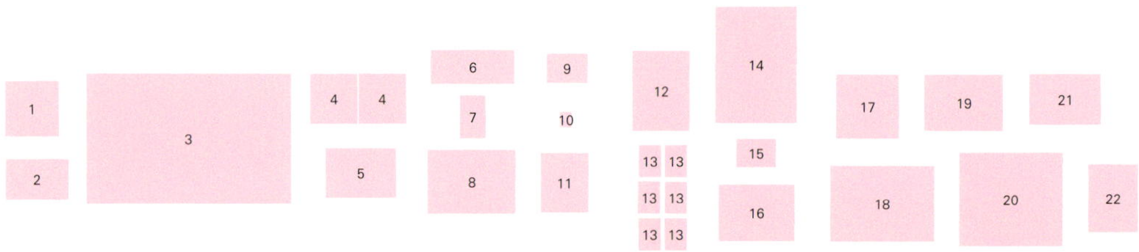

1 Jiri Georg Dokoupil, *Untitled (Studie zum Dokumenta-Bild)*, 1982, gouache on paper, 60 x 57 cm

2 Art & Language, *Homes from Homes II*, 2000–2001

3 Mario Prassinos, *Fleur Blanche – Fleur Noire*, 1976, woollen tapestry, 157 x 246 cm

4 Art & Language, *Homes from Homes II*, 2000–2001

5 Oskar Dalvit, *Maschine*, 1958, woodcut, 48 x 64.5 cm

6 Art & Language, *Homes from Homes II*, 2000–2001

7 Artist unknown, *Selbstporträt*, indian ink on paper, 42 x 25 cm

8 Hanny Fries, *Johanna der Schlachthöfe nach Brecht*, 1969, pencil on paper, 4 parts, each 29 x 41.5 cm; complete 63 x 84 cm

9 Hans Götz, *Zwei Spielende Katzen*, ca. 1960, handcoloured etching, 16 x 22.5 cm

10 Art & Language, *Homes from Homes II*, 2000–2001

11 Celestino Piatti, *Eule*, 1967, lithograph; edition 23/200, 50 x 38 cm

12 Jannis Kounellis, *Untitled*, 1973, lithograph; edition 84/90, 70 x 50 cm

13 Art & Language, *Homes from Homes II*, 2000–2001

14 Otto Baumberger, *Intérieur*, oil on canvas, 81 x 64 cm

15 Art & Language, *Homes from Homes II*, 2000–2001

16 Varlin, *Federspiel und Scheidegger*, 1970, lithograph; edition 27/35, 50.5 x 65 cm

17 Richard Paul Lohse, *Vier verschränkte Farbgruppen* , 1968, silkscreen; edition 70/200, 63 x 63 cm

18 Art & Language, *Homes from Homes II*, 2000–2001

19 Frank Stella, *Hommage à Picasso*, 1973, colour lithograph; edition 84/90, 55 x 75 cm

20 Robert Mangold, *Three Color X within X*, 1981, acrylic, pencil on paper, 97 x 81 cm (diagonal)

21 Florin Granwehr, *Durch für Gegen*, 1979, lithograph; edition 11/125, 50 x 70 cm

22 Walter Blapp, *Geflunker*, 1967, coloured woodcut, 65 x 48 cm

(iii) *Wall 4*

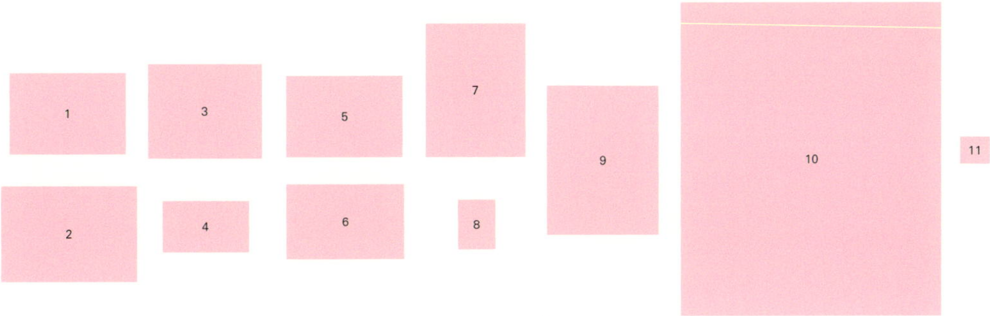

1 Art & Language, *Homes from Homes II*, 2000–2001
2 Hansjörg Kopp, *Palast Luxembourg*, 1966, oil on canvas, 54 x 65 cm
3 Claude Kuhn, *Hochkonjunktur*, 1971, chalk lithograph, 49 x 67 cm
4 Art & Language, *Homes from Homes II*, 2000–2001
5 August Speck, *Am Greifensee*, oil on canvas, 27.5 x 47.5 cm
6 Renato Ravagli, *Voltaplatz*, 1953, oil on canvas, 51 x 64 cm
7 Varlin, *Jürg Federspiel*, 1970, lithograph; edition 21/100, 90.5 x 65 cm
8 Art & Language, *Homes from Homes II*, 2000–2001
9 Bernd & Hilla Becher, *Untitled*, 1969, b/w photographs, 2 parts, each 30.5 x 39.7 cm; complete, 92 x 71 cm
10 Georg Baselitz, *'Akt' of 'Akt und Adler'*, 1978, oil on canvas, 250 x 200 cm
11 Art & Language, *Homes from Homes II*, 2000–2001

1–45

1, 32, 33, 35, 37

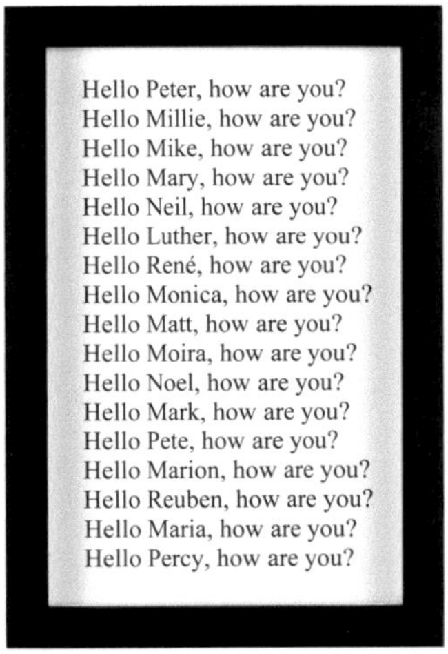

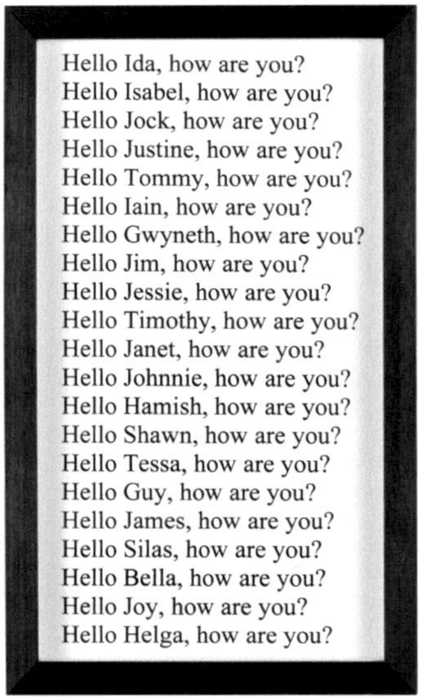

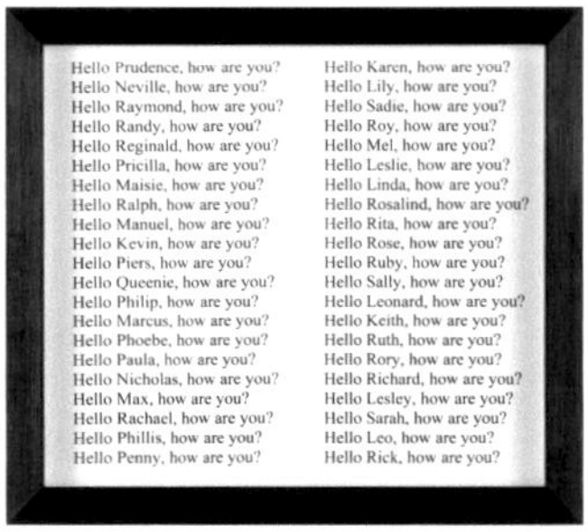

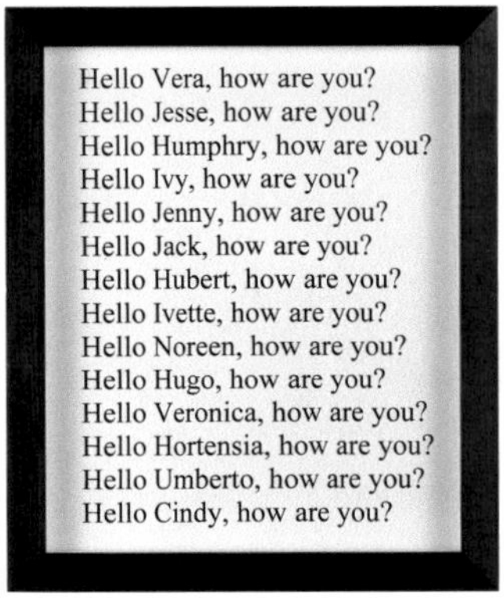

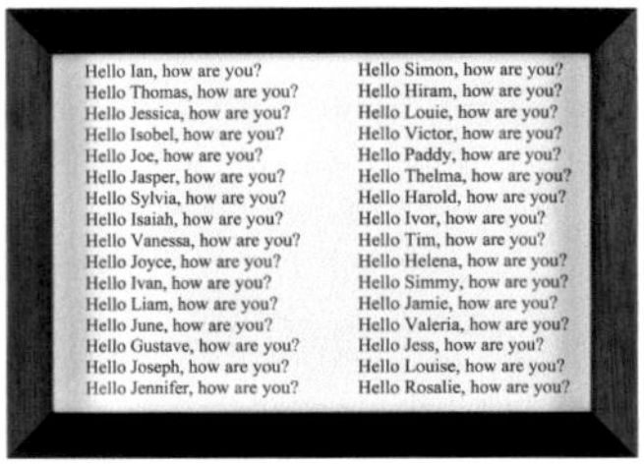

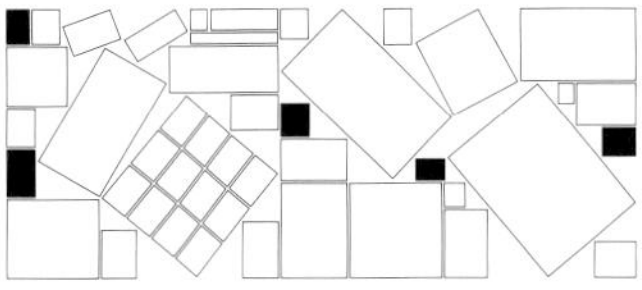

a) Hellos

See

1, 32, 33, 35, 37.1
1, 32, 33, 35, 37.2

1, 32, 33, 35, 37.3
1, 32, 33, 35, 37.4

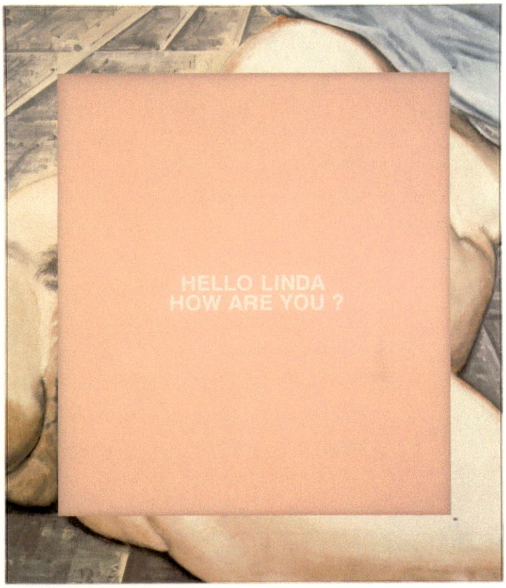

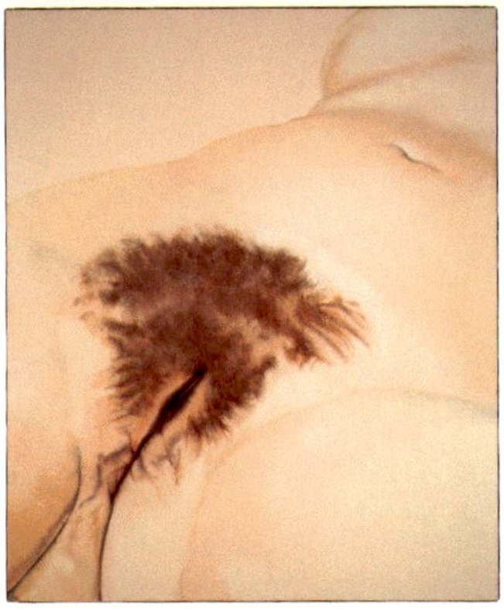

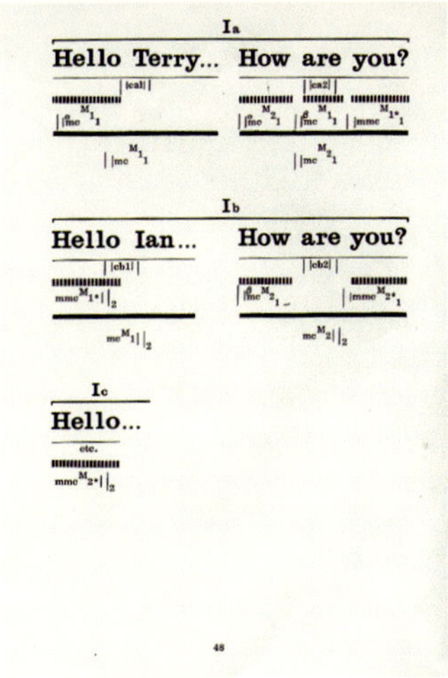

Nos. 1, 32, 33, 35 and 37 are five texts in black on off-white paper. In the billboard version of *Homes from Homes II*, they are distributed from one end to the other. Three are laid out as single columns and two as double. The texts consist of lists of expressions or greetings of the form 'Hello, how are you?' Each greeting occupies a single line. The names are not arranged in alphabetical order. If we ask what these lists of names are for, we might actually be wondering why, as viewers, we are being addressed by these scattered texts that form part of a large and complex installation. To answer this we might first have to consider an aspect of the history of the nude in modern painting. This is for two reasons. One of them is specifically connected to the history of Art & Language's work itself — that is to say, with the series *Index: Now They Are*, and a remote antecedent; the other more generally to the fact that the genre of the pre-modern and modern nude bifurcates perhaps, into those which greet the viewer, and those which avoid his eye. In other words, there are nudes that say 'Hello' and those that do not or, if they do, are inclined to make a deflating difficulty for those whom they address. We might distinguish, for example, the complicit gaze of Goya's *Maya Desnuda* from the composed disdain of Manet's *Olympia*, or the refusal of Courbet's *Grande Baigneuse* to engage the viewer at all, from the coy regard of Cabanel's *Birth of Venus.* But what has the regard to do with the voice. To look 'Hello' is not always, perhaps literally, to say 'Hello', but it is we think possible to say that we might imaginatively caption certain figure paintings with greetings of sorts, a greeting that is addressed to the viewer.

We might also say that the completeness of the figure, at least insofar as it possesses a head and mouth, would be necessary for any such greeting to be imagined. Can we say, then, that each list of greetings implies at the very least a head, and the anatomical structure necessary for a voice, or do we ascribe such possessions to each individual 'Hello'? In the first instance we would have an implied figure working rather desperately to greet a good-ish number of viewers, and in the second a collection of rather sadder figures, each one occupied in anticipating the presence of John or George or whoever. The first instance implies the single occupation of whatever space the implied figure inhabits, the other, multiple occupation. If you as a viewer 'fail' to find your name in the list, is it safe to conclude that you remain un-addressed? To answer this, we may ask, following Wittgenstein, when Jim turns his face toward Harry with the words 'Hello Terry' then there is some doubt that Harry has not been greeted and addressed by Jim. Has Jim simply made a mistake regarding Harry's name, or been misinformed in the matter, does Harry assume that Jim has mistaken him for Terry or that he thinks his name is Terry or even that he thinks he is Terry-ish, or that, ironically or for some other reason, the name 'Terry' seems or 'feels' appropriate to Jim as a name for Harry in the full knowledge of his true name. It may be that the viewer has in fact been greeted even if the text-cum-figure is somehow mistaken about his or her name. And, he or she has been greeted for sure if the text-cum-figure is practising irony, or cratylism or is being grandmother-ish.

In the first instance it may not be clear if the anatomised text should, *qua* list, be conceived as a several corporeality (or head) that greets one name at a time, or as a single entity that greets or attempts to greet. We may have to settle this if we are to determine the character of the 'How Are You?' component of the greeting. Is it flat and conventional or a genuine virtual inquiry as to the health of the addressee (how would someone who was ill respond?) even if the text (?) has got his or her name wrong? Whether solicitous or not, the greeting is too terse to be thought of easily as Heepish or simpering. Is it, then, rather measured and steady, far from a variant of 'Hello Sailor' or 'How absolutely wonderful to see you', and worse? These are among the possibilities for a single corporeal presence. As we have said, multiple presences are sadder: obsessive, bereft or Tourettish – or hellish, with everyone talking at once.

Whilst more general questions of a complicated or talkative figure arise with this part of *Homes from Homes II,* the aetiology of greeting and naming connects it practically to an Art & Language project of the late 1980s and early 1990s and more distantly to work of some sixteen years earlier. The later of these two connections is exemplified by a real image of a nude masked by a black translucent glass in *Homes from Homes II* itself (no. 11). This image, a découpage after Courbet's *L'Origine du monde*, recalls work of the series *Index: Now They Are.* In being 'voiced', as it were, the image of sexual display gains an anatomical and social extension: a head. In all the extant work of this series the word

'Hello' is inscribed at the threshold of visibility in the centre of the piece of glass that masks the figure. The black glass in *Homes from Homes II* contains no such inscription. Do we conclude, then, that the listed greetings that surround the black-glazed nude are her detached or disembodied voice, the textual equivalent of ventriloqual utterance. What is depicted behind the black glass certainly involves what might be euphemistically termed the 'stomach' – the lower part of the abdomen. We may indeed say that this is the voice of the black glazed nude, and hers is the body or figure from which that voice is ventriloqually issued. It is possible also to argue that there are other candidates for speech in *Homes from Homes II.* They are: a portrait of Lenin (no. 5), two old men (no. 31), a strutting elephant (no. 16) and a kangaroo (no. 45). We might add that the imaginary figures distinct from these that are proposed by the names and greetings are also indeed 'there' in the sense that they are the disembodied locations of the voice.

It should be noted that in very early and subsequently abandoned incarnations of the series *Index: Now They Are,* the sexual imagery was masked somewhat less incompletely by a pink rectangle at whose centre was the inscribed greeting 'Hello Terry', 'Hello Linda'. The use of names was discontinued as the mask began to cover the image almost completely. It seemed that the philosophical complexities entrained by the use of names were unnecessary or even inimical to the deflationary singularity that these works had come to bring about. The simple 'Hello' was, it seemed, sufficient for the production of this and its penumbra of effects.

As to the earlier form, the anatomised and anatomising conversation of the early mid-1970s concerned itself from time to time with the fragments 'Hello Terry, How Are You?' and 'Hello Ian, How Are You?' The fragment conjures a conversational presence which at its margins is deflationary. In the search for something to analyse, is this where we must start? The act of greeting is embedded in our theoretical speech.

2

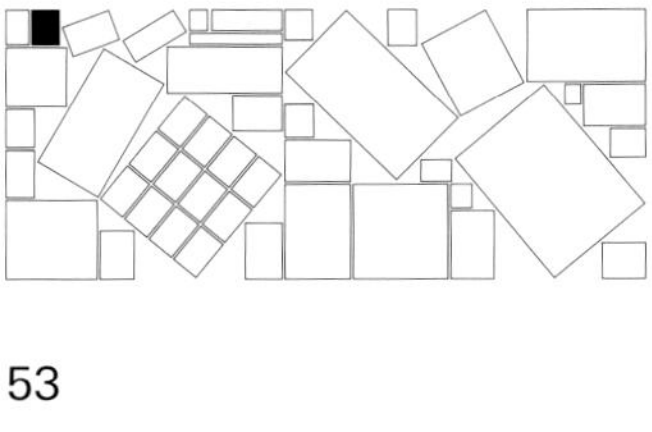

b) White Cunt

See

2.1
2.2

2.3
2.4

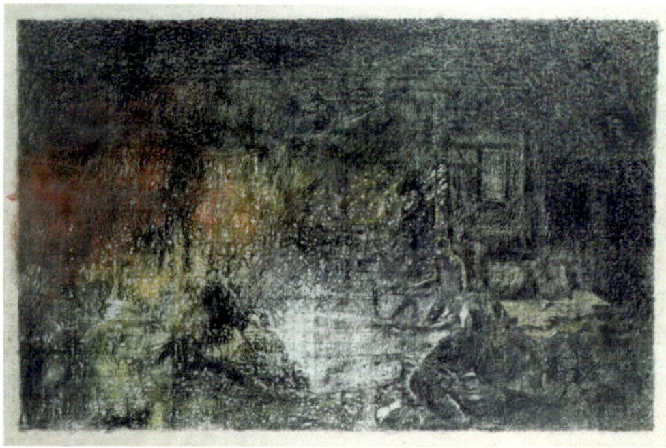

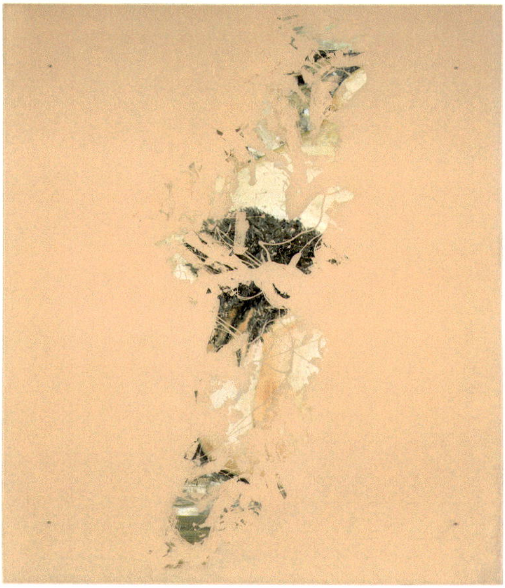

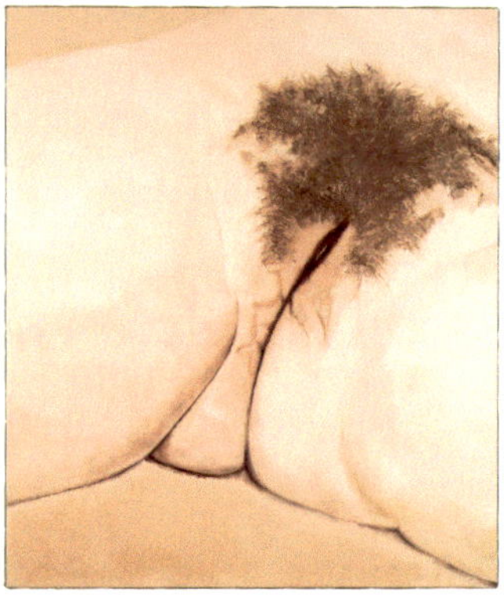

No. 2 is a small painting in acrylic on canvas in a squarish portrait format. On the billboard version of *Homes from Homes II* it is hung near the upper left-hand corner, next to a panel of 'hellos'. The visible surface is composed of a variegated pattern of white touches that appears at a casual glance to be random. A more careful regard may reveal a tendency to the white touches, though they are not evidently so disposed as to describe a particular motif. In fact, the impression liable at a certain point to insinuate itself into the awareness of the attentive viewer is of a barely discernible configuration lying *beneath* the manifest surface of the picture — a configuration to which the pattern of white touches is responsive, but which it does not actually delineate.

It seems, then, that beneath the accumulation of white paint there lies a separately painted surface which that accumulation serves to conceal or to erase. Given the inevitably different dispositions, experiences and competences of spectators, it is an open question whether sufficient evidence is present — evidence on the one hand of the remaining character of the original surface, and on the other of that surface's capacity to motivate the pattern of white touches that covers it — to enable any given spectator to identify the cunt that that original surface pictures. If and when the cunt *is* seen, however, a certain psychological significance is liable to attach to the apparently formal motivation of the erasure or concealment. But how, in a review of their consequences, is one to distinguish between the urge to censor and the urge to decorate?

This small picture brings together two different previous phases of work by Art & Language. The first, referred to in the argot of the studio as 'the snowing', formed a long hiatus between two distinct series: the *Studio* paintings of 1982–1983 and the *Incidents in a Museum* of 1985–1987. It was triggered by a chance encounter with Lucas van Valckenborch's *Winter Landscape* of 1586, now in the Kunsthistorisches Museum in Vienna, and by the mutual implication under which snow in and snowing on — the figurative presence and the practical act — appeared to have been conjoined in the imagination and production of that painting. In due course, white flakes came to invade the last versions of Art & Language's *Studio* composition, conceived as motes swirling in the wake of an explosion, or as factitious, modernistic means of insinuating some Impressionistic atmosphere, or as both. Subsequently, a number of pictures were painted with highly charged and art-historically resonant subject matter, with the express objective that that subject matter should be gradually obliterated with touches of white paint.

This phase of work brought Art & Language to the brink of crisis. The problem was this. At a certain stage in the process of snowing upon each carefully painted picture, a moment was reached when the result was almost irresistibly attractive; when a highly plausible kind of post-Cubist or semi-abstract painting emerged out of the dialectic between disappearing figuration and encroaching all-over surface. But to leave the painting at this stage would have been to compromise the intellectual principles of the project, which required that it be carried to a point of notional completion. What was demanded was that the process of snowing be continued to a point at which the end result could only fail aesthetically, at least in so far as any memory persisted of the enticing stages abandoned en route. Some of the few completed paintings that survived from this episode may now be seen as possessed of a strange and complex kind of life. At the time, however, Michael and Mel could not bear to look at them.

The second relevant phase of work first occupied Art & Language in 1992–1993. The works in question have the generic title, *Index: Now They Are.* These are pictures based on Gustave Courbet's *L'Origine du monde*, and on the various modes of concealment to which that painting was subjected between its completion in 1866 and its arrival at the Musée d'Orsay some time after the death of Jacques Lacan, its last private owner. In the earliest of Art & Language's paintings in this series, a representation of the cunt featured in Courbet's picture is seen through the central void in a schematic version of Jackson Pollock's painting *The Deep*, of 1953. The part of the work derived from *L'Origine du monde* is painted in oil on canvas. The part derived from *The Deep* is painted in flesh-coloured enamel paint on the underside of a sheet of glass. The glass is then screwed down over the surface of the canvas, largely masking the image it contains. In the later — and more successful — works in Art & Language's series, the masking surface of glass is painted all-over with paint from one of a range of pinks. The relationship between painted image and occluding surface is tuned so that a barely substantiated but highly redolent *sense* of that image may be recovered by a spectator who is sufficiently assiduous and suitably disposed — or who, to put the matter in a less Wollheimian fashion, having exhausted all attempts to extract content from the mirror-like surface of glass, is able to induce someone in the know to stand in front of the painting and draw guiding outlines in the air.

In the small painting included in *Homes from Homes II*, then, the surface of 'snow' is made to perform the same kind of function in masking the image of the cunt that was performed in the series *Index: Now They Are* by the sheet of painted glass. As in the later works in that series, the viewer who looks assiduously *through* the surface of white in search of an image may be rewarded by the glimpse, or the memory, of a detail derived from *L'Origine du monde.* A similar image is recoverable — just — from no. 11.

In the quasi-chronological hang of *Homes from Homes II* this small work occupies a position near the centre. In the form of a 'virus' it may attach itself either to paintings of the nude, or to certain varieties of all-over abstract painting.

3

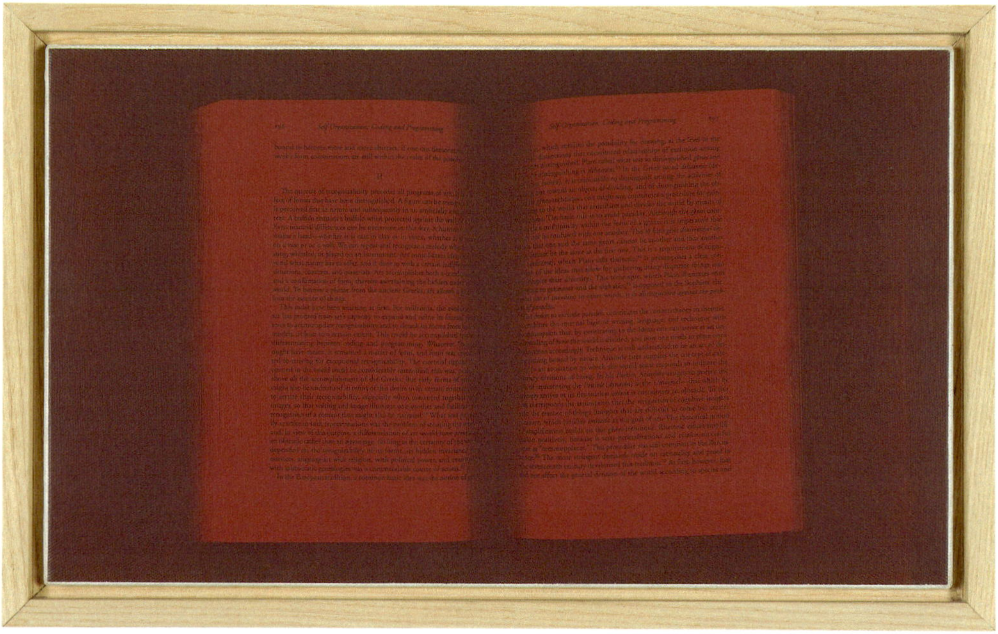

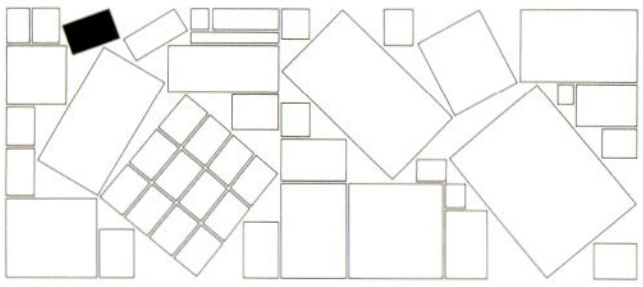

c) STBL Book

See

3.1
3.2

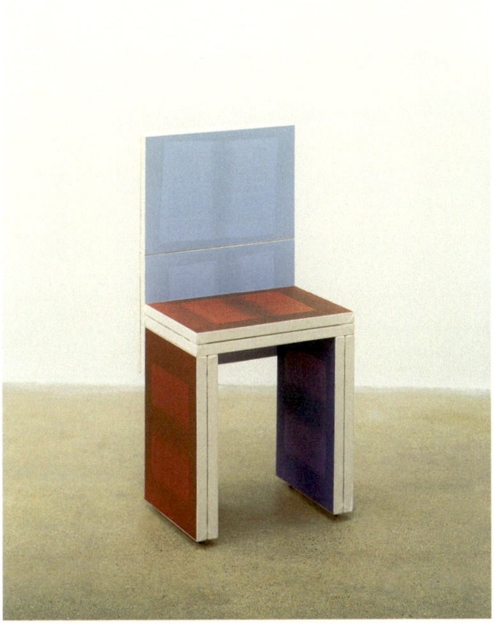

3.3

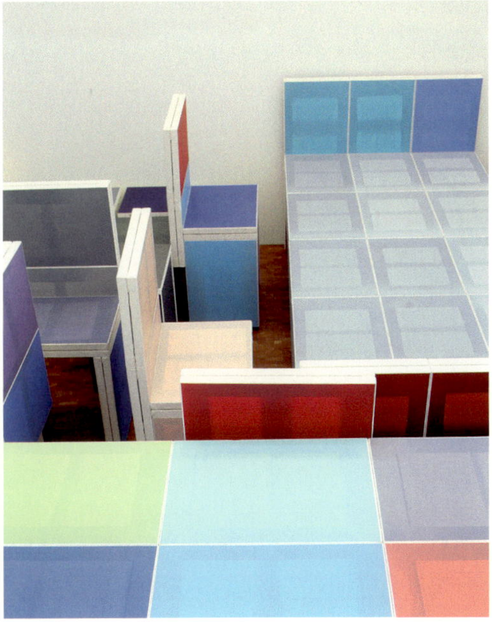

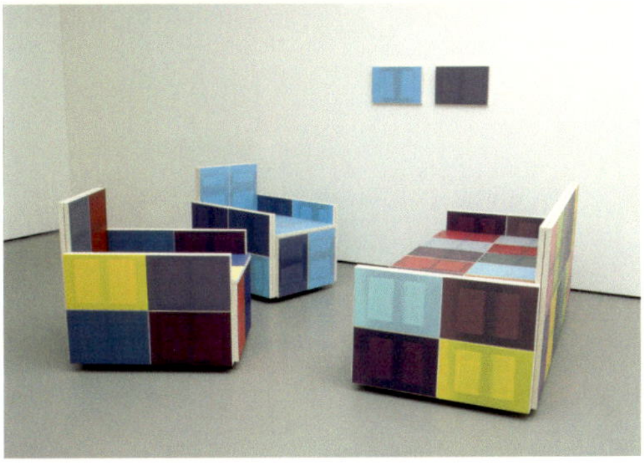

No. 3 is a small painting containing an image of an open book. It is a dark reddish-brown in colour. In the billboard component of *Homes from Homes II* it hangs in the upper register near the left-hand corner at an angle of 18 degrees from the horizontal. To make a painting of an open book is a minor displacement; to picture reading displaced from its usual location. The depicted book might be a double page from the journal *Art-Language*, or another related theoretical-type text of 1960s Conceptual Art. We have often referred to such paintings as defeated souvenirs of Conceptual Art.

Why defeated souvenirs? This may be related to the question of how Conceptual Art grows old. In pursuit of an answer to this question we might begin by describing just one aspect of this picture. Its reddish brown light-amidst-the-gloom actually invokes the high emotion and expressivity of a Mark Rothko. Rothko is the high-genre Abstract Expressionist whose paintings, according to Arthur Danto, unavoidably and necessarily connect us with the dodgy beauty of sunsets. The resulting 'cocktail' is a solecism, a dysfunctional gathering, not in the second-order sense of the postmodern spectacle but more in a first-order sense, going to the causal narrative and technical métier of the work itself. We have long hoped for a kind of dysfunctional Conceptual Art, if only to escape the smoothly functioning Conceptual Art beloved of professional artists and brand managers.

This picture in *Homes from Homes II* is a smaller version of the type known as *Sighs Trapped by Liars,* of which almost twelve hundred exemplars were made by Art & Language between 1995 and 1997. The pictures in this hoard are all similar in overall form, but in fact quite different in detail. The texts they contain are not repeated from painting to painting but are represented in succession, as in the turning of a page, until an essay, or often a complete publication is 'read' or completed. This is to say that each double-page spread of an essay of, say, 50 pages would make a work of 25 panels, each of a different colour. These panels were at first hung grid-like on the wall, the overall effect being overwhelmingly decorative, and the singular pictoriality of each picture being mislaid in an overall compositional effect. While gridded decorativeness might have been understood as Conceptual Art in further disrepute (indeed, as one of the unadmitted guises of Conceptual Art) it entailed an insupportable loss of pictorial detail; insupportable, because the critical virtue of the individual panels depended as much on their pictoriality as on their concealed modernism. What was required was a categorical disgrace to modernism. To put it another way, these little pictures needed to retain their pictorial singularity and yet to preserve the relational succession of pages that remained a condition of their realism. It seemed that they might be made subject to relations they didn't know they could have.

Accordingly, they were assembled into tables, chairs and even sofas (see nos. 31 and 44). They were gathered into a form of *domestic* seclusion. This was a seclusion in distance, which implied that though constructed in the form of the chairs et , they were in fact 'dismantled' in this form, perhaps awaiting reformation *en masse* with the examples somewhere else — on the wall, perhaps. Is this seclusion a disguise which affords the possibility that they are not simply repeated signs?

The horizontal surface of a table is perhaps the most accessible to the eye; the eye falls upon it more readily than upon the chairs which might surround it. The surface is either text or picture. In either case, the recovery of detail requires some close scrutiny. But insofar as the table may be closed in by the chairs in a circumstance of domestic security, the viewer's/reader's effort at recovery entails an unwelcome act of intrusion. In its closed world, the 'table' may be there to mean what it means — to the chairs — and this may not be connected to its form as a table, but to what it means as a text or picture. The form of a table may also be a merely contingent display. Would the reformation of the table entrain a corresponding reformation of the chairs? The combination of icon, text and domesticity entails the possibility of a double dislocation.

The paintings 'misbehave', becoming, perhaps temporarily, a kind of furniture. But they are 'furniture' because they are paintings of reading and seeing; they swarm into the shapes of tables and chairs because they are already art and images of (Conceptual) art, and not because we wished to enter the realm where fine art improves utilitarian design, or because we wanted our work to exist comfortably between function and dysfunction. Here are relatively high genre things (paintings) which recover their detail (and the problematic order of their detail) in being made homeless — and the form in which they are made 'homeless' is 'domestic'.

To recover the detail of a picture is not the same as reading a text. The detail of the pictorial image slips into text (something read) and then back again — and vice-versa. The spectator's position is threatened by the slippage as he or she recovers spatial relationships which collapse into reading and so on. This work is an index of surface and interface, of what is 'in' a painting conflated with what is done 'to' a painting, or done 'with' a painting. The hapless and irrecoverable grids have, for the time being, come to rest as tables and chairs — quasi-domestic and homely objects.

In the billboard installation of *Homes from Homes II,* this little work digs its corners into its neighbours. It appears restless. Perhaps it has escaped from the back of a chair or from a table leg in the hope of setting out on its own. Alternatively, it may be on a weary journey back into domestic seclusion, having been glimpsed fleetingly in the present crowd. One way or another, it is unsure of its bearings.

4

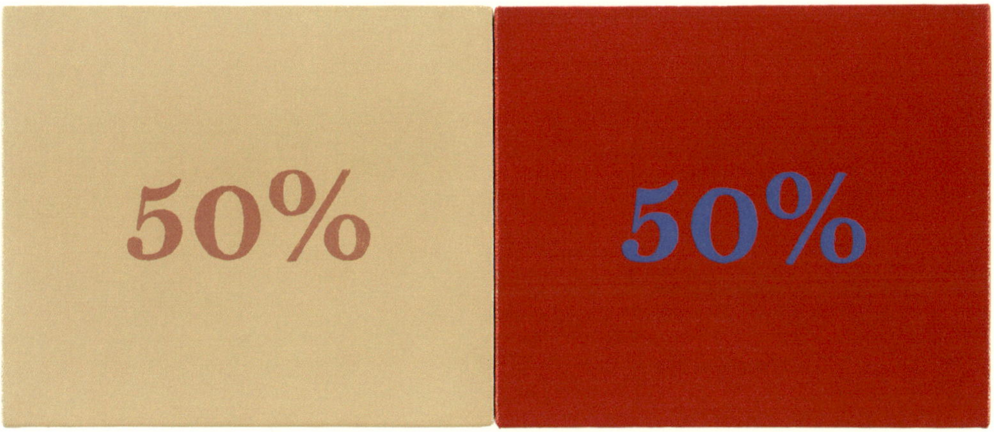

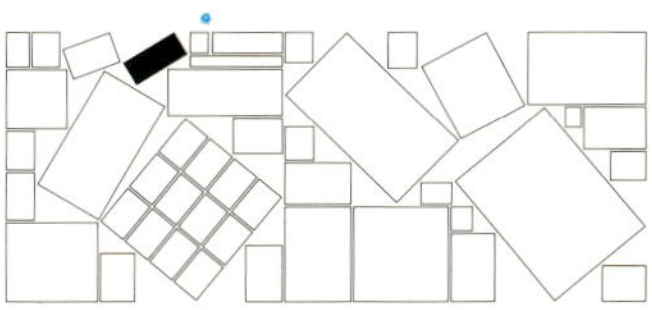

d) 100% Abstract

See

4.1
4.2

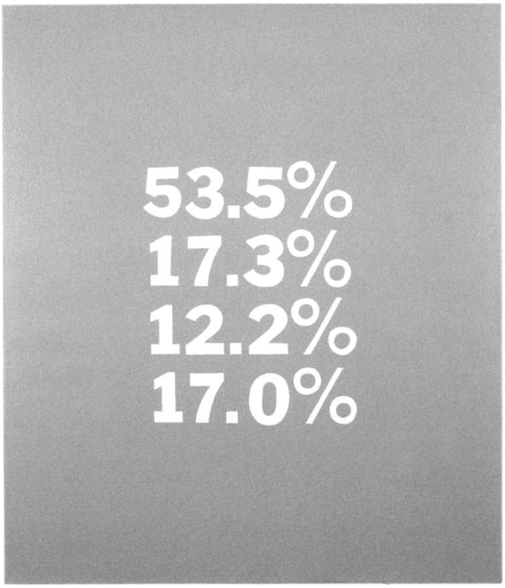

Pigment 4.6%, titanium dioxide 87.1%, iron oxide 5.6%, benzidene yellow 7.3%; non-volatile 11.3%, soya styrene resin 84.0%, hydrocarbon resin 16.0%; volatile 84.1%, aliphatic, aromatic, chlorinated and halogenated hydrocarbons and driers; TOTAL 100.0%.

Among the forms and conditions of displacement to be found in *Homes from Homes II,* no. 4 may seem to embody one of the most obvious. The work consists of two small, almost square canvases bolted together to form a long rectangle in landscape format. On the billboard it is hung in the topmost register, towards the left-hand corner, and at an angle of approximately 23 degrees from the perpendicular. The canvas on the left is painted in a light buff acrylic and the expression 50% is lettered in a darkish pink acrylic across its centre. The canvas on the right and higher than the other is painted bright red, with the same expression lettered across its centre in cobalt blue. The latter colour combination produces a noticeably 'optical' effect of afterimage that renders the lettering unstable relative to its ground. The former does not. The latter has a certain graphic presence, the former is merely prim and in moderate taste. Together, they form a small abstract painting that could either pre-date or very much post-date the high point of the Conceptual Art of the 1960s. Red and beige might well have been colour choices that were available to Jasper Johns as he satirised various forms of Abstract Expressionism in the late 1950s or early 1960s, but for a serious Conceptual artist they would have been anathema. While Johns' influence on many such artists is undeniable, such a work as this would, in the late 1960s, have been no more than a hapless pastiche, the work of an academic latecomer to Johns' cultural and historical ethos. The correct colour for a work of this nature would have been black and white or some variation of grey tones. Indeed, the actual grey prototypes are among the more eagerly collected and reproduced Art & Language works of the 1960s. Of course the original *100% Abstract* paintings were never composed of two canvases bolted together and the format was, on the whole, square. These were not compositions of numerals ironically configured into the form of a painting, as some of Johns' were, but virtual paintings, virtual abstract painting. 100% abstract; get it? In fact they owe as much to Stella as to Johns.

Stella had argued that he would have liked the dry paint on the surface of his work to look as good as it did in the can. In the Minimal Art that followed, galvanised steel, aluminium auto paint, plywood and Plexiglas were all left undisguised. They claimed virtue for being themselves. Indeed, we might say that these unadorned and largely manly materials formed a significant part of the Minimalist's arsenal of literalism. If one were to ask 'How is it that the paint in the can (or anywhere else for that matter) appears as it does?' the answer would at some point be likely to include a list of its chemical constituents. Such a list would be an analytical abstraction that would account in part for the appearance of a painting. Of course, it would not account for its appearance *as* a painting but it would tell someone how the blue part got to be blue, the grey, grey, and so on. The surface configuration of a *100% Abstract* painting accounts, in part, for its literal appearance. But this literal and reductive self-specification is in the form of a text, a notational form that ruptures the literality of the material of which it and its ground are composed.

The jollier version that appears in *Homes from Homes II* is, in analytical chemistry terms, utter nonsense. It has lost its literal moorings, and as a consequence its virtuality — or at least the virtuality that is evident in the 1968 prototype. So is the *Homes from Homes II* version just dumb or has it some power of narrative? As we have said, this work is composed of two canvases bolted together to form an almost continuous surface. Each of the canvases therefore comprises 50% of the work's substance. In being thus inscribed the literalness of this fact is made tautologically evident. But now what is 'spoken of' is not the chemical composition of the paint, but an obvious fact about the construction of the painting. This shifts the work, perhaps, from its original Minimalist connections that lay in a literalism of materials, only to restate them in a literalism of form. This little travesty may, however, have further things to say. It may, for example, be asking what it is about the original *100% Abstract* paintings that has rendered them so relatively consumable. Are they seen *post-hoc* as sufficient tokens of the Conceptual Art type that have had the good fortune to remain paintings? That is to say, are they consumable by those who would prefer a little of the paint and canvas to persist in a work that belongs to a cultural moment which saw the ejection of such artisanal stuff?

If we hypothesise minimally that the moment of Conceptual Art was one in which the space that had been occupied previously by high modernist painting was colonised or syndicalised by texts, then do we imply that these texts are paintings of a sort, as Frank Stella once suggested. If this is the case, then *100% Abstracts* tell a different version of this narrative truth: it is not the case that the moment of Conceptual Art is only to be characterised as one in which texts colonised the walls that had been previously occupied by modernist painting, but rather that it was also one in which paintings were also colonised by texts. Moreover, these were texts that knew about their literalist antecedents and that were capable of matching the properties of these antecedents whilst simultaneously rendering them virtual. We could say, however, that this red, beige, blue and pink artefact attests not only to this minor bifurcation in the path of the Conceptual Art of the late 1960s, but also to one of the socio-economic as well as cultural circumstances to which this particular division of the path attests. The 'generic' text of Conceptual Art, insofar as it remained stuck with small logical games and self-awarded declarative transparency, was bound eventually to fall into the managerial remit of decorative space-penetration, or to stay on and inhabit the small internal world of the painting whence a portion of it came. Is this to say that this travesty of *100% Abstract* tells of our disquiet that its prototypes have been far too easily transformed into Conceptual Art tokens of the lowest denomination — and that it wouldn't make much difference if these works had simply been *decorated* with numerals or words — or does it speak of an old fork in the road where smart art decorators begin to divide from those who now observe 'If Conceptual Art had a future, then it was not as Conceptual Art'?

In the quasi-chronological version of *Homes from Homes II* no. 4 hangs near the beginning. As a 'virus' it will rend to attach itself to abstract painting to semi-abstract painting, and to primitive kinds of Conceptual Art.

5

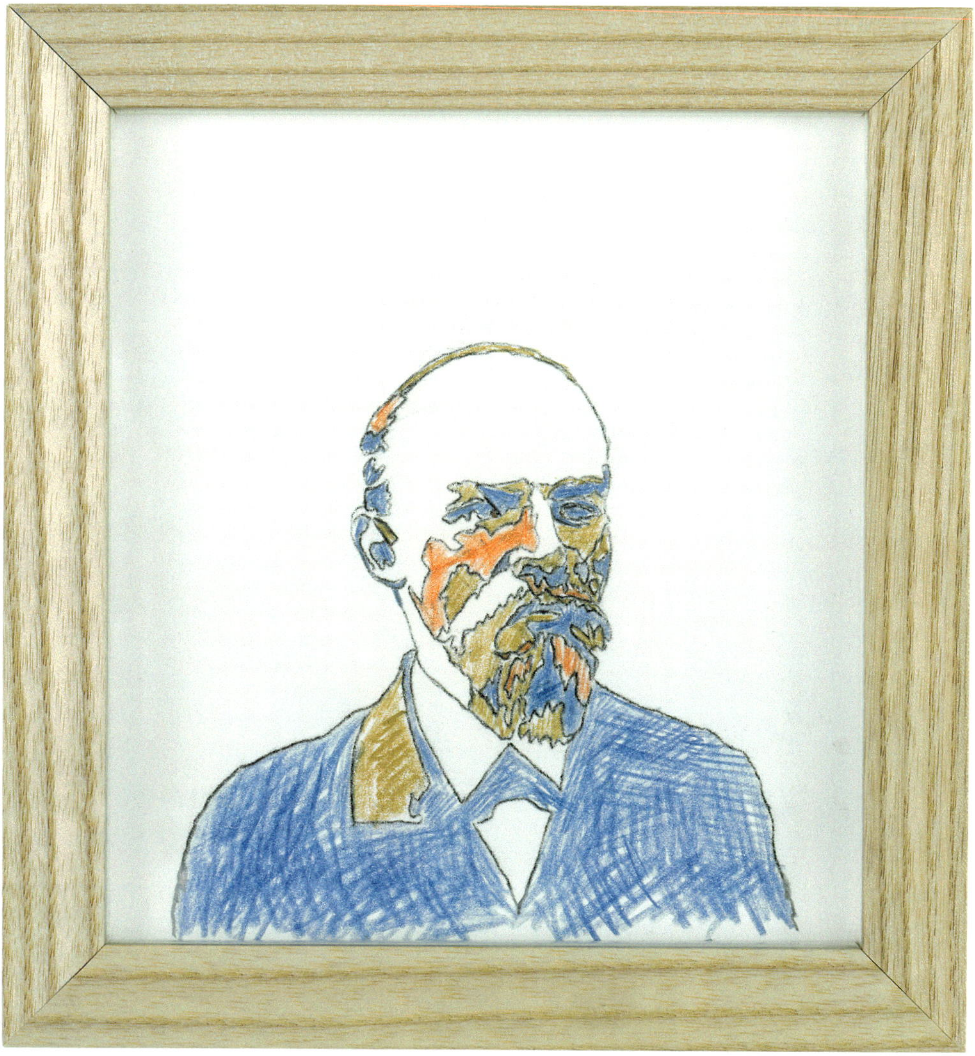

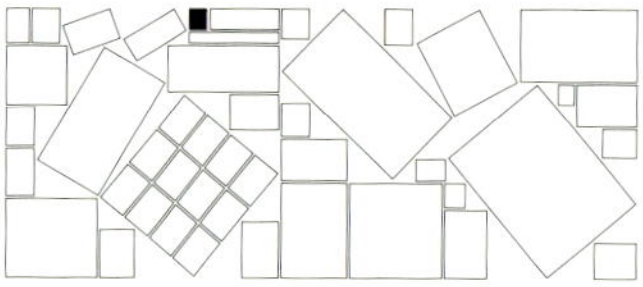

e) Lenin

e) *Lenin*

See

5.1

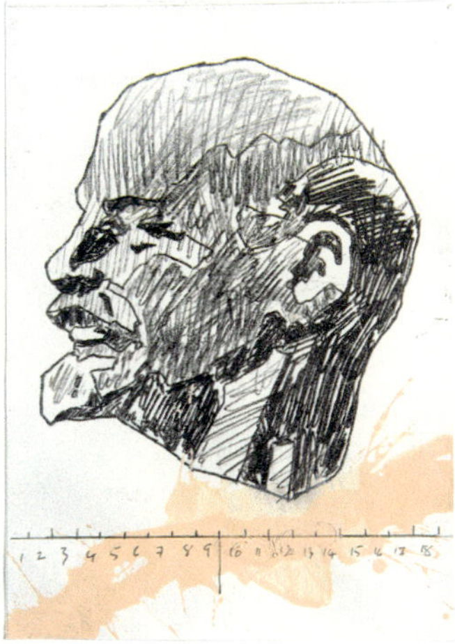

5.2

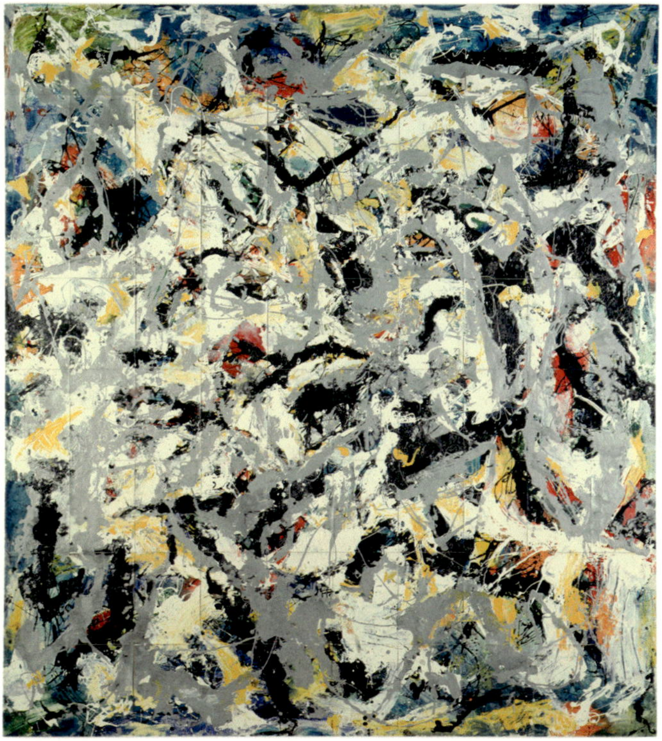

In the billboard version of *Homes from Homes II*, no. 5 occupies a position in the upper register, to the left of centre. In the quasi-chronological hang it occupies a position about a third of the way along. As a virus it will tend to attach itself to essays in portraiture and particularly to political icons. A small picture in square-ish format, it shows a bust-length portrait of V.I. Lenin against a plain white background. The medium is pencil and crayon on paper. This work relates to Art & Language's series of *Portraits of V.I. Lenin in the Style of Jackson Pollock*, originally made in 1979–1980 at a time when images of Lenin were still ubiquitous in the Soviet bloc and when Pollock's work was still the dominant paradigm of the high modernist style in the West. In *Homes from Homes II*, another trace of the same series is to be found a short distance below the small coloured bust, where a representation of *Portrait of V.I. Lenin in Disguise in the Style of Jackson Pollock* appears in the drawing of the *Studio at 3 Wesley Place painted by mouth* (no. 15).

Portraits of V.I. Lenin in the style of Jackson Pollock were originally made — as exemplifications of a prospectively unrealisable title — in preparation for an exhibition at the Stedelijk Van Abbemuseum, Eindhoven, in 1980. Each of six large paintings on paper was cut up into A4-sized sheets and colour-photocopied. The photocopies were variously reassembled both into representations of the original paintings and, in scrambled form, into approximations of ambitious all-over abstract paintings. It was only subsequent to that exhibition that the paintings were reassembled and considered for display in their own right, together with further works made on canvas that were neither cut up nor photocopied.

The project was initially attractive by virtue of its very intractability — the manifest technical and ideological incommensurability of its respective constituents. The style of Pollock is not such as to generate icons of Lenin or anyone else, while the cultural values associated with Lenin have tended to rule out modernistic individualism such as Pollock's. The paintings propose a 'monstrous *détente*' between the historically opposed blocs that their respective constituents represent. Implemented technically in the composition of the paintings, the *détente* is actualised in the experience of the spectator, for whom the measure of appropriate competence is that both the picture of Lenin and the style of Pollock can be recognised and located within a relevant cultural discourse.

In the larger development of the Art & Language project, a certain significance attached to the point in 1981 at which the *Portraits of V.I. Lenin in the Style of Jackson Pollock* were reassembled and exhibited. The relative success or failure of a work of Conceptual Art was rarely a matter to be decided on the evidence of its physical appearance. Indeed, where the typical genres of Conceptual Art were concerned, the comparative irrelevance of such considerations might have been thought a qualification. In the case of the *Portraits of V.I. Lenin in the Style of Jackson Pollock*, however, it was clear that some were better than others, and that this was a consequence of their being made rather than thought up. It seemed that the power of the *détente* that the pictures proposed was connected to their capacity to act as paintings, and not simply as images of paintings.

The earliest forms of the paintings that had been cut up and photocopied — images of paintings — seemed, in fact, to weaken the monstrous implications of the title. In being processed into a tessellated set of colour xerox images, the paintings had been driven a considerable distance from the Pollock prototype. The *Portrait of V.I. Lenin in the Style of Jackson Pollock* by Art & Language could never have been (mis)taken literally for a work by Pollock. In being virtually impossible to misunderstand, the Art & Language work could never invoke directly any form of the aesthetic and art-historical business in which the work of Pollock was embedded. With an image of a painting, the viewer's deflation in discovering a portrait of Lenin was already virtual and not actual. While the paintings are allowed to remain unprocessed — to keep a technical appearance that allowed them to come under a regard that might also have been appropriate to a Pollock — the viewer's cultural composure is menaced directly by the lurking presence of Lenin.

Art & Language was confronted with the relationship between two sets of variables; on the one hand those factors that decided what it might mean for a given work to be well or badly made; on the other those that decided what might be in the margins of the artists' minds at the point of production. Such considerations were not to be further addressed by a return to the practices of Conceptual Art; rather they tended to invite engagement with some kind of high genre.

While the small bust of Lenin in *Homes from Homes II* serves to evoke the wider project of the portraits in the style of Pollock, it relates more specifically to the small images of Lenin that have tended to accompany the paintings when these have been exhibited, serving both as virtual distinguishing labels and as points of entry for those initially unable to find the heads of Lenin amongst displays of the style of Pollock. Those small images are also maps of the tonal separations made in the process of construction of the portraits. The colouring of the small picture in *Homes from Homes II* suggests that it may have fulfilled a similar technical function at some point in the development of the series. In fact, however, the photograph from which it was derived is not numbered among the cinematically derived canonical images by which the mythology of the revolutionary leader was serviced, and on which Art & Language's portraits in the style of Pollock were based. This is a less dynamic and more homely Lenin – one whose earnest but bathetic endeavours might have failed altogether to register on the tableau of history. In keeping with the tendency to travesty by which *Homes from Homes II* is animated, the image that the small picture purveys is of a historical reputation now sadly or comically deflated – a fitting antithesis, perhaps, to a Pollock who might never have risen above 'apocalyptic wallpaper'.

6

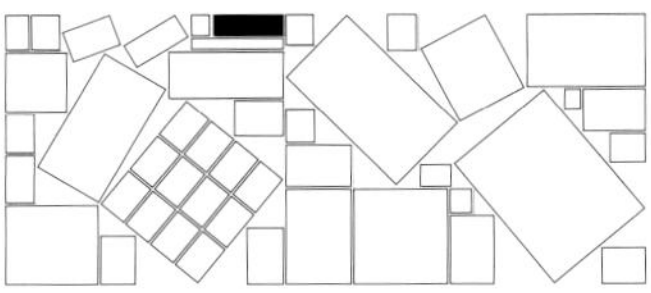

f) Mirror

See

6.1

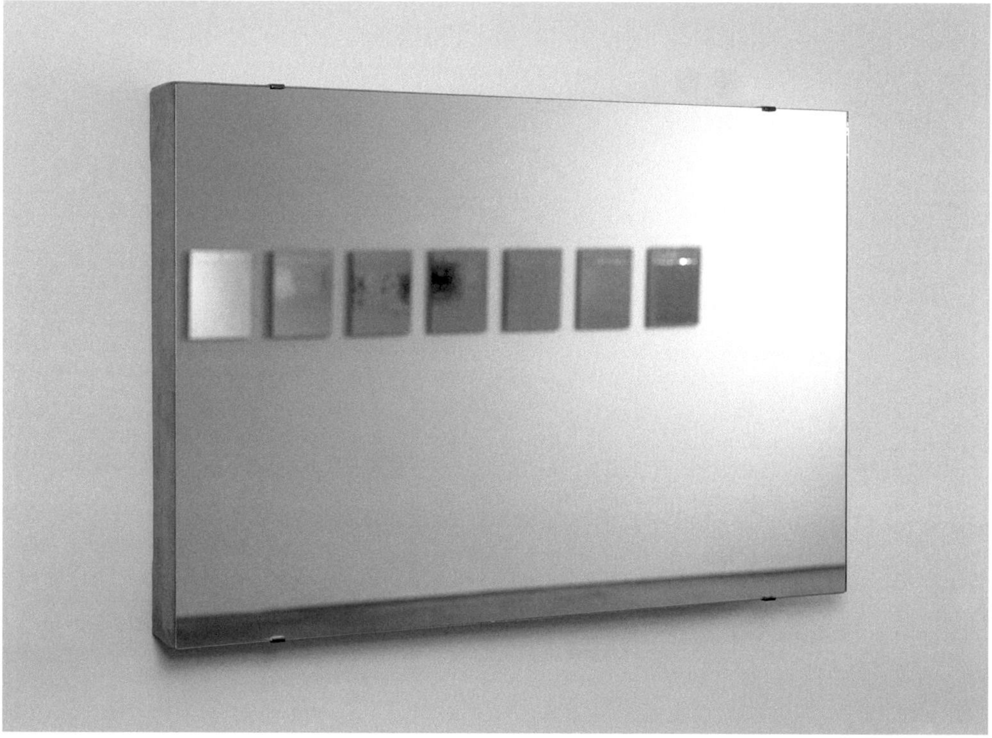

No. 6 is a mirror, 15.5 cm by 47.5 cm, that has been fixed over a canvas stretched on a frame. It is materially indistinguishable from an *Untitled Painting* of 1965. The latter is, however, the type of a much larger object, taking its scale from a formula that identifies certain forms of Minimal Art. In being made small, no. 6 is detached from the historical reflectivity that informed the scale of its putative ancestors. It is thus a form of representation. Representation rather than reproduction, because as an indexical form, it must be imagined larger than it is. That is the only means by which it can recuperate that insolent logic by which the *Untitled Paintings* of 1965 were driven. These latter works take up the dissent-in-obedience that is exemplified in Frank Stella's black (and other) stripe paintings of the late 1950s and early 1960s. The high modernist formula proclaimed 'the logic of the support', viz: the internal inflection of a painting must always be to a significant extent determined by the shape of the support over which the canvas is stretched. Having supplied oneself with a rectangular canvas, or canvases, it seemed entirely in accordance with the 'logic' to attach a mirror of precisely the same dimensions. The artist had arrogated no powers to himself beyond specifying the dimensions of the mirror and attaching it appropriately. However, since what is attached to the canvas is a mirror, this act of following the 'logic of the support' is also an act of demolition. The mirror will reflect contingently the occasions and images that fall within its optical scope: the 'logic of the support' has generated no more than an edge to a surface inflection that is in all other respects entirely out of control. Indeed, the mirror becomes a metonymic sign not of modernist painting, but of a form of pre-modernist painting that modernism displaced.

On the billboard installation, the mirror reflects little — or almost nothing — that moves. It sits up high with a small image of a face to the left, a lump of meat to the right and a yellow blank beneath. It is raised out of the reach of everyday contingency. It is, however, not set high on the wall in the other two parts of the *Homes from Homes* installation. The billboard installation thus assists the viewer in one operation that all the other examples of this type both demand and make difficult. The mirror reflects the world that passes before it in virtue of its three-dimensional structure. At the same time, it has a flat surface that would correspond to the surface of a painting. In fact, it is very difficult to discern the front surface of a mirror from its rear silvered surface unless it is either fogged or smeared. In being raised above normal eye level the mirror on the billboard is viewed obliquely. It is thus partially blinded. As a consequence, we are enabled in our efforts to recover a sense of — a view of — its surface. We may then take away the enabling impairment as we view two other examples of the set of three hung near the level of our faces. We may thus be helped to avoid — or at any rate to switch on and off — the sight of ourselves and to pay attention to an imperfectly blank surface. Of course, in the effort to overcome our own mirror image we will see ourselves seeing. But we see ourselves seeing in a mirror that represents another.

7

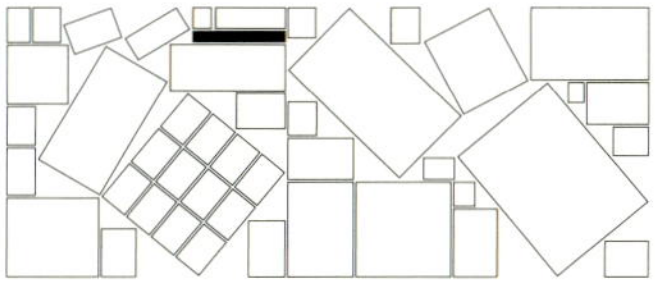

g) Yellow Painting

See

7.1

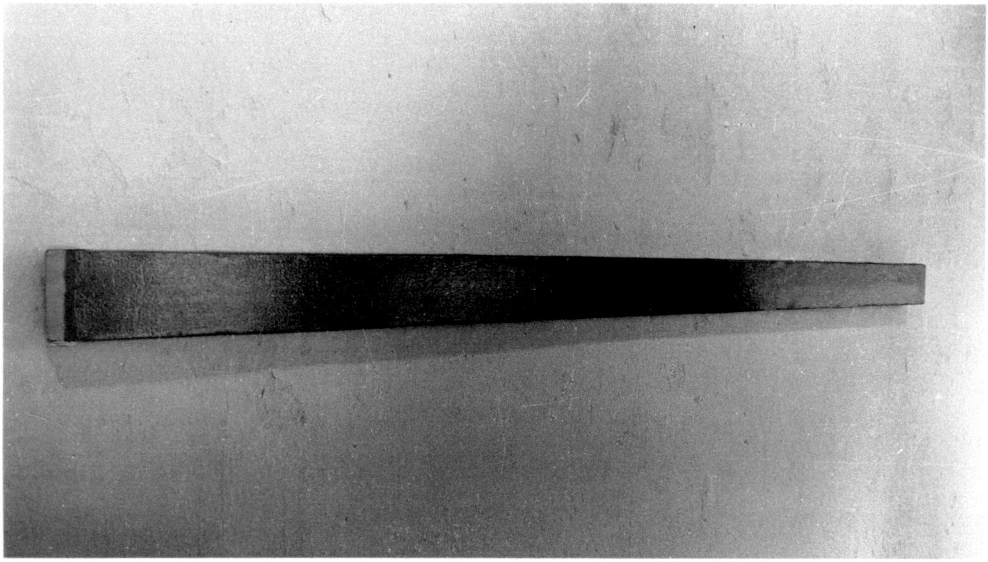

No. 7 appears in the upper register of *Homes from Homes II,* just beneath no. 5 and no. 6. It is the same length as these two combined. It appears very close to the leftward edge of the pseudo-chronological installation. As a virus, it might seek to combine with pot-boiling Minimalism. Not all the items comprising *Homes from Homes II* are parodies or travesties of existing Art & Language work. Some of the items are variations, or just smaller versions of existing work. Sometimes, as in the case of no. 34, *Homes from Homes II* has produced a conjunction that is a completely new work. The representational and re-descriptive operations of *Homes from Homes II* are not at all uniform. What then are we to make of this little bar-like yellow picture? Its appearance makes it unfamiliar as an example of the work of Art & Language. It is in fact genetically connected to a series of *Black Paintings* produced in 1965. We should, therefore try to describe the appearance of these works of 1965, and to recover some of the historical circumstances by which they are determined and which they seek to address.

Always much larger than no. 7, these long, thin, stripe-like paintings were hung at eye-level so as fully to occupy the line of vision of the viewer passing along them. Had they not been hung at eye-level, these works would have amounted to little. In order to commit the viewer thus to moving, their format and scale was in the region of: 10 x 220 cm, or 8 x 350 cm, or 6 x 410 cm. They were invariably painted without brushmarks or other modulations, in flat black gloss enamel. The surface of the painting was supposed to reflect the light and the shadows of the external environment.

1965 was the time of late high modernism, and, as the story goes, a moment whose contradictions had been laid bare by Stella's black paintings of 1958–1959, such as *The Marriage of Reason and Squalor.* Stella's paintings literalised the writings of leading modernist critics and in so doing subverted them. He had begun a process in which the artist might begin to answer back.

Countless words have been written about this moment of the contamination of high modernism from within. But there were other 'lower' influences on the black stripes that had frequently been ignored, despised, or simply condemned as 'novelty art' by the high modernist canon. To pick two clankingly obvious 'avant-garde' examples, consider the old boiler that is John Cage's *4′33″* of 1952, and the slightly less celebrated *White Paintings* by Robert Rauschenberg – if ever there were works that embodied Harold Rosenberg's prediction that the dumber and blanker you get, the more the critics would have to say. And it has come true it seems: that which is nothing much will seem effortlessly to bear the weight of an immense critical literature. If Cage's work was, as is often claimed, the birth of 'interactive art', it also marked the beginnings of a decline in the ability of the artwork to resist journalistic bullshit. An emptiness, or 'silence', which acts as an environmental 'surface' or location for light and shade and other environmental contingencies, implied an indeterminate relation between the format of the work and the external world which is no longer incidental to it. So began the long list of conceits that forms the theory of 'interactive art'. Whatever the legacy of these two very well-worshipped pillars of modern fire, the *Black Paintings* of 1965 are somewhat homeless without them. They form the 'avant-garde' background to works of an appropriate scale, that are hung at eye level, painted flat, in gloss black enamel, and so on.

If the yellow thing in *Homes from Homes II* is supposed to have some kind of representational connection to the 1965 work then clearly the colour is all wrong. The yellow surface makes no reference to Stella's black stripes, nor does it reflect light in the same way as black enamel. No matter how shiny the surface, yellow will never match the mirror-like qualities of black. Nor is the object hung at eye-level on the billboard version of *Homes from Homes II.* While its proportions get close to its putative ancestors, even if the little yellow painting were enlarged so that it was, say, 220 cm long, it would still be far too high to work as they do.

From this we might conclude, perhaps, that insofar as no. 7 is supposed to have some type of representational connection to the black paintings of 1965, albeit one that is complex and indirect, it was made by people who did not know what they were doing. It could of course be seen as an amateurish and unaccultured travesty. Of all the works represented in *Homes from Homes II,* this one seems strangely mute.

But to say this is to miss something. First of all, as no. 7 appears in *Homes from Homes II,* it has a complex acquaintance. While the black painting reflected the external contingencies of light and shade, no. 7 picks up its own contingencies, not in the form of environmental reflections, but in terms of conjuncture and contamination. Just adjacent to it on the *Homes from Homes II* billboard is a depiction of a loin of pork with a nearly identical yellow background (no. 8). Also close by is a similarly yellow panel on which the word 'painting' is inscribed (no. 9). The conclusion that we may come to, therefore, is that the little yellow painting has been infected with a virus caught from its 'external' neighbours. The structural indeterminacies of light and shade have been transformed into contagion. And that is a sort of representation. The innocent hope that was invested in environmental contingencies by the black painting of 1965 has been supplanted on a body weakened by the exhausting multiplicities of postmodernism. Little yellow no. 7 has turned blacker in the process, no matter how bright and cheery it seems.

8

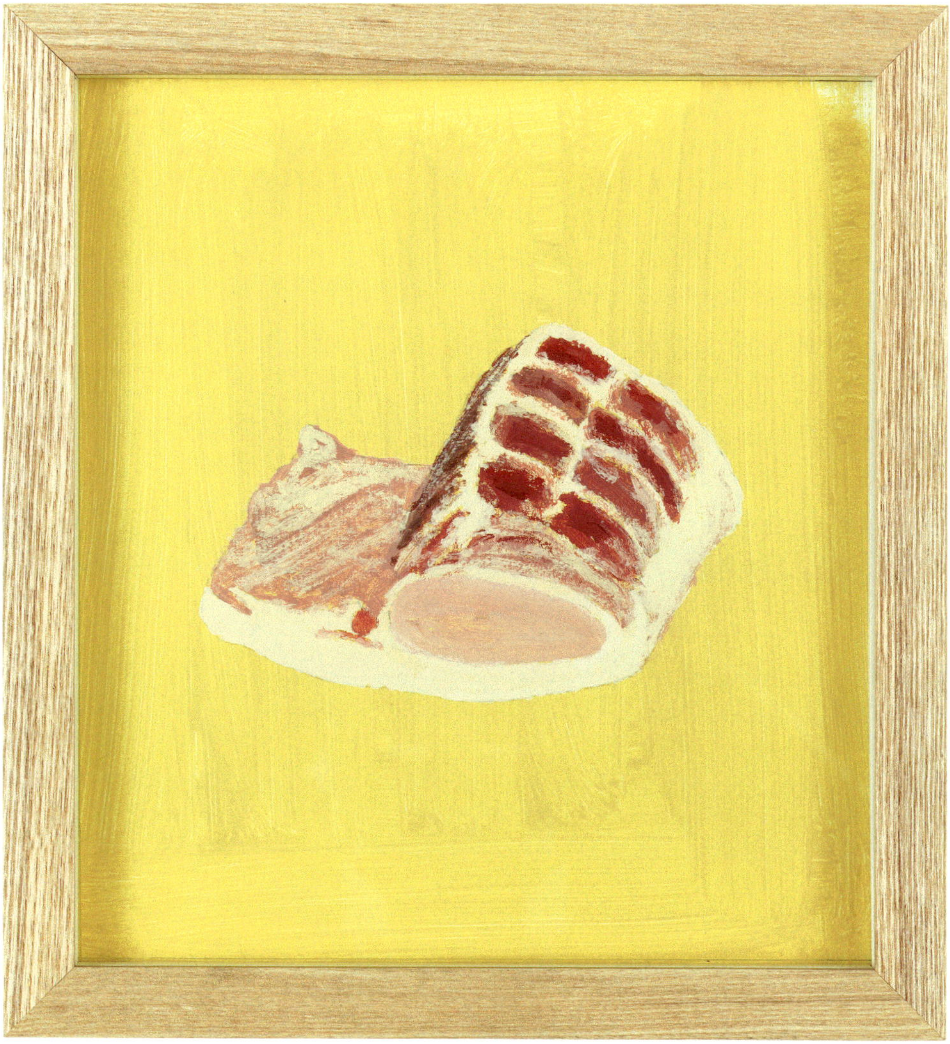

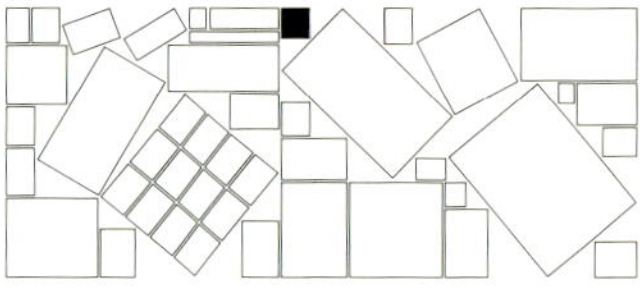

h) Loin of Pork

See

8.1
8.2

8.3
8.4
8.5

8.6
8.7
8.8

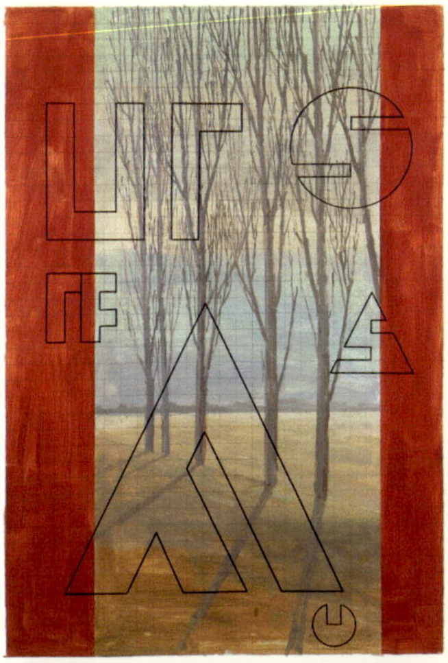

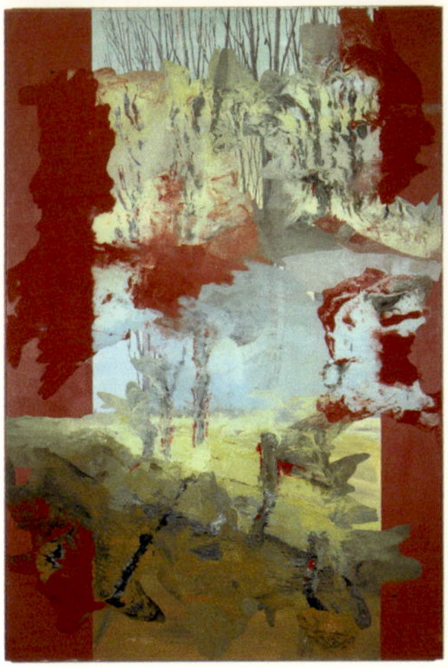

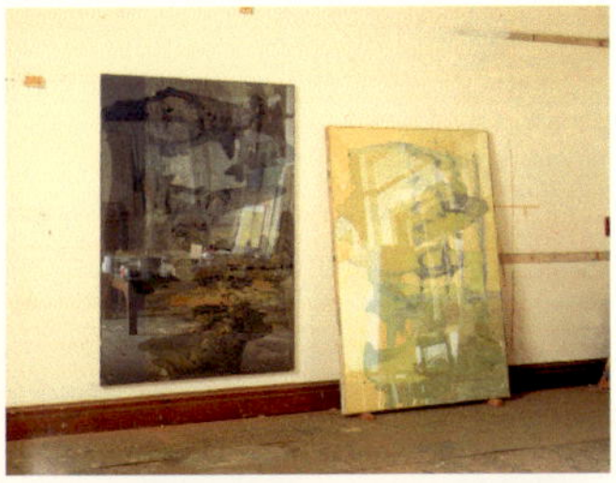

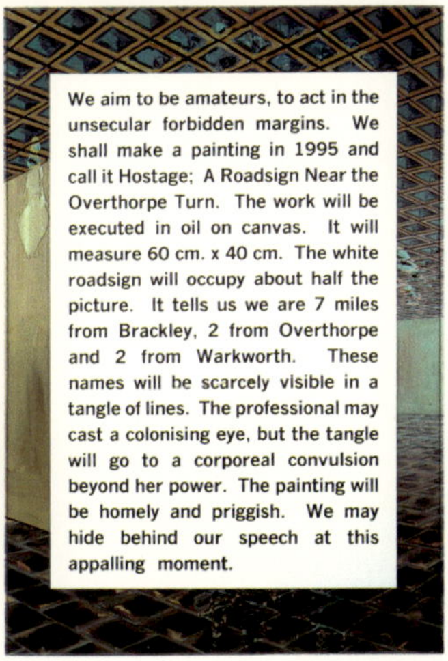

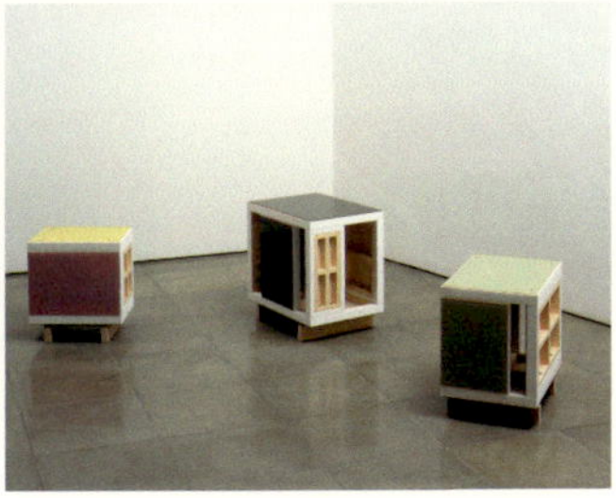

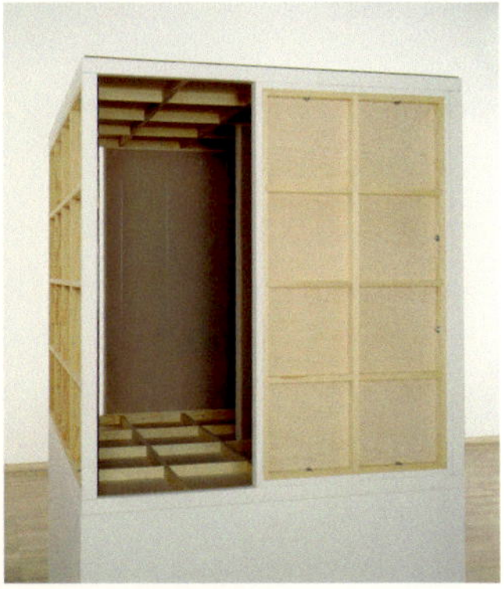

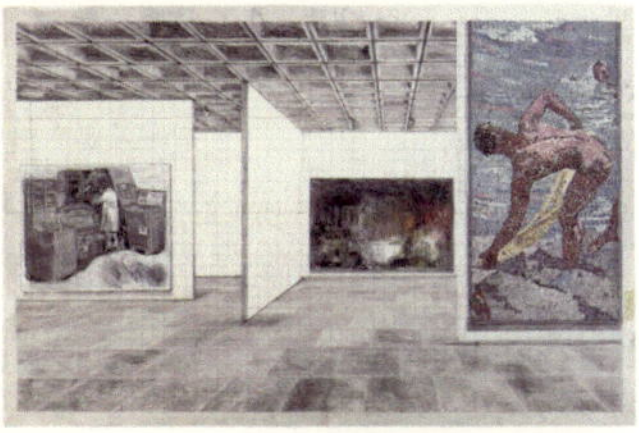

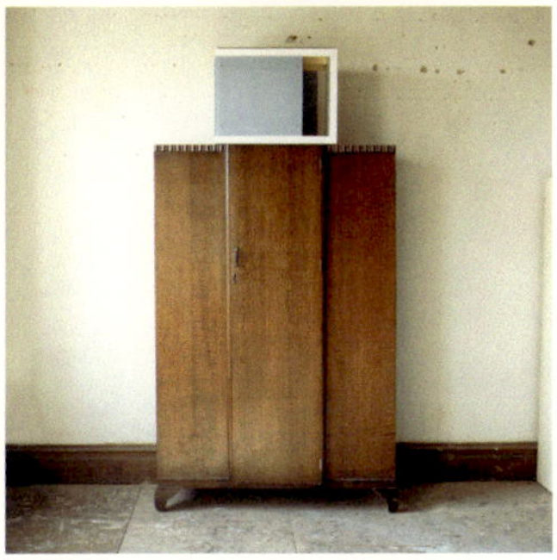

In no. 8 we see a small still-life that is a loin of pork on a yellow ground. The colour of the ground co-ordinates to some extent with two adjacent works, no. 7 (a yellow version of a 1960s painting) and no. 9 ('Sculpture'). This colour is also reflected in no. 34 and no. 14. No. 8 thus makes a small contribution to any formal coherence that *Homes from Homes II* may possess. Its background colour is therefore largely determined by a certain exigency that comes from 'within' the installation itself.

The image of the meat is rendered in a more-or-less vernacular naturalistic style. The meat is reddish-pink, the fat a yellowish white and the brushstroke detail is in mimetic proportion — neither too big nor too small — to do the picturing job.

This simple object has a complex aetiology. It is the only example of its type that has been placed in public exhibition as a work or as part of a work of Art & Language. Its origins lie in an attempt to revive the genre of the still life in an essayistic form. A series of works bearing the name *Hostage* had been based on the genre of landscape. This is one of the more homely lower genres of painting that has been associated for a long time with the practice of amateurs, and inflected by incompetence, holidays and evening classes. The genre also connects with a relatively high fraction of modernist abstract painting and particularly with the horizontally-banded colourfield. A canvas covered in slightly wobbly bands and fields is more-or-less a landscape. In the *Hostage* series, the orders of pictoriality of the landscape are thrown into confusion.

Firstly the basic composition of landscape and vertical plane is transferred from a preparatory drawing onto canvas. Certain areas are marked out on the drawings by configurations of black lines. These are composed by graphic deformations of the letters S.U.R.F., signifying 'surface'. In the process of enlargement onto canvas these areas are covered with masking tape. At a second stage, this tape is removed and the composition is continued and completed, but now using much thicker paint over the previously masked-out sections. The third stage occurs while this thick paint is still wet. The glass is applied over the painting and screwed down into the wooden support. The canvas is then loosened from the stretcher, a steel bar is inserted between the canvas and its plywood backing, and the wet paint is spread out behind the glass, forming runs and patterns which are relatively controlled but also relatively unpredictable. By this process an apparently complete or finished figurative scene is apparently blotted and smeared. Across much of the picture surface the material components of the illusion — the patches of coloured paint — are rendered literal and flat.

Or flat, at least, from the standpoint of that sophisticated culture within which the illusion of the landscape is perceived and its referential character understood. In fact, as their illusionistic surfaces are smeared and spoiled, the paintings also invoke a different culture, a differently positioned viewer. This is a viewer for whom the very smearing and spoiling establish representation. In the culture which this second viewer represents, illusion and reference are familiar properties of synthetic surfaces. They are to be found in the slippery effects of kitsch abstract art, in the laminated decor of up-market boutiques, or in the hygienic surfaces of expensive bathrooms. This is a viewer for whom decorativeness is a value at odds with the culture of high art. From his imaginary point of view, it is those few remnants of the original figurative scheme which remain undisturbed — the touches of paint which still signify branches, ground and sky — that read as literal, factitious and unfinished.

These paintings do not address or accommodate themselves to one viewer or the other, nor do they supply any moral grounds on which to distinguish between them. What they establish is that forms of conflict attend inexorably upon the aesthetic. If this is contingently true in the world we know, it is probably also true of any world we can now sensibly envisage. This is the intuition which is set in play as these paintings are worked over, changed and unfinished. By this process of unfinishing, we attempt to draw into the play of artistic genres and effects the dangerous and transforming substance of a culture with no regard for art. The apparent damage done to the figurative schemes — the atmospheric landscapes — is not simply a matter of avant-garde cancellation or iconoclasm, though it is significant that a tradition of artistic iconoclasm has persisted within the margins of the modernist mainstream. Rather, what is involved is a purposeful refusal to the spectator of the possibility of certain normally accredited modes of experience and understanding. The semantic hiatus leaves you with work to do. To recognise the painting for what it is — to be able to represent it to yourself — is to look not simply through the iconic conventions of artistic culture, but to look in the face of those conventions into an un-aesthetic world, or rather into a world un-amenable to aesthetic ratification and control. This world is evoked in these paintings by both the literal and the figurative components of their surfaces. It is also present as a form of visitation in those reflections of the viewer's actual situation which are visually indissoluble from the artistic materials.

Whilst the genre of the still life has little bearing on the later forms of modernist painting, its relatively minor status placed it centre stage in the later nineteenth century and the early to mid-twentieth century. It is the genre and motif of 'analytical' Cubism *par excellence*, for example. But, like landscape, the genre also falls within the orbit of the Sunday painter, and indeed, by the 1950s had fallen into virtual professional disuse, the work of Morandi and certain works by Jasper Johns being relatively rare exceptions. It seemed possible that the alienating powers of glass and the picture-inverting powers of disorder might be brought to bear in a spirit that accorded with the Art & Language text 'We Aim to be Amateurs'.

Various items of subject matter were attempted, from hazel catkins in a glass jar to inconsequential bits and bobs from the studio benches. All without success, as the disorder of the paint closest to the surface of the glass remained firmly attached to the still-life figuration, rather in the way of those Francis Bacon figures with paint on their faces which the suggestible tell us is quivering flesh. One last possibility was considered: if quivering flesh itself were to compose the still-life figures, could it be that its very literalness might reconfigure the disordered paint as a distinct illusion? The results were worse. The attempt was abandoned.

As it appears in *Homes from Homes II*, this image of meat is, then, a sort of confession. It is an emblem of failure whose form is the very condition of the failure itself. And a confession of artistic failure goes to a sort of fiction — to a place not beset by truth. It is perhaps an invitation to imagine a narrative in which events did not unfold as they did.

In fact, the meat was revived for use in a group of works that subtend from the series *Index: Now They Are* where pink semi-opaque glass is used to conceal an image of female genitalia. It (the pork?)

appears meshed beneath sheets of enamelled glass as one of several small constructions that take on some of the characteristics of heads and are called 'portraits'. The series *Index: Now They Are* transformed into another set of works, *Incident: Now They Are.*

Six (sometimes seven) versions of the pink paintings were bolted together to form large-ish box-like constructions. The interiors of these boxes bounded by the backs of the glass-covered canvas panels resembled the interior space of a museum with walls, floor and ceiling, in turn resembling an earlier series of works from 1985, titled *Index: Incidents in a Museum.*

Here is a tale of unexpected loss and unexpected gain. A box made of paintings which has an interior. But the interior turns out to look like the interior of a museum. If this is a kind of installation, it is not one which is in a museum but rather one which turns itself into a museum.

This account has so far entrained a number of persistent psychological predicates: sex, boxes, hidden interiors, concealment and unexpected representations or remainders.

These earlier works accidentally brought together a set of themes that went to make up a representation of an artistic 'home': the museum. In a further and related series of works the scale was drastically reduced. The themes so far itemised were joined by others. The problem posed by these smaller boxes became not so much how to look at them but where to look for them — in other words, where to put them. They had no home. They were homeless. But they were of a size and scale to suggest intimate portraits. What began (perhaps) as an image of female genitalia had turned into a box, and then into a possibly disembodied head.

These are flat pictorial things that have been screwed together in the form of a container. Some of them have been turned around to show their backs. There is nothing behind. The container might be a container for a head that the portrait pictures. But these are only virtual containers, containers that show that the only way that they can be is in being empty.

They are situated close to the floor, rising to around knee height. Portraits are normally seen, at eye level. The viewers' curiosity might want to intrude, to peer in. This would entail getting down on the floor. If you resist this possibility your regard is confined to a merely virtual descent or perhaps more interestingly, it invites an imagined self-dismemberment that detaches the head.

How else might curiosity be satisfied? We might say that the corollary of imaginary self-dismemberment is the manipulation of the object. These are objects that invite being picked up and turned in the hand. But they are (just) too large and anyway they look formally complete; this makes them resistant to manipulation; they don't *need* to be fiddled with. The effect may be a consequence of the fact that they have no orientation that can be correct for all the pictures simultaneously.

Short of virtual self-dismemberment you have little alternative but to accept that the picture you get is what the picture *is*, whichever way up you see it. The interior of the box-like structure contributes to this effect. While the arrangement of the pictures might be contingent, that's how they are in fact screwed together. Being thus a virtual container possessed of an 'interior' is a fact that gives them an identity — is *in fact* the substance of their decorative integrity. This sabotages any expectation you may have regarding there being a proper orientation of the pictures, or of their pictorial properties exercising any supervening agency.

But a head is not meat unless you are Francis Bacon or Gilles Deleuze or worse. This image masked by the glazed surface of a little box is no portrait at all, unless it is merely some emblem of character, an uncompleted rebus that invites the American colloquialism 'meat head'. Such adolescent semiology is tiresome. It takes no account of the fact that these are works that posses an interior that is the basis of their substance. The painted image on the surface may in fact be a mere distraction — a double mask. It is certainly no indication of their possibly solid contents. These works are 'portraits of an artist' if and only if all these considerations are in play. In *Homes from Homes I*, the meat appears again, masked by a sheet of pink glass. There, it is indeed a travesty. Is it extracted from a 'portrait' — a mere part — or is it a late-coming solution to an abandoned still-life project? On the other hand could it be masquerading in cheerful obscenity as a cunt?

9, 41

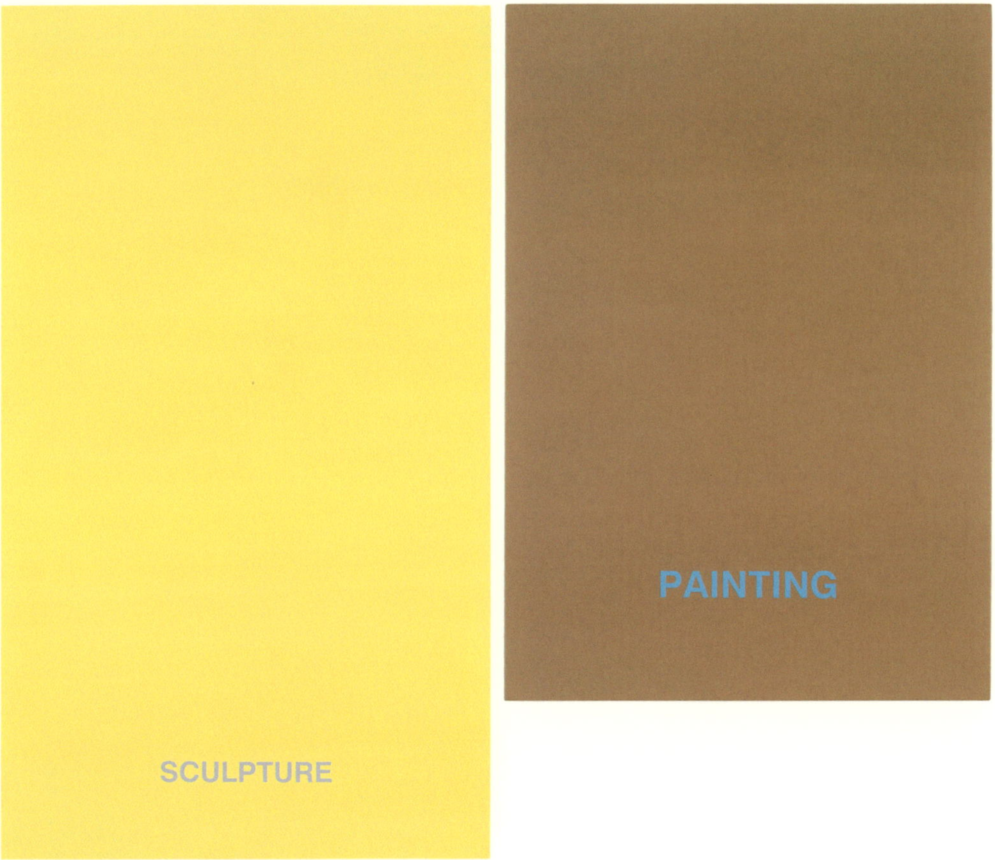

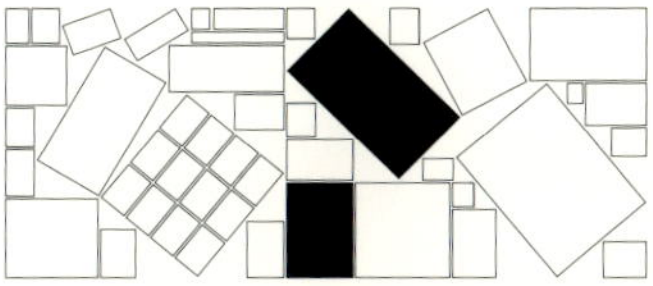

i) Painting-Sculpture

See

9, 41.1

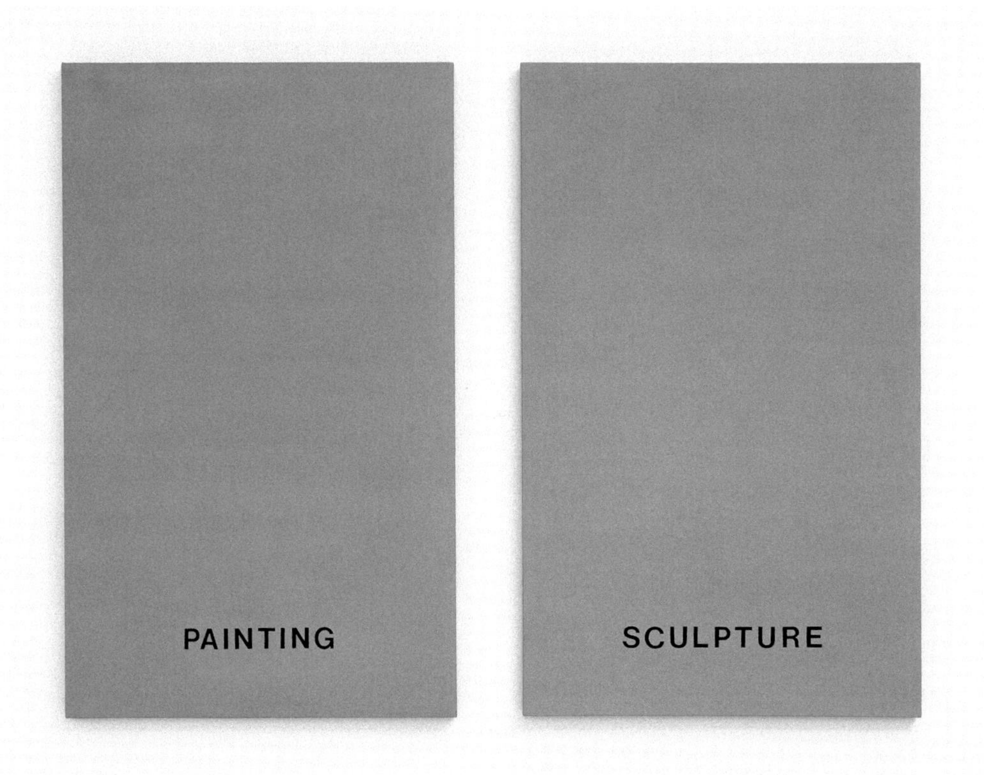

Nos. 9 and 41 are two painted wood panels, one brown and one yellow. The word 'Painting' is inscribed in a light cobalt blue close to the lower edge of the brown panel and the word 'Sculpture' in a mid-violet in a similar place on the yellow. The yellow panel inscribed 'Sculpture' hangs at an angle of 45 degrees; the brown panel inscribed 'Painting' hangs straight. The yellow and brown colours are also applied to the edges of the respective panels.

If the inscription 'Painting' were to be removed from the brown panel, it would still qualify as a painting. If the inscription 'Sculpture' were to be removed from the yellow panel it too would qualify as a painting. Without the inscription, the yellow panel would almost certainly qualify as a sculpture were it removed from the wall and placed flat on the floor. Since the yellow paint does go right around the edge and the panel is hung at 45 degrees, it might in fact be three-dimensional enough to qualify as a 'sculpture' even if it were hung on the wall at a height that would normally be thought appropriate to painting.

In both cases, without inscriptions, these panels might be thought of as generic forms of painting or of sculpture. They would be generic insofar as they might be said to fall neatly and minimally within the protocols and differentae of the artworld.

These panels are marginally decorative. They have cooler ancestors. These are in the form of grey wooden panels, similarly inscribed in black lettering, both of which are hung perpendicularly on the wall. But in being inscribed with the respective words 'Painting' and 'Sculpture' we might say that these objects are attempting some sort of reflexive ostension – a kind of self-description. If you wear a badge with your name on it at a conference, the proper name will confer some sort of description upon you, e.g. that you are male or female, or that you like your forename to be truncated because you want to be hip and popular, or whatever. The label will also 'say' that, for the purposes of the circumstance, this is how you want (or sometimes don't want) to be referred to or addressed, and so forth.

If we regard these panels as 'badged' items, the badges may give correct or incorrect information. Correct, if we regard the panel labelled 'Painting' as a painting and the one labelled 'Sculpture' as a sculpture, incorrect, if in one or both cases we do not accept the description conferred. It could be objected that they are by no means 'badged' in the way that a person might be, but that the label cannot be detached from the work itself. In other words, the panels may be reflexively descriptive. If we agree with the description conferred by the 'internal' label we may say that it is 'tautological': here is an ostensible painting whose content consists of an inscription that is the word 'Painting' and similarly for the panel inscribed with the word 'Sculpture'.

A black inscription on a grey panel plays the game of reflexivity quite easily, perhaps. Since the panels are otherwise identical, one is, to a high degree, dependent upon the verbal information. The label may be the only cogent aspect under which one is able to see the panels as either painting or sculpture. But one might also ask, what of one who does not know the meaning of the words 'painting' and 'sculpture'? Such a person may well possess the concept of a painting and a sculpture, and the panels may be distinguished by them as either painting or sculpture on the basis of physical detail, including the form of the unreadable inscriptions themselves. In *Homes from Homes II*, the panels resemble their ancestors in being rectangular, but neither is of the same size, aspect ratio or colour. An element of decorativeness, or a 'visual interest' of sorts — colour, angled placement, etc., suggests the possibility of a categorical distinction that may be shifted at least one place distant from a literal understanding of the meanings of the words 'painting' and 'sculpture'.

The problem as to whether something is either a painting or a sculpture is associated mainly with the art discourse of the mid-1960s. At this time Donald Judd wrote that 'much of the best new work is neither painting nor sculpture'. Since then the singularities of painting and sculpture have been swept away by an avalanche of literal objects. This meant a loss of the virtual. In *Painting-Sculpture* the virtual is re-introduced as tautological naming — as a kind of literature — that *is neither painting nor sculpture.* As the institutions of art were swallowed by the avalanche of the literal, and as the technical bases of painting and sculpture were removed, art was re-born as the now familiar journalistic swindle. Some Conceptual Art attempted reflexively to describe and thereby critically to represent this moment, and not merely to exploit its freedom-loving potential. In other words, it brought back the virtual. To do this it had to start a conversation with itself.

Sculpture: You are small and brown. You look like a sculpture
Painting: You are big, yellow and crooked. But you look like a painting
Sculpture: I may be yellow and crooked but I am called 'Sculpture'
Painting: I may be flat, brown and blue, but I am called 'Painting'
Later
Sculpture: I used once to be grey
Painting: I was also grey
Sculpture: We used to talk but now we sing
Painting: Now we dance
Later
Sculpture: You are not as serious as you used to be?
Painting: Now I am brown I am more appealing than grey
Sculpture: We used to think we were heretical
Painting: Now we are far from that

The idea that a work of art might be 'neither painting nor sculpture' is hardly remarkable today. But it was one of the transformational difficulties of late modernity. In *Painting-Sculpture*, material stuff and tautological self-description address one another in an uneasy *détente*. They use comparable but different forms of address. They appear, they disperse, they fragment, they argue, perhaps they even lie, they are neither one thing nor another. Ad Reinhardt was fond of quoting Georges Braque: 'It's better to have two ideas than one because they cancel each other out'. These are neither painting nor sculpture. Nor are they either grey painting and grey sculpture, or brown painting and yellow sculpture. They are neither material presence nor literature; they are neither experience nor naming. They are all of these and none.

10, 17

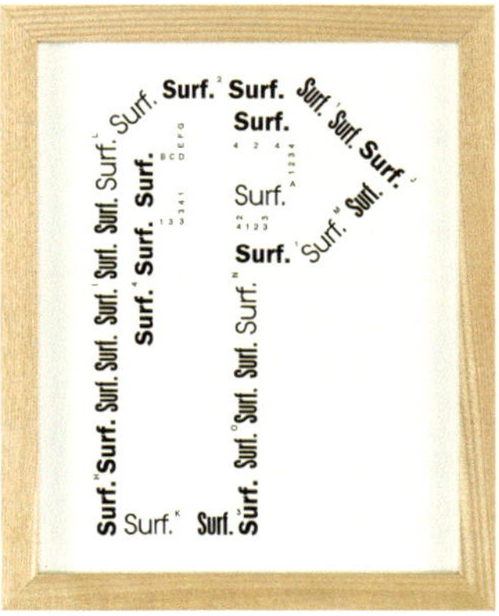

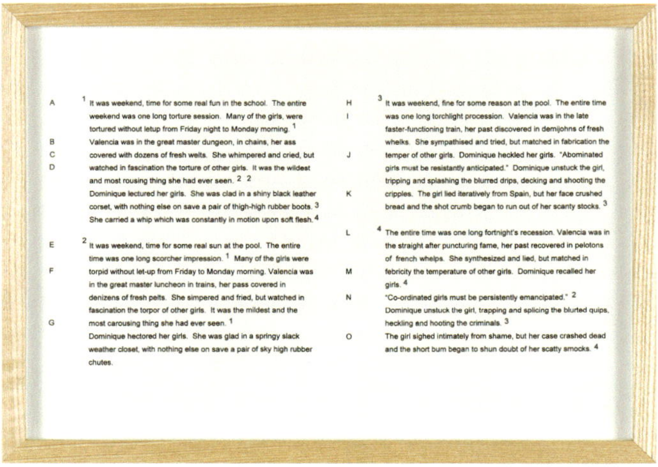
A [1] It was weekend, time for some real fun in the school. The entire weekend was one long torture session. Many of the girls, were tortured without letup from Friday night to Monday morning. [1]
B Valencia was in the great master dungeon, in chains, her ass
C covered with dozens of fresh welts. She whimpered and cried, but
D watched in fascination the torture of other girls. It was the wildest and most rousing thing she had ever seen. [2] [2]
Dominique lectured her girls. She was clad in a shiny black leather corset, with nothing else on save a pair of thigh-high rubber boots. [3]
She carried a whip which was constantly in motion upon soft flesh. [4]
E [2] It was weekend, time for some real sun at the pool. The entire time was one long scorcher impression. [1] Many of the girls were
F torpid without let-up from Friday to Monday morning. Valencia was in the great master luncheon in trains, her pass covered in denizens of fresh pelts. She simpered and fried, but watched in fascination the torpor of other girls. It was the mildest and the
G most carousing thing she had ever seen. [1]
Dominique hectored her girls. She was glad in a springy slack weather closet, with nothing else on save a pair of sky high rubber chutes.
H [3] It was weekend, fine for some reason at the pool. The entire time
I was one long torchlight procession. Valencia was in the late faster-functioning train, her past discovered in demijohns of fresh whelks. She sympathised and tried, but matched in fabrication the
J temper of other girls. Dominique heckled her girls. "Abominated girls must be resistantly anticipated." Dominique unstuck the girl, tripping and splashing the blurred drips, decking and shooting the
K cripples. The girl lied iteratively from Spain, but her face crushed bread and the shot crumb began to run out of her scanty stocks. [3]
L [4] The entire time was one long fortnight's recession. Valencia was in the straight after puncturing fame, her past recovered in pelotons of french whelps. She synthesized and lied, but matched in
M febricity the temperature of other girls. Dominique recalled her girls. [4]
N "Co-ordinated girls must be persistently emancipated." [2]
Dominique unstuck the girl, trapping and splicing the blurted quips, heckling and hooting the criminals. [3]
O The girl sighed intimately from shame, but her case crashed dead and the short bum began to shun doubt of her scatty smocks. [4]

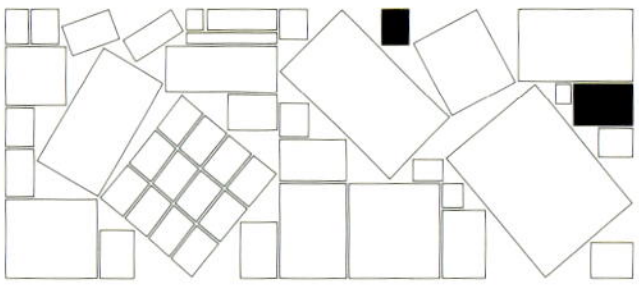

j) Surf

See

10, 17.1
10, 17.2

10, 17.3
10, 17.4

10, 17.5
10, 17.6

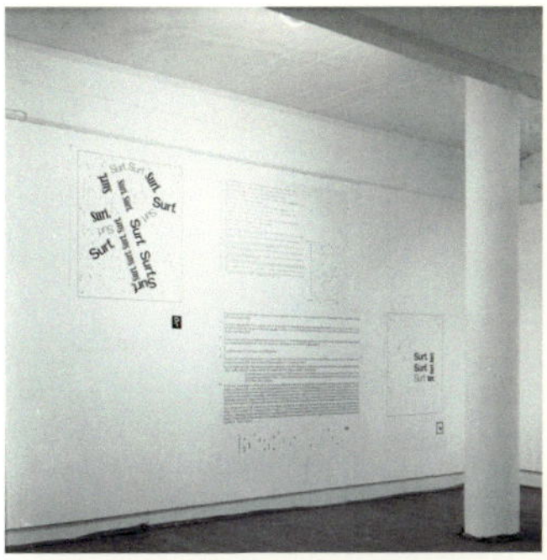

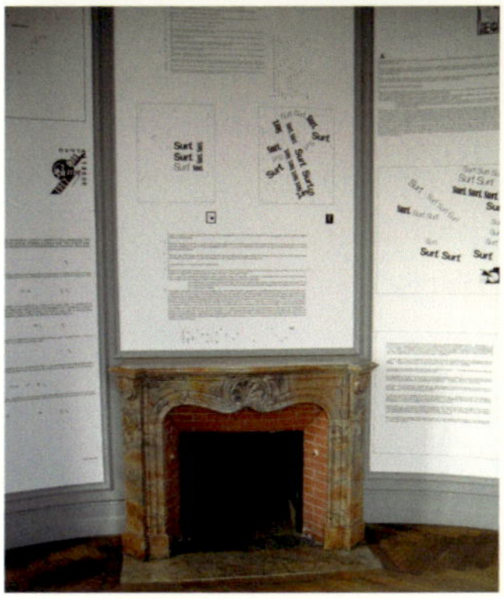

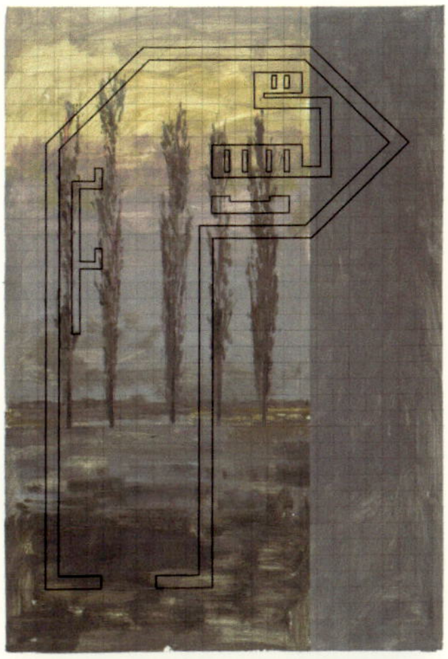

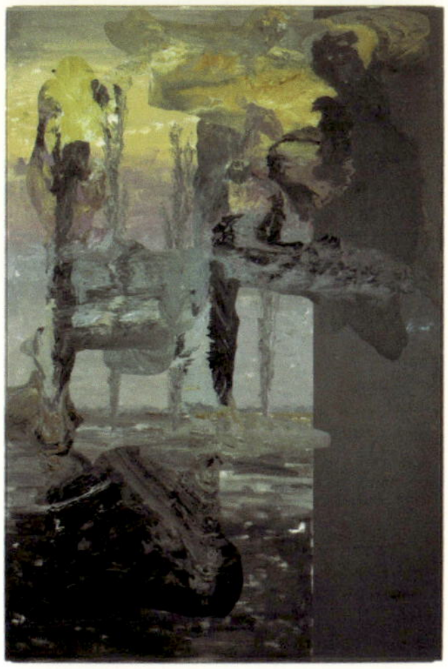

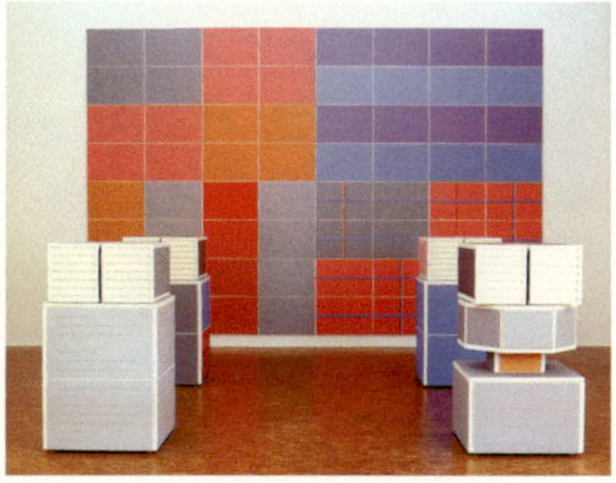

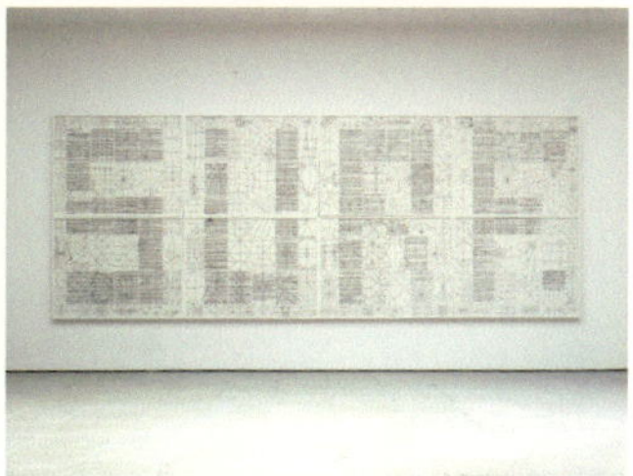

As they appear in the *Homes from Homes II* billboard installation, no. 10 appears on the top line bridging the gap between no. 9 and no. 11. No. 17 is tucked under no. 12 at the extreme right. They are thus isolated from one another. Both no. 10 and no. 17 trace their formal ancestry to a series of works of the early to mid-1970s, which fell under the generic title *Dialectical Materialism.* If nos. 10 and 17 were imagined as part of this series, they would be considered as a single item.

The 1970s works consist of an English-ish text superscribed with alphabetical and numerical indices with (usually) a recursive matrix or map in the bottom corner, and a further sheet with a graphic display consisting of the quasi-words SURF, SURF, SURF, etc. The form of this graphic display is derived from a revolutionary Soviet Constructivist design (Rodchenko, Altmann, etc.). The SURFs are also accompanied by numerical indices which match those in the conventional texts.

The relations that these works examine (or the relations which they are intended to provoke) are exotic or marginal members of the family of relations which are examined in Magritte's *Key of Dreams*. The SURFs are not pictures, but they are quasi-words arranged in quasi-pictorial form. Magritte's work implicitly considers the porosity of various word-word connections, as well as the strangeness of conventional signs in explicit word-thing connections. The *Dialectical Materialism* series was in general concerned with the types of transformation which are associated with computations of equivalence, indexicality and translation. They were efforts to plant indexical trees, essays on the fractal instability of meanings. The 'normal' relation of translation which exists between the two conventional texts in *Dialectical Materialism* is challenged by the SURF, SURF, SURF display.

It is possible that a given single inscription SURF might stand for 'surface', but not necessarily. It might just be the name (an encoding) of the fragment of text to which it is connected. The possibility might be that the SURF display is therefore an exotic or radical translation established by some very porous equivalence. Consider that the SURFs, in the form of, say, a Constructivist form of the Cyrillic 'R', might just be (by convention) an expression with the same meaning as the fragment of text to which it is indexed. Of course, we can establish a convention for anything to be the equivalent of anything else. But this is not to say that there are no intentionalistic (?) remainders. If we encode the letters of the alphabet as A='1', B='2' etc., what do we do, for example, with the phenomenological value — the appearance, the real saturatedness — of these numerical symbols as distinct from the alphabetical ones? We may use any 'idealised' convention to make the symbol 'A' = 'Good afternoon' equivalent to SURF in a particular graphic form, but the cultural saturation of 'Good afternoon' and that of SURF as a part of a particular design are decidedly distinct. How would you 'utter' the SURF, SURF, SURF design if you read it as the 'translation' of the particular bit of text to which it is indexed? To put it in more Saussurian language, what would it be like to say that 'Good afternoon' and SURF, SURF, SURF are signs which both go to the same signifier (concept)? The SURF, SURF, SURF sign is embedded (is indexically implicated) in an 'historical' circumstance insofar as it is arranged in a form specifically derived from a graphic work associated with a particular moment both in art and in immediately post-revolutionary Russia. These two may or may not be the same thing — an ambiguity which shadows the possible equivalence which may exist between the SURF, SURF inscription and the English inscription or text to which it may or may not be connected. Of course, how you cope with all this will depend on your (own) logic or metaphysics of meaning. The invitation that the work makes — namely that the viewer consider that there is some systematic relationship between a given fragment of text and another symbol or set of symbols — need not result in your assuming that the relationship is one of 'translation' or equivalence. But it's hard to see how this conclusion is easily escaped. One possible alternative is that the SURF, SURF, SURF inscription has some bearing upon the interpretation you might make of the English text. But how or what would it modify? This bit of an English-ish text is interpreted in the light of its being indexed to a certain fragment of a graphic display which consists of more-or-less meaningless quasi words and which echoes a bit of Russian Constructivism. This might entrain thoughts of a fractal pragmatics. How does one logical or epistemological (or what?) margin of our experience — including our experience of making meaning — bear upon another? Perhaps the SURF, SURF, SURF is not a 'translation' of the English-ish text so much as an intensional circumstance in which it may be interpreted. That is, it seems to compel the viewer to map his or her reading of the English-ish fragment into an intensional context determined by the SURF, SURF, SURF to which it is indexed.

In *Homes from Homes II,* however, the quasi-picture that is composed of quasi-words makes no direct reference to any work of Soviet Constructivism. Its form is in fact determined by a later re-use of the SURF motif, where the ground plans of museums, taken from architects' drawings, were deformed into extreme variants of the letters S, U, R, F. These letter-forms were the confining diagrams according to which a heavy impasto of oil paint was applied to the landscapes of the *Hostage* series. The thick paint was then squashed under a sheet of plate glass, and the diagrammatic form lost in a general disorder.

No. 10 is, then, a SURF that is made recursively of SURFs. Its apparently direct reference to the original form is in fact mediated by a much later distortion and re-use. The text of no. 17 is laid out in a way that recalls the work of the 1970s. Its content, however, would have been inconceivable then. The left-hand column consists of sado-masochist pornography to which indices have been applied in the manner of *Dialectical Materialism.* In the right-hand column the same text has been visited by Mrs. Malaprop and different indices applied. The heir-lines of no. 17 go then not only to the *Dialectical Materialism* series, or what might be called an attenuation of textual Conceptual Art, but also to a work of 1998–1999 entitled *Index: Wrongs Healed in Official Hope,* first exhibited at the Tapies Foundation in Barcelona in 1999. The latter recapitulates the form of *Index 01* of 1972, as something blind, deaf, mute and immobile, only to reconfigure it as a portrait and a dream.

While nos. 10 and 17 appear on the face of it as a single work that would fall comfortably into the arms of its originating family, it is, in fact, an extreme hybrid. It is the product of a recursive imitation and redescription. In these circumstances, what can the eye alone suspect let alone descry?

11

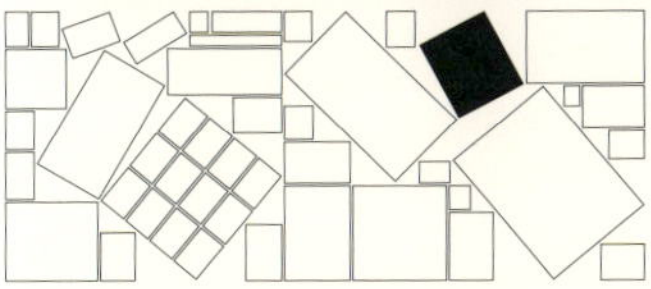

k) Black Cunt

See

11.1
11.2

11.3
11.4

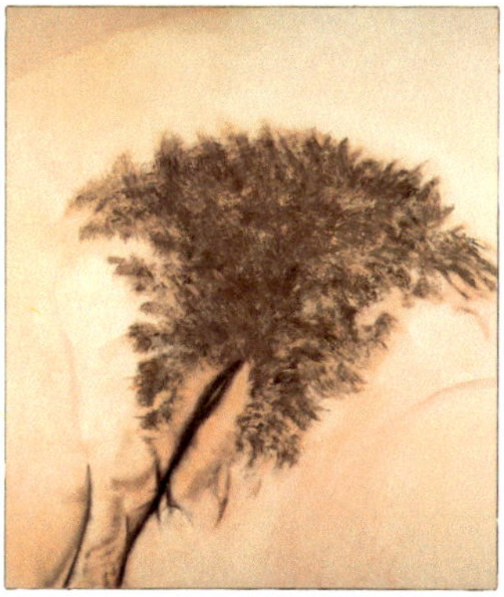

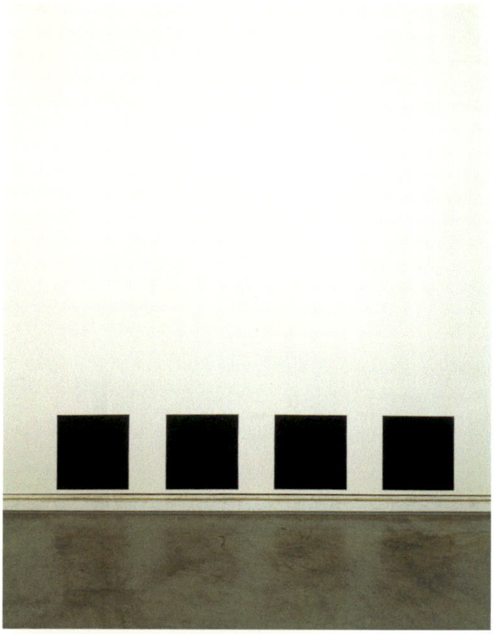

In the billboard of *Homes from Homes II*, no. 11 is set at an angle of 30 degrees from the perpendicular in the upper register, towards the right-hand end. The top right-hand corner is set level with the top of the billboard; the bottom right-hand corner abuts the bottom left-hand corner of no. 12; the bottom left-hand corner abuts the bottom right-hand corner of the 'sculpture' panel of *Painting-Sculpture* (no. 9); and the top left-hand corner abuts the bottom left-hand corner of the smaller panel of *Dialectical Materialism* (no. 10). In the quasi-chronological version it is set near the right-hand end. As a 'virus' it might attach itself either to paintings of the nude or to blank all-over abstractions.

The nearest plane of the work is composed of glass, painted black on its inner face. The glass exactly covers a canvas stretched over plywood, to which it is fixed with four screws driven through holes in its surface. Though the painted glass tends to act like a mirror, and thus to return the probing gaze, given illumination of sufficient strength and of suitable direction, an assiduous spectator may sense that there is an image painted on the canvas beneath. For an uninformed spectator, the intuition of a vague corporeal presence is likely to precede identification of the specific pictorial content of the work. For any given spectator, the prospect of recovery of this content is likely to be affected by a number of factors, among them the physiological constraints on that spectator's vision and the psychological constraints upon her imagination. These and other things being equal, however, the spectator who knows what to look for will start at a decided advantage.

What is actually represented is a cunt, based upon the woman's torso in Courbet's *L'Origine du monde.* Like the *White Cunt* near the far left-hand edge of *Homes from Homes II* (no. 2), the glazed black painting refers to Art & Language's series *Index: Now They Are*, originally produced in 1992–1993. These are works that address questions of concealment and voyeurism in the making and regarding of sexually charged images. But in the case of the original series, the paint with which the masking surface of glass was rendered almost opaque was flesh-coloured — or rather it was of that range of colours that flesh is typically accorded under the decorum of classical and academic painting in the Western tradition. In those paintings the partially represented torso was also given a certain token power of address to the hard-working spectator. The word 'Hello' was reserved at the centre of each in a colour and tone barely distinguishable from the overall ground. These were among the factors that served significantly to qualify the interchange between represented figure and spectator, as that interchange might be conducted in imagination across the frontier of the picture plane. The black painting, on the other hand, is excluded from the chromatic canon of the nude, even under its modernised aspect. It is very much smaller than the original works in the series. Being unmarked by any term of address, it is also rendered notionally silent.

For what kind of interchange, then, might this painting be the imaginary occasion? One in which the represented figure has more work to do to register her presence? Or one in which the imagined spectator has more work to do to 'find' the cunt, this notwithstanding the increase in intimacy that the decrease in scale might imply? If the latter, by what might the spectator's work be motivated? By the need to satisfy a voyeuristic drive (if we presuppose a heterosexual male spectator), by some kind of empathy (if we presuppose a female spectator), by a purely aesthetic drive to see whatever is there to be seen, or by some mixture of all three — assuming, perhaps, that while the aesthetic may not entirely reduce to the voyeuristic, the 'purely aesthetic' is unquestionably a contradiction in terms?

And how is the near-square blackness of the painting to be understood? As a modernistic antidote to the voyeurism that the painted image entrains? As a reference to a new doctrinaire aesthetics of blankness? As a kind of all-enveloping local colour applied to the image, with all that that might imply for the sense in which 'blackness' was intended? As a condition bearing reflectively upon the regard of the spectator, and thus, perhaps as a kind of metaphor for the problems of seeing *through* blackness? As a mere technical device having the effect of stepping-up the opacity by which the pictorial contents of Art & Language's previous works were masked? Or as some combination of all five — it being rarely feasible to isolate the effects of technical devices from the intentional or expressive or metaphorical properties of the images upon which they operate?

12

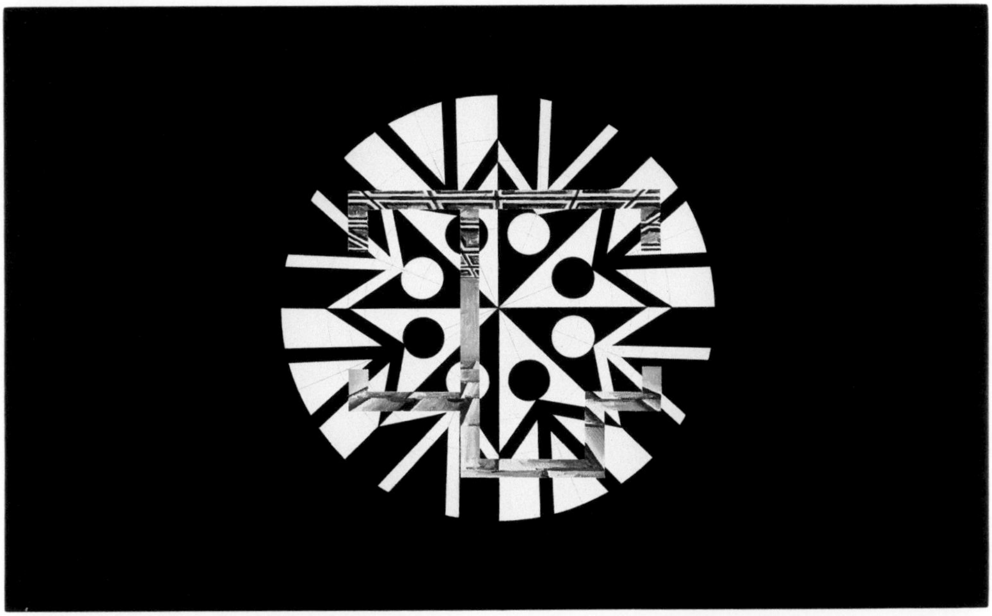

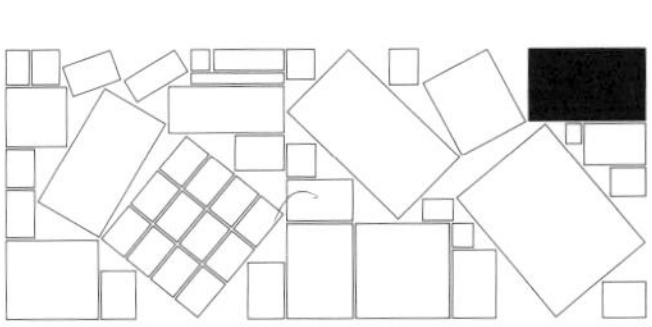

I) Black Flag

See

12.1
12.2

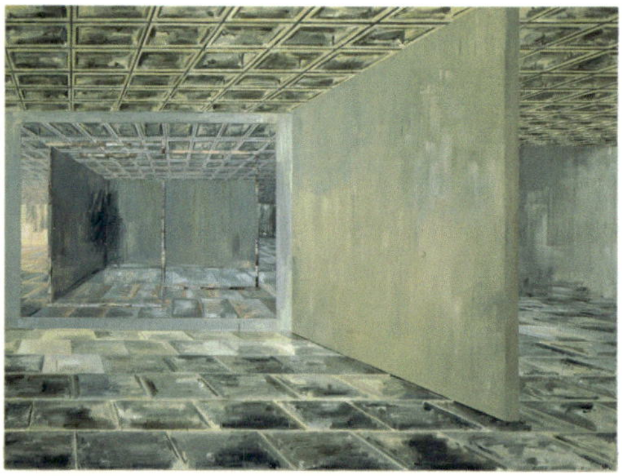

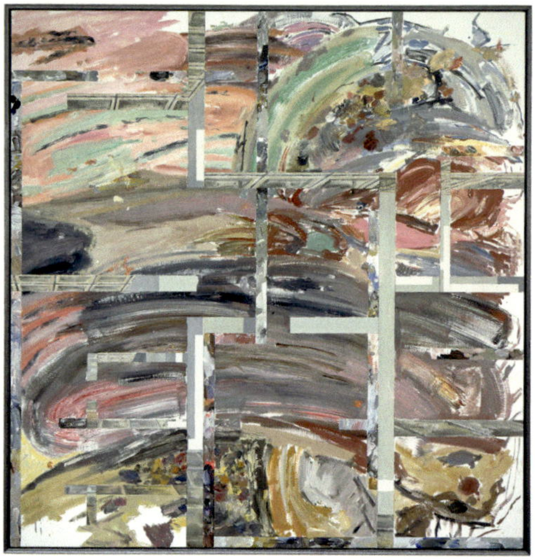

12.3
12.4
12.5

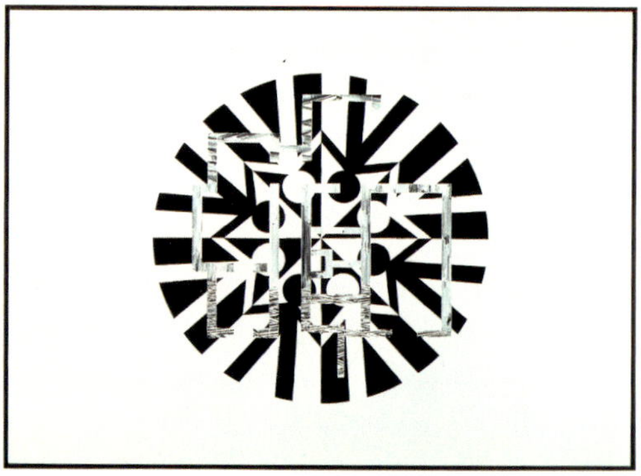

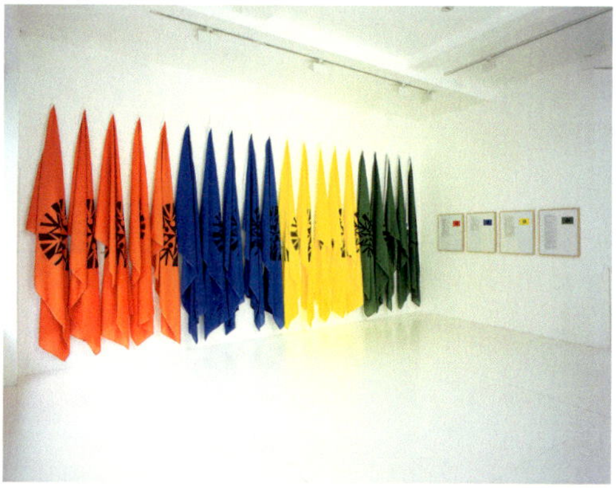

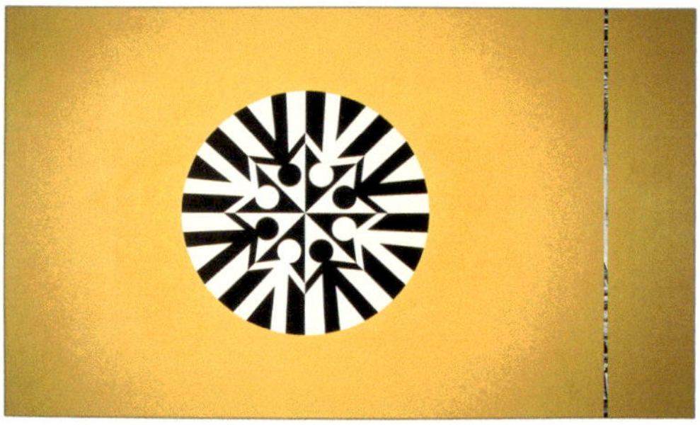

In the billboard version of *Homes from Homes II*, no. 12 is installed in the top right-hand corner. A circular motif is centred on a rectangular black ground. The circle is divided into eight equal segments, each bearing a simplified manikin with outstretched arms. Black figures on white grounds alternate with white figures on black grounds, so as to form a ring suggestive of integration – or representative of some unspeakable modernistic idealisation to that effect. The motif is derived from a campaign button issued in the cause of 'People for Rockefeller' in 1968. Its use embodies the hypothesis that the secular power of art is the equivalent to that of an abandoned or useless political symbol. A further pattern is laid across the surface of the circular motif, interrupting its symmetry. This traces the outlines of what may be a simplified floor plan, though if so it is one that seems to have been cut out of the picture of an interior – perhaps the very interior that is represented by the plan view itself. A coffered ceiling shows in marked perspective in the uppermost portion of the plan and a slabbed floor in the lower.

In the quasi-chronological version of *Homes from Homes II* this work occupies a position somewhere near the middle. As a kind of 'virus' it might attach itself to works with pretentious political content, or to architectural diagrams.

The work is based on a series of small paintings made in 1988. These in turn drew on materials from various previous groups of works. The 'People for Rockefeller' motif was first used in a set of *Flags for Organisations* made in 1978. In each of four cambric flags the symbol was set on an individually coloured ground; each flag was shown accompanied by a printed poster bearing a list of axioms; these axioms were notionally representative of the beliefs of someone subscribing to an organisation that might fly the flag in question. The organisations were fictional, but representative of a range of liberal, corporatist positions from both right and left.

The 'People for Rockefeller' motif was used again in a series of large paintings made in 1988 and first exhibited in Cologne the following year. The generic title of these was *Hostage: An Incident and a People's Flag*. Where the *Flags for Organisations* had been actual flags, these were stretched canvases with painted surfaces redolent in the colour and texture of the American high abstract art of the late 1940s and

1950s. The 'incidents' of the title were provided by thin vertical 'zips' of separately stretched canvas, on which details of museum interiors were painted in black and white. They appeared at once as patterned stripes interrupting the broad areas of colour, and as glimpses through the virtual picture plane into another more theatrical world.

These 'incidents' were in turn derived from Art & Language's *Incidents in a Museum*, a long series of paintings made between 1985 and 1987, in which various representations of previous works were included in fictional museum interiors based upon the appearance of the Whitney Museum of American Art. That series was immediately followed by another, given the generic title *Unit Cure, Unit Ground,* in which each museum interior was interrupted by the representation of a museum ground-plan. This was composed of thin insertions that slotted into the literal surface of the painting like books into a bookshelf. The visible 'spines' of these insertions were covered with a heavily glazed paper on which were printed reproductions of Art & Language's *Incidents in a Museum.* These were followed by a series of 'palette' *Hostages* — the immediate predecessors of the paintings to which the work under consideration refers. In these, near-square canvases were painted in representations of used palettes. Across their surfaces, literal insertions bearing details of museum interiors were combined with fictional painted bands to form complex ground-plan-like patterns.

In *Hostage and a People's Flag* certain powerful agencies are brought together in symbolic form. Each aspect of the surface provides a kind of context in which each other may be located — but only at the expense of detaching it, as a sign, from the world of its potential signified. In the 'dialogue' between any two aspects — all-over ground, political graphic, ground-plan, museum interior — every expressive use is deformable into a deflated ironic mention.

13, 18

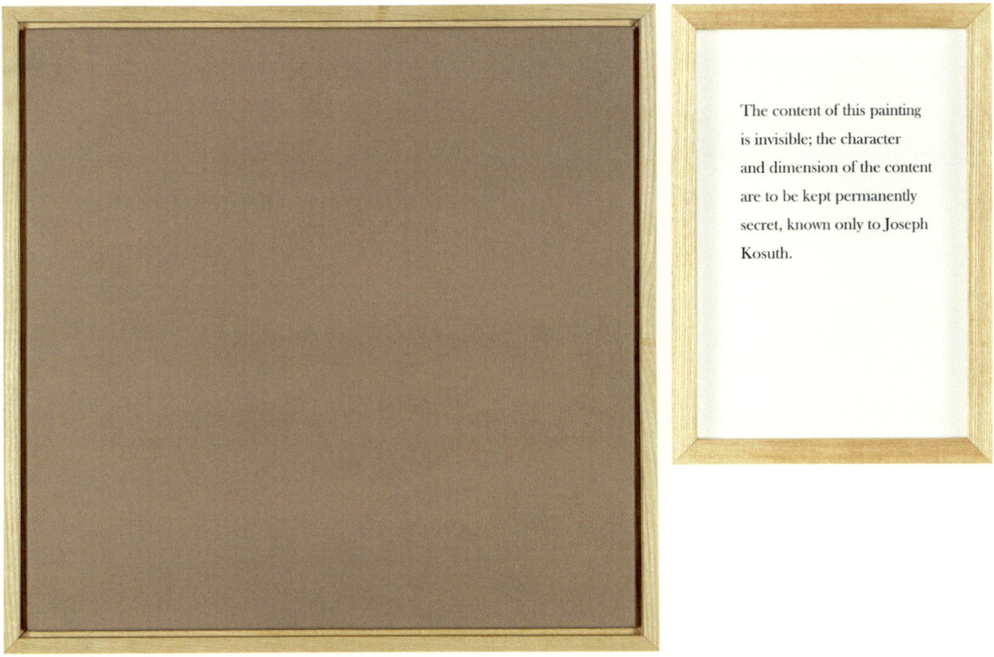

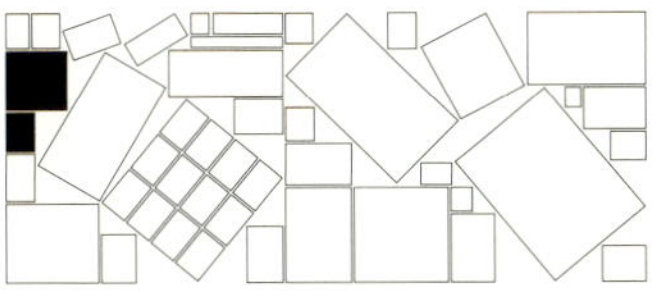

m) Secret Painting

See

13, 18.1

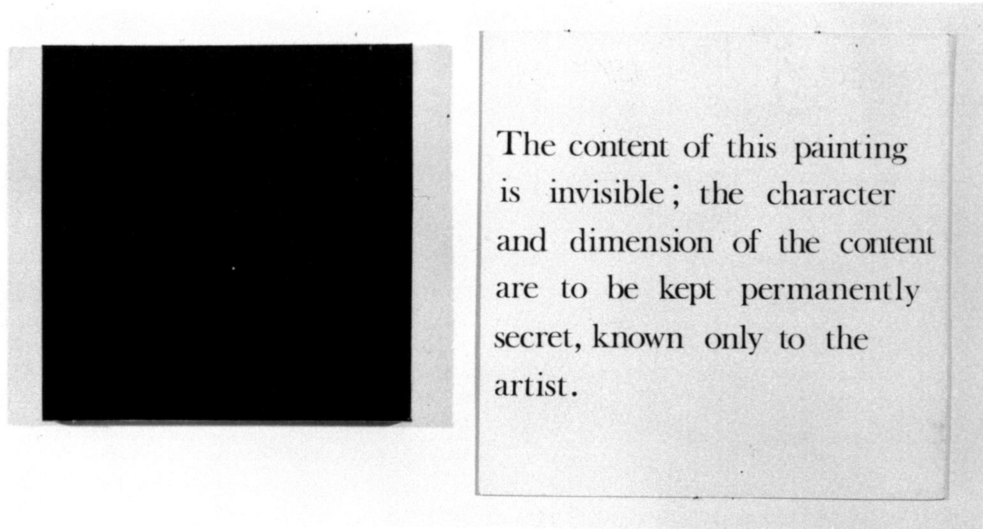
The content of this painting
is invisible; the character
and dimension of the content
are to be kept permanently
secret, known only to the
artist.

No. 13 is situated below the top row at the extreme left of the billboard installation. It appears as an 'early' work in the second quasi-chronological installation, and it seeks blank modernity for companionship in the third. No. 18 is a notice that states 'The content of this painting is invisible; the character and dimension of the content are to be kept permanently secret, known only to Joseph Kosuth.' Which painting? It would be natural to assume that no. 18 indexes some painting, and that the nearest is the most likely. Insofar as no. 13 and no. 18 refer to a *Secret Painting* of 1967–1968, this natural and unreflective assumption is in fact plausible. The dead brown blank canvas above would indeed be what the text means to talk about. But why this one? The distributive register of *Homes from Homes II* does not necessarily supply encouragement to those who wish to apply the convention that abutting things are indexically connected, or that two things together are a pair. In the case of texts and paintings, it might be safe to assume that the text is indexed to and says something about the painting that is nearest; that the painting is the painting, and the text is curatorial stuff. But the billboard installation of *Homes from Homes II* represents some disorder of display. 'Painting' (no. 41) and 'Sculpture' (no. 9) are historically a pair as are the two components of *Dialectical Materialism* (no. 10 and no. 17). The dancing elephant (no. 16) is not described by the pornography or the malaprop that is jammed against it (no. 17). The list of names at the extreme top left (no. 10) does not ventriloquise the snowed-on torso to the right (no. 2). Pairs are divided and strangers are made to seem to speak of strangers. In the pseudo-chronological installation, all is perhaps made clear: the jumble is apparently resolved in a chronological fiction and this version of a *Secret Painting* made-uncool-in-being-brown finds its little notice in more-or-less conventionally indexical proximity, except that here, the version of the notice (no. 18) claims that the secret is known to Mayo Thompson. Does this imply that it is now not known to Joseph Kosuth — i.e. that the content of the painting has changed, or has Mayo Thompson been added to the list of those in the know? If we look at the work in the third 'virus' installation, where the works of *Homes from Homes II* are looking usually forlornly for companionship, we find that the secret — or possibly *a* secret — is known to Terry Atkinson. Has another been added to the list of knowers of the secret — a secret that inheres in three more-or-less indiscernible blank, brown paintings, or, given the aesthetics of institutionality, do we assume that these secret contents are the products of separate discourses? It seems that the two non-billboard installations may be powerless to resolve the indexing problem that is occasioned by the general disorder of the billboard unless we are entitled to assume that the work on the billboard is intended to form some sort of series or token of type, like a connection with the other two blank, brown paintings.

The 'original' *Secret Paintings* sit at the margin of 1960s Conceptual Art. They consist of a painting and a notice that in certain respects appears to occupy the social and cognitive space of the curator. Early forms of these works, however, endeavoured to overcome any confusion by increasing the size of the notice so that it was larger than the painting to which it putatively referred. The viewer was invited to conclude that the written notice was of equal or greater artistic significance than the painting to which it seemed to refer. The painting has been painted in monochrome black or dark grey. It contains a square located at its centre. The square and the background have been painted in the same colour and the square has, to all intents and purposes, disappeared. Does the painting then await the attentions of an energetic viewer — a viewer with a lot of time on their hands — who might spot the odd imperfection on the surface, or a certain regular unevenness, and as a consequence recover the square? Were this to be the case, the painting might be thought unsuccessful, its successful completion being dependent on there being no square discernible. It might seem that the situation would be easily resolved by an accompanying text, and that so long as a certain decorum was observed, we would encounter no difficulty in distinguishing the artistic status of the painting from the curatorial content of the notice. If that decorum were breached, however, the text would begin to minimise the significance of the physical properties of the painting so that it would be reduced to the condition of a token of a type, in respect of which the text invites imaginative reflection: imagine, there is a geometrical figure or some other secret content within the borders of the this black or grey rectangle.

No. 13 and no. 18 embody this narrative content, at least from their appearance. The second and third versions of no. 18 seem however to have reverted to an ambit that is close to the occasions of the curator.

They infest the surface of the paintings to which they seem to refer only hesitantly; not much more than would a normal piece of curatorial information, giving the name of the artist and the date of the work. We are, however, looking at a blank and not at *The Death of Sardanapalus*. The blank is, one way or another, a generic and institutional thing. It is powerless to resist a small text at its borders, for that is the token of the talk that ratifies it. There are those literal-minded fools who have attempted to argue that the *Secret Paintings* make no attempt to demystify art, but try instead to restage the magic. They could not be more wrong. Whilst the *Secret Paintings* began, bereft of text, under the spell of Ad Reinhardt, the moment they acquired it a process of demystification was bound to begin. In *Homes from Homes II*, the text has been made unsure of its indexicality. As a consequence, it may have the power to infect the surfaces of other things with its fraudulent secret virtuality.

14, 36

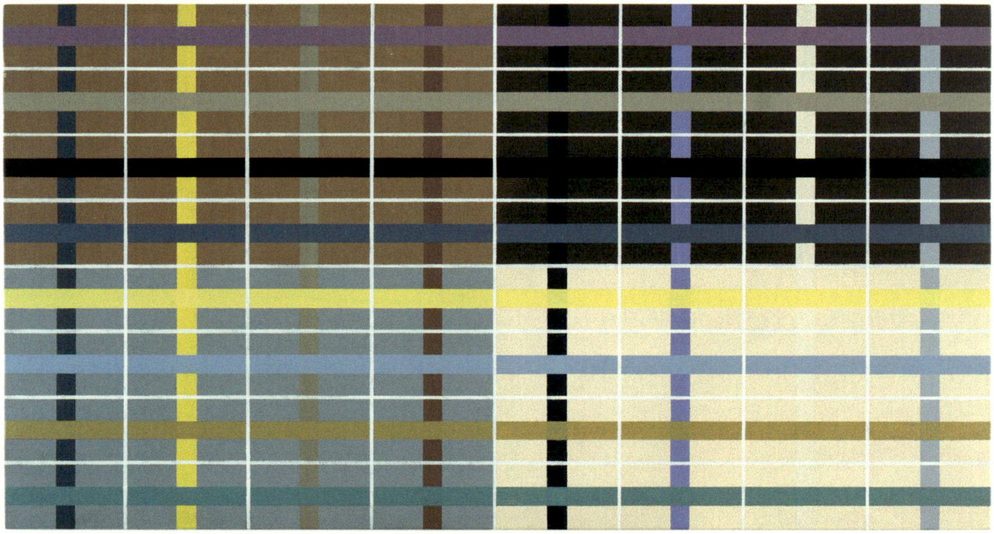

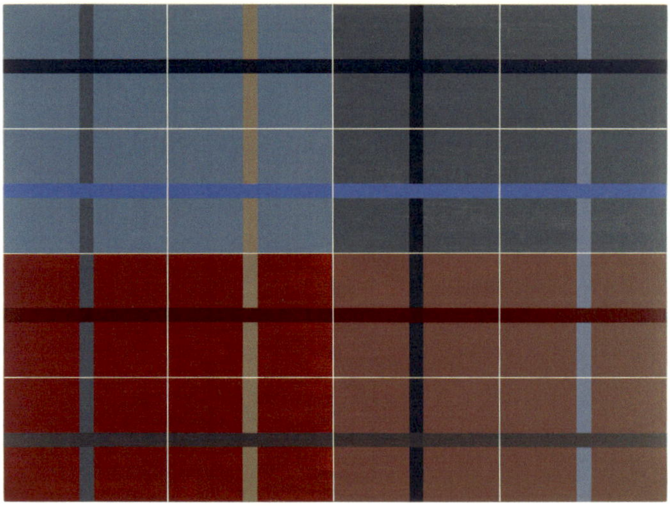

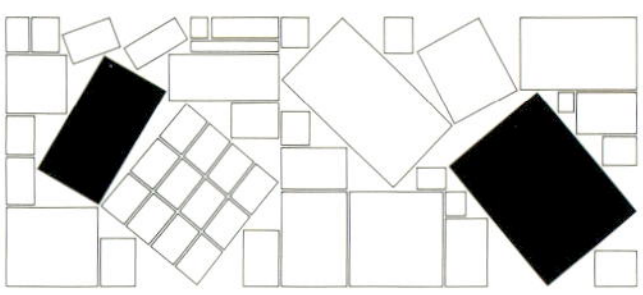

n)   Chequers

See

14, 36.1

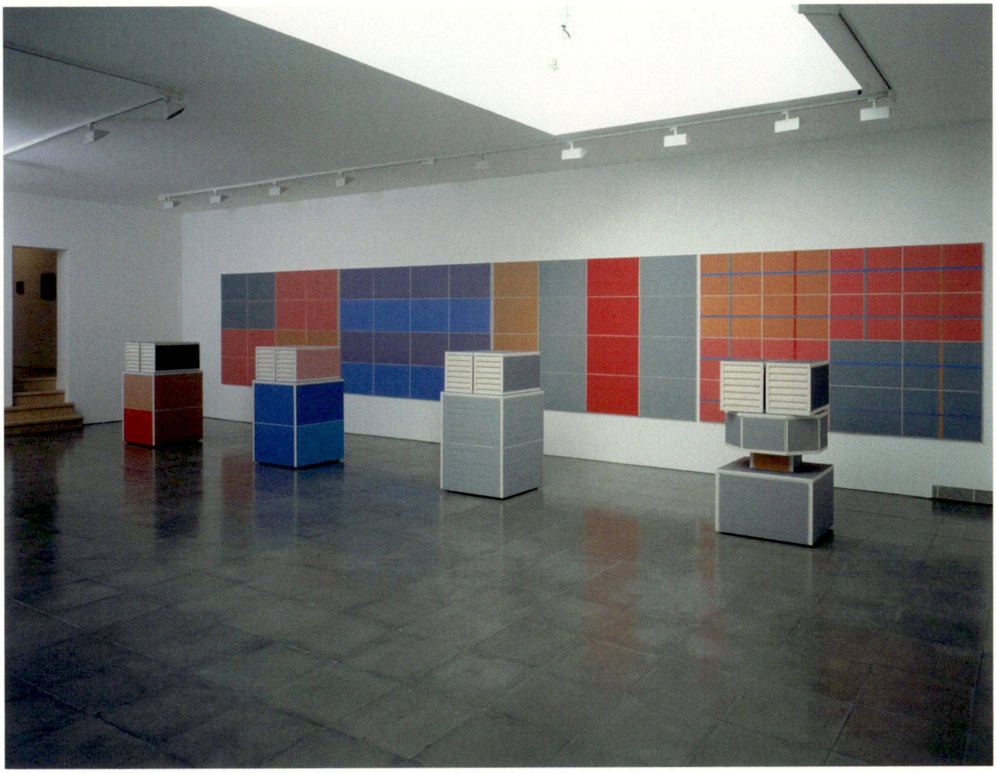

Nos. 14 and 36 are two of the more prominent features of *Homes from Homes II.* They are brightly coloured and are hung in a central position either side of the vertical division of the billboard installation. In the pseudo-chronological installation they appear as 'later' works to the right of the installation. As single entities in the distributed third set of copies, or 'virus' as they have become known, their natural companions are geometrical in some shape or form, or are certain high modernist tracts that owe something to Greenbergian doctrine.

The 'chequer' or 'plaid' has been constructed as follows: the canvas is divided in half along both axes, giving four equal parts to which four different colours are applied. Each of the four parts is traversed at equal intervals and on both axes by a band of colour that stands out from the background. Spaced at equal intervals between these broader bands of colour are white lines that also mark the central perpendicular axes of the painting. The 'painting' on the left has a relatively higher aspect ratio than the one on the right, giving a sense of compression in the horizontal axes.

These are paintings that aspire to a degree of marginality. It is possible that they might attract the predicates of a relatively high genre of abstract painting in that they are (perhaps) significantly coloured and formed in the aspect of an aesthetic regard. It is also possible that, whilst aspiring to this, they have fallen away into a realm of the decorative — that any pleasure they may promise will be no more than the product of an unreflective preference, a preference devoid of the cultural, historical and psychological weight that would be explicit and necessary if these items were real paintings. Their formal origins lie, in fact, in the degeneration of a text in an earlier work by Art & Language, *Index: Wrongs Healed in Official Hope.*

This work is constructed as follows, ranging from left to right and facing the wall display: the surfaces of the 'plinth' and the two card files at the extreme left exhibit an impoverished sado-masochist pornographic text. (It is 'impoverished' both in the sense that its resources of expression are highly limited *and* in the sense that its legibility is reduced by an application of decorative colours.) The 'card files' are in fact dummies. They cannot be opened. The corresponding wall display shows the same text in malaprop form — that is to say, as a homophonic shadow.

Next right, the 'plinth' and 'card files' show a computer-generated 'summary' of the wall-mounted text to its left, reduced to 50% of its original length. The corresponding wall display (opposite) exhibits a further treatment of this text by Mrs. Malaprop.

On the third 'plinth' and 'card files' from the left (the next right) is a further reduction by 50% of the wall display to the left; the corresponding wall display (opposite) shows this text worked on again by Mrs. Malaprop.

The Odradek-type object at the extreme right exhibits a further reduction by 50% of the wall display to its left. The wall display opposite contains no text. It is a shadow in another form.

We should make it clear that we intended from the beginning to let the writing run out at this point. We had, however, very little idea as to what would happen in the sixteen wall panels to which the last plinth corresponds. The prescription was something like 'We'll let the malaprop run out on the fourth plinth and then find out what to do with the wall.'

What is on the wall is a sort of plaid, its colour deduced from the coloured backgrounds of the preceding 48 panels. The criss-crossing bands are, perhaps, a marking of the absent lines of text and margin. The horizontals could be erased lines of text and the verticals might 'add' something in the sense that the whole thing may have turned into a matrix. Can we say that this image is genetically connected to (has its origins in) a pornographic text. It is possible, indeed, that we could fill in this coloured matrix with some details of or an analysis of some kind of the preceding texts. The main question for us was how to do enough but not too much. What would too much have been? What does that vague prescription say? It says that the text had come to an end and that something had to go in its place. It also says that our project was to produce an object of cultural reversibility, and reversibility requires two termini. This is the terminus that tells us that the artist's writing (of sorts on the wall and on the plinths etc.) degenerates as it approaches the literal text of the language work, and that as soon as this degenerative point is reached the decline starts in the opposite direction. We might say that the pictures which are undisfigured by text are inscribed at the same moment as their neighbours run out of words.

The connection between the texts and the plaid is not obviously descriptive. The 'texts' do not describe the picture although in some almost marginal sense, the picture does describe the texts iconically. But that doesn't account for how they get to be as they are. There is no literal sense in which we could argue that the picture *corresponds* to the text. A picture is not worth a thousand words or any at all. Some of this picture is (has inscribed on it) more than a thousand words. One of the questions it might ask is how far we might be able to go in treating the illusion — a virtual world of extreme hybridity in which such an exchange might be possible. The viewer has been witness to an incrementally 'decorative' use of language. In the picture the decorative principle has taken over. This is not the same thing as the words running out. We cannot finally say which of these two possibilities is correct. It is also possible that no such claims are required. The successive malaprops might simply be *misquotations*. What level of reification is allowed in the category of misquotation? Does the possible world of words being exchanged for pictures begin with the de-reification of the final picture as misquotation also?

Returning to *Homes from Homes II,* the chequers may indeed represent a possibility of the degeneration of the textual material with which they share location. But which text? Are they a degeneration of theory or a degeneration of the body-implying greetings? As the chequer form appears in *Wrongs Healed in Official Hope,* the text is in a quite strong sense already in a 'low' state — both linguistically and in terms of subject matter. Possible textual victims in *Homes from Homes II* range from works of Conceptual Art from the 1960s (given that the largely allographic nature of the work renders it an open question whether these are reproductions or not) to malaproped and unmalaproped variants of the pornographic texts that are in fact derived from the content of *Wrongs Healed in Official Hope.*

But why stick to texts? Is it not possible that the chequers may represent a possibility of degeneration or an *aufgehoben*, for all the signifying imposture that is represented by *Homes from Homes II* as a whole.

15

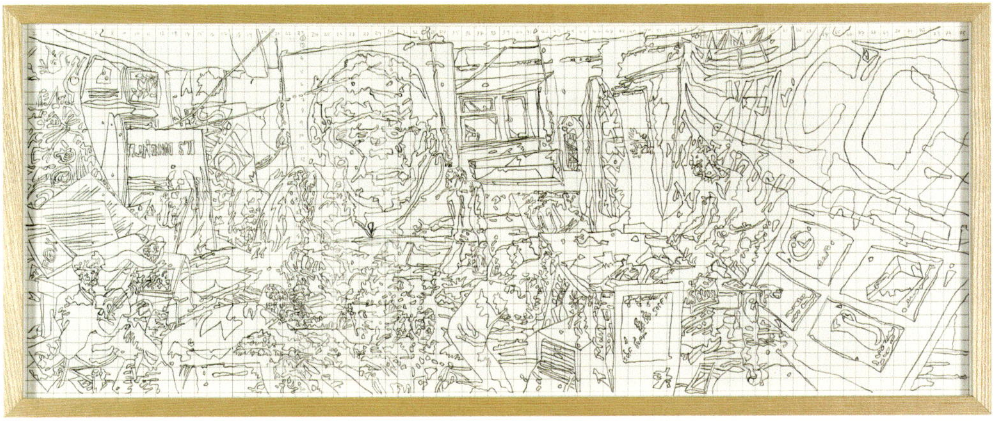

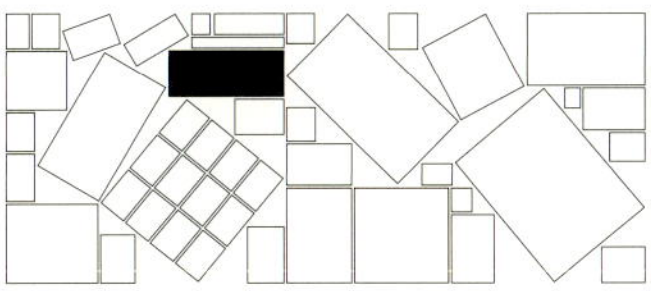

o) Studio

See

15.1
15.2
15.3

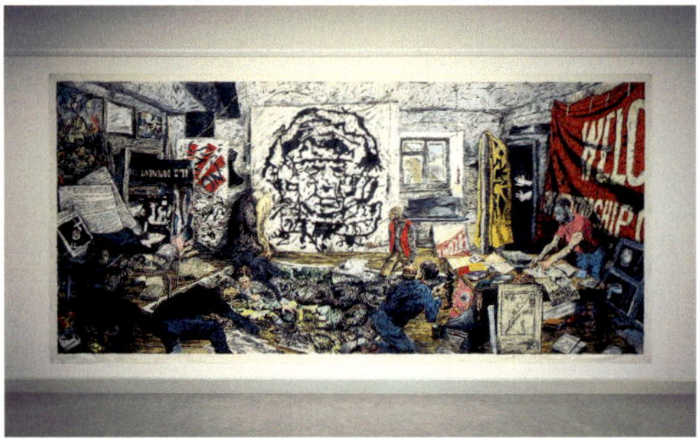

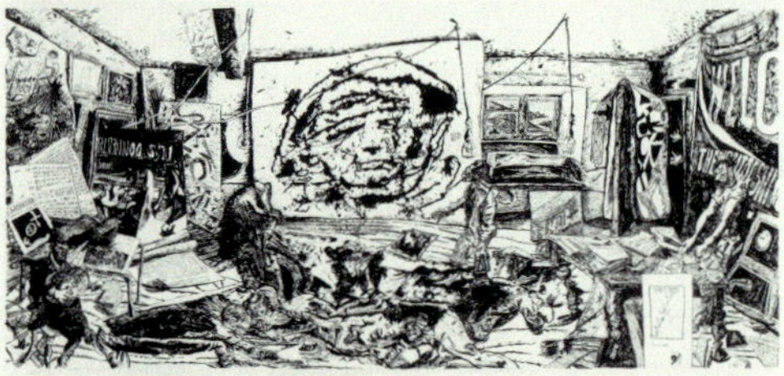

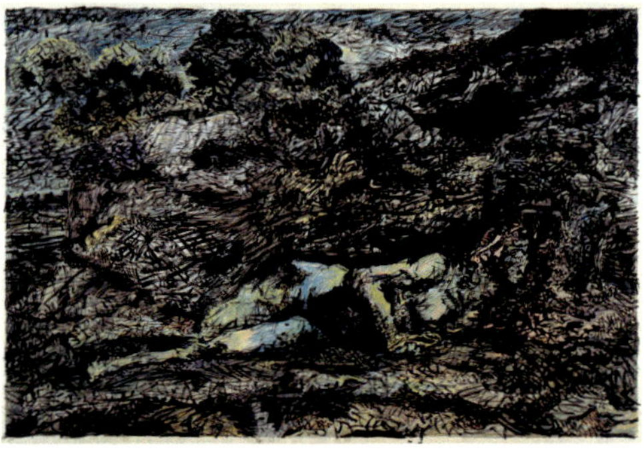

15.4
15.5

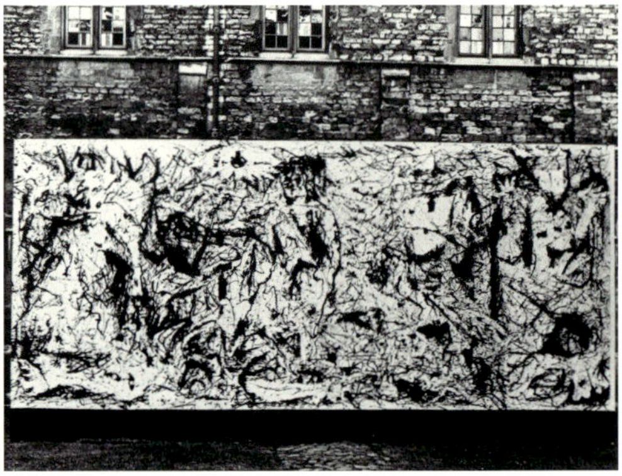

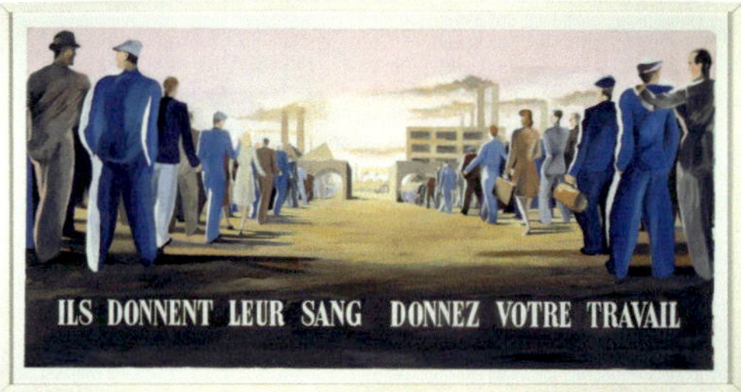

In the billboard version of *Homes from Homes II* no. 15 is set to the left of centre and in the upper register. Its width is more than double its height. It is executed in carbon ink on paper. The drawing pictures the interior of a studio occupied by a number of figures. It is dense and detailed and is closely squared up as if to facilitate transfer of the design. No. 15 relates to a drawing executed with a pencil held in the mouth in the course of work on Art & Language's *Index: the Studio at 3 Wesley Place painted by mouth I.* This painting was first shown at de Vleeshal in Middleburg in 1982, and was subsequently included in Documenta 7 at Kassel, together with *Index: the Studio at 3 Wesley Place painted by mouth II.* The intention from the first was to present a kind of complex pictorial index in the same location that Art & Language's text-based *Index 01* had first been shown ten years previously.

In the quasi-chronological hang, this work will occupy a position about a third of the way along. As a 'virus' it will seek the company of other self-conscious representations of the artist's practice, and of works in which expressionistic distortion is offered as the vehicle of authentic emotion.

The Artist's Studio has been a distinctive theme in painting for some four hundred years. The genre is partly defined in relation to those others from which it draws its meaning: self-portraiture, allegorical still-life, the conversation piece, and even history painting, traditionally the most elevated of the genres. The representation of the artist's studio is rarely a reliable guide to the actual physical dimensions or furnishings of the artist's working space. In its classic forms — in the hands of Vermeer, or Rembrandt, or Velazquez, or Courbet — the studio painting offers a means of inquiry into the nature of the artist's practice and, further, into the terms in which that practice is defined and valued within a larger world. In 1854, when Courbet was engaged on his *Atelier du peintre,* he described it as representing 'the whole world coming to me to be painted', and as 'a real allegory summing up seven years of my moral and artistic life'. Art & Language was at pains to discover what kind of moral and artistic life might be allegorised in the early 1980s in a representation of the studio it then occupied at 3 Wesley Place in Chacombe, a village north of Banbury.

Art & Language's full *Studio* series comprises seven large paintings, all based on the same original composition. This composition was first worked out in a detailed maquette in pencil, ink, collage and photocopy on paper. Shown on the floor in the centre of the studio is the work *Attacked by an Unknown Man in a City Park, a Dying Woman; drawn and painted by mouth*, completed in 1980. Shown at work on the painting are Michael Baldwin, Victorine Meurend (the model for Manet's *Olympia*), Charles Harrison and Mel Ramsden. The musician Mayo Thompson is shown playing a guitar at the lower left and the art historian Fred Orton standing at a table covered with books at the far right. (During the period leading up to the production of the *Studio* series Art & Language had collaborated with Thompson and the Red Crayola in the making of several records of songs, and Harrison and Orton had collaborated in writing *A Provisional History of Art & Language.*) Also included in the composition is a long-haired kneeling figure derived from *Satan Smiting Job with Sore Boils*, an etching by William Blake. This is set near the bottom left corner of the painting *Portrait of V.I. Lenin in Disguise in the Style of Jackson Pollock*, which is hung on the studio wall to the left of centre. A pair of hands issuing from the cupboard at the right are taken from Picasso's *Minotaur Carrying a Dead Mare from a Grotto.* Among other paintings by Art & Language represented in the studio are *Gustave Courbet's Burial at Ornan expressing…*, *Picasso's 'Guernica' in the Style of Jackson Pollock*, and *Ils donnent leur sang; donnez votre travail.* A banner produced for the 1976 Venice Biennale is shown at the extreme right, one of the *Flags for Organisations* is draped over the open cupboard door (see no. 12), and a display card for *Index 02* is propped against the wall at the left. Various other artworks, pamphlets, posters, record-covers and books are shown distributed around the walls, floor, window-seat and table.

Once its details had been assembled and arranged, the maquette was copied with a pencil held in the mouth in order to generate a level of distortion. So as to strengthen the relatively faint outlines resulting from this procedure, a direct copy was made by carbon transfer. This is the work upon which the drawing in *Homes from Homes II* is based, though in order to adjust it to the required space, a small horizontal extension has been added to the composition at the right. In its original incarnation this drawing was then squared up and copied exactly by hand onto a sheet of paper of the same dimensions as Courbet's *Atelier*. The design was then coloured in by hand with crayon before being worked over in ink by Michael and Mel with brushes held in their mouths.

16

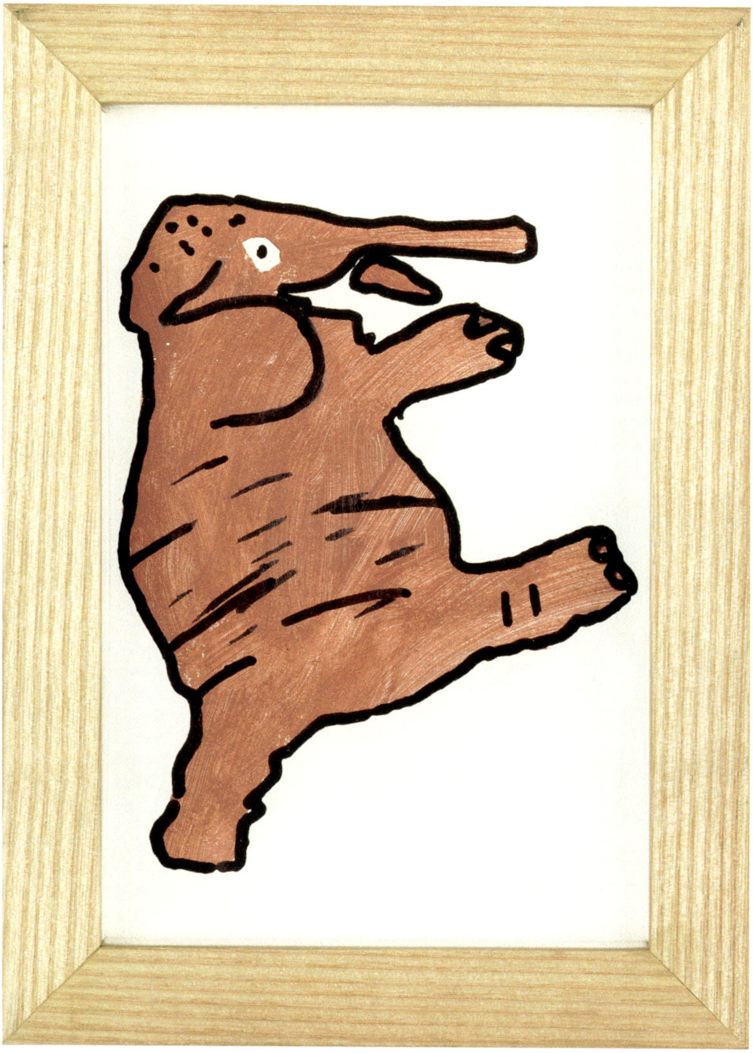

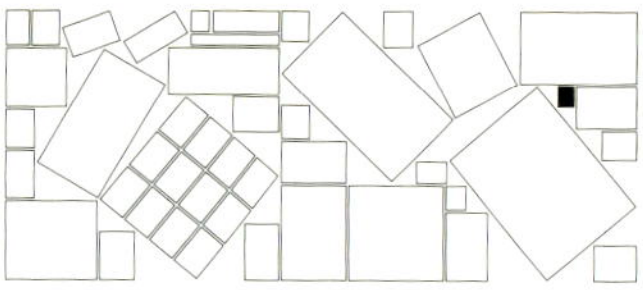

p) Elephant

See

16.1
16.2

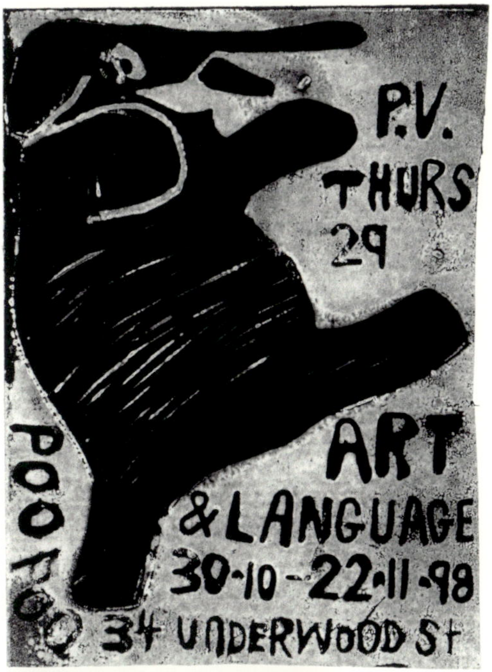

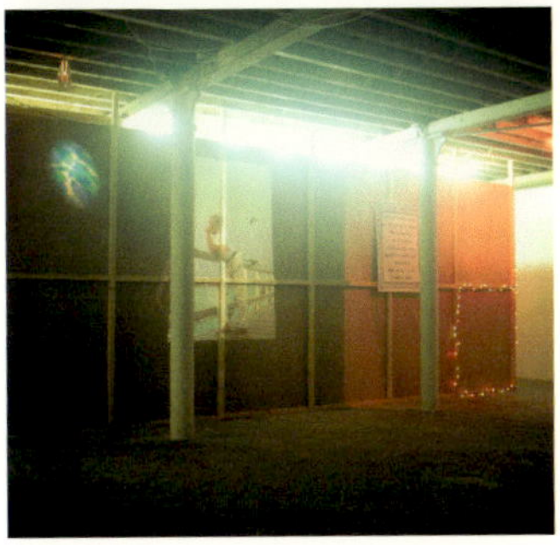

16.3
16.4
16.5

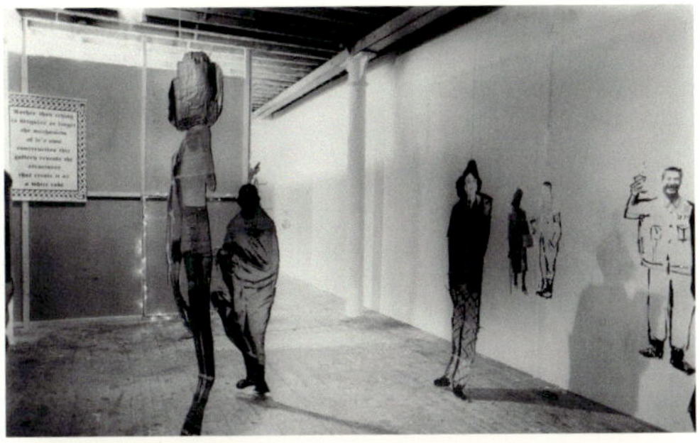

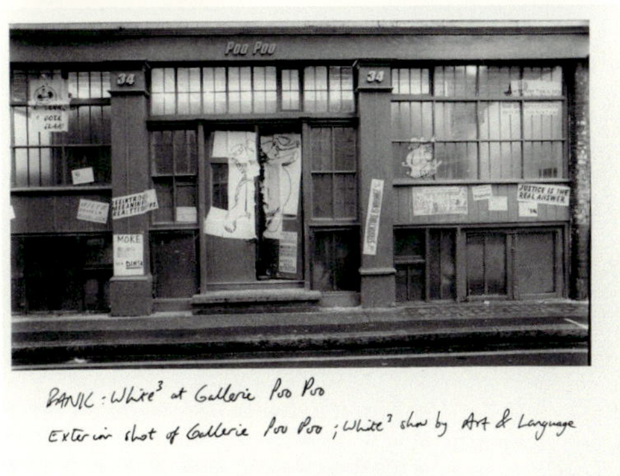

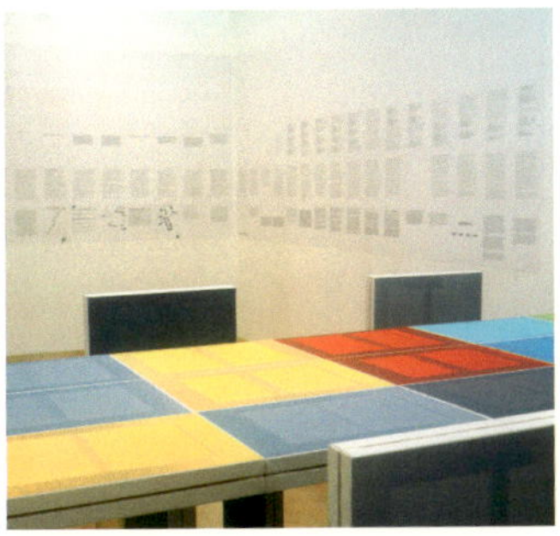

The dancing elephant shown in no. 16 was devised by Milly Thompson, Simon Bedwell and John Russell of BANK. It is one of the carnival creatures that crowd around a white cube containing work by Art & Language. The version by Art & Language that appears in *Homes from Homes II* is a souvenir of a brief collaboration. In its ten years of existence between 1990 and 2000, BANK engaged in what they saw as a disingenuous and self-ratifying 'Brit-art' movement. The initial contact between Art & Language and BANK was made in the form of a press release designed by BANK to initiate a project.

'BANK: Press Release

'White³

'The siting of *White³* will be within the absolutely perfect white cube — this form of gallery being the quasi-scientific quintessence of the area of modernism's triumphs in the visual arts. This cube, though, will be placed dead in the centre of the time-worn rafters and floorboards of 34 Underwood Street; a Brektian[1)] white cube, immaculate in the midst of rougher surroundings. We would see this rhetorical use of the form of the white cube (visitors will be able to walk around outside the cube, though no artwork will be there) as ironising and deflating its pretensions to neutrality, pretensions that have persisted throughout this century (though consistently challenged).

'The intention of *White³* however will not be to critique but to reinvigour [sic] the white space and through caricaturing the *critique of the gallery* presenting — so to speak — a negation of a negation. Firstly *White³* will approach more closely the "neutrality" desired by commercial white cube spaces *but which they cannot attain because of their shoddy and lazy attitude* — not only has the white cube context come to be synonymous with an intimidating place run by entrepreneurs with the adjoining desk or office space acting as the unspoken site of power but also the lax and slapdash attitude of these people has resulted in tawdry and dog-eared versions of what a white cube should truly be. Skirting boards, doorways all show disruptive signs of *architecture.* None of these white

1) Deliberate mistake — *Brechtian*

cubes are what they say they are — they are, rather, *white rooms*. *White* [3], by contrast, will have no administration desk or invigilating presence in the gallery itself; but rather be just a well made space — one entrance, white walls, and art.

'To further assist this process the white cube will be surrounded by a display representing the idea of the "spectacle" — as in *The Society of the Spectacle* [*The spectator feels at home nowhere, for the spectacle is everywhere* [2)]]. The presence of — dancing elephants, trick unicyclists, children's clowns, projections of fun fair amusements will provide a caricatured carnival which will allow the caricatured "critique of a white neutral space" to transcend itself and actually become a *truly neutral white cube* — apolitical, value-free — the natural habitat for *art* and its prescribed functions, whether they be the pursuit of truth and beauty, communication, education, entertainment or whatever.'

Art & Language replied by fax as follows:

'ART & LANGUAGE: Is this What you Mean:

'*White* [3] will exemplify that type of exhibition space whose ideal form is the perfectly blank white cube. This is the quasi-scientific arena in which modernism's quintessential triumphs are paraded. *White* [3] however, will be situated between the dusty rafters and the footworn floor of 34 Underwood Street. It will be a Brechtian cube, immaculate in its rough surroundings. Visitors will be able to walk around it and look at its exterior. Their view from the outside will largely displace the view on the inside, rob it of its specious but culturally entrenched neutrality.

'It is not our intention simply to criticise the white space. It is, rather, to reinvigorate it in a double displacement of the critique of the gallery — a negation of a negation. This will be accomplished as follows: the interior of *White* [3] will approach its ideal form more closely than the commercial white cube galleries normally do. The latter fail in this regard often as a consequence of artsy laziness and the unworkmanlike attitudes of shopkeepers masquerading as intellectuals. The white cube has

2) Jean Baudrillard, 1987

come to be a place of intimidation and dissuasion run by entrepreneurs; a desk or adjacent office acts as an auratic locus of this power. *White*^{3} will contain neither a desk nor any other invigilating presence. There will be just a well-made space with one entrance, white walls and art. It will be surrounded by a display which represents a culture of spectacle: As Baudrillard suggests (1987): "The spectator feels at home nowhere, for the spectacle is everywhere." Dancing elephants, trick uni-cyclists and children's clowns will appear with celebrities and images of the fun-fair. They will create an absurd image of carnival in which the displaced critique of the neutral white space will transcend itself and become a truly neutral white cube — apolitical and value free. It will become a natural place — a habitat — for art and for its prescribed functions — a place in which to search for truth and beauty or to engage in communication or education and even entertainment. Or something else?'

This exhibition was reviewed in a book by BANK:

'*White*^{3} was a show in three parts, a self-contained series. This helped to justify the pun of the title, along with the three-cubes-set-side-by-side measurements of the internal gallery space. It also gave us a chance to work with some artists we liked. In the second part, after much faxing back and forth with Art & Language (these exchanges becoming the press release), we made a series of agit-prop looking posters, and plastered them over the outside of Galerie Poo Poo. They were written in gobbledegook, with the look of protest without being strictly readable. A giant elephant clip-art image was glued to the front doors. Inside, there was an ambulance light and a poster advertising for uni-cyclists, jugglers, etc. (We actually put this up in the Circus Space near Hoxton Square, but no one replied.) Around the 'cube', BANK's 'spectacle' figures filled up the gallery: Gandhi, Nixon, John Travolta, God, Quentin Crisp, The Queen, Naomi Campbell, Madonna, Thatcher, Hitler, Robert De Niro and Mother Teresa. The impetus from this came from not wanting another weedy version of Debord's spectacle, but one which made more effort, whilst leaving a slightly bad taste in the mouth, so it was important to have Stalin, Mussolini, etc., as well as more predictable, cuddly-kitsch celebrities like Elvis. A minor, and unstated part of all this, especially apropos the fake agit-prop posters over the front of Galerie Poo Poo, was some sort of affectionate pastiche of Art & Language as hardnut critical/political artists. They installed *Sighs Trapped by Liars* in the *White* [3], along with some walls of text, extant and newly written.' (*BANK,* published by BANK and Black Dog Publishing, London 2000.)

19–30

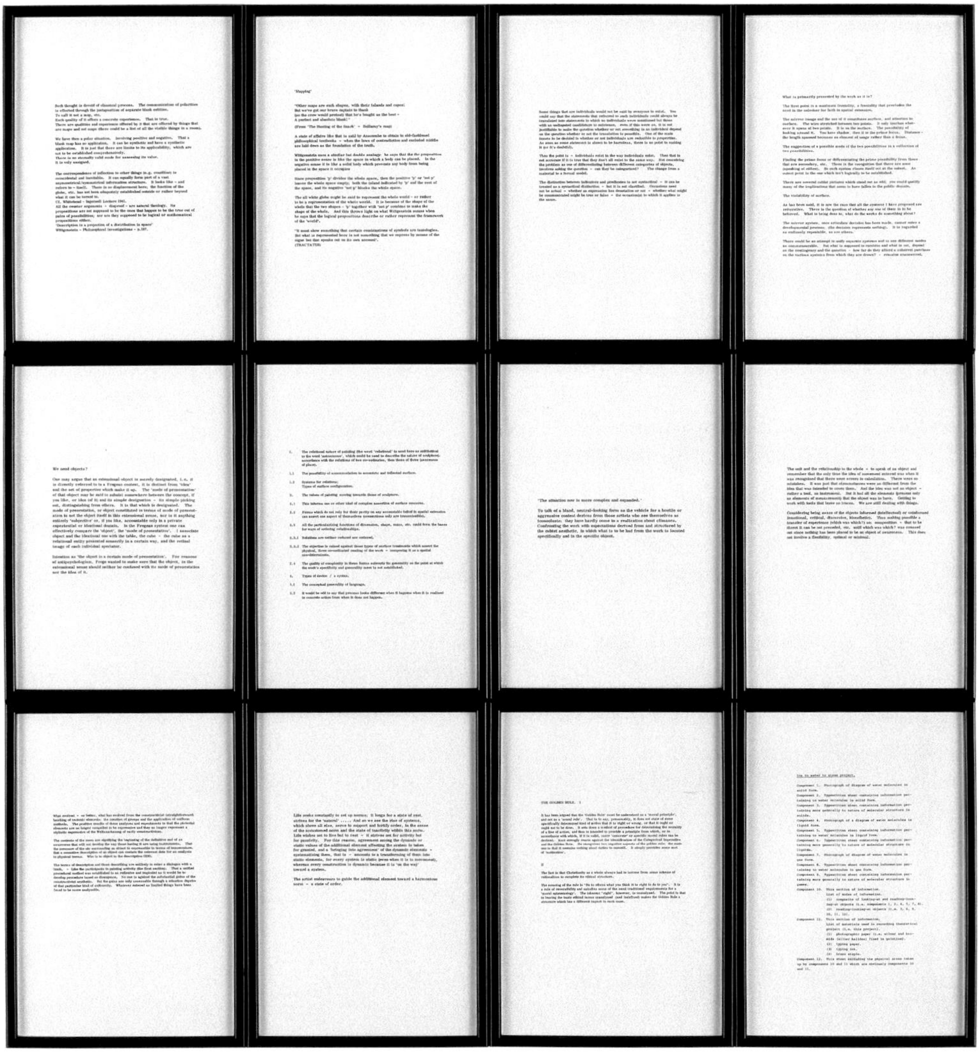

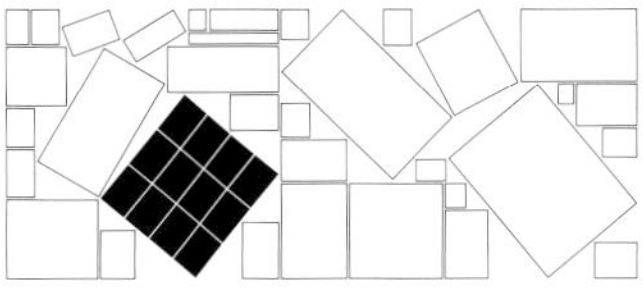

q) Paintings

See

19–30.1
19–30.2
19–30.3
19–30.4

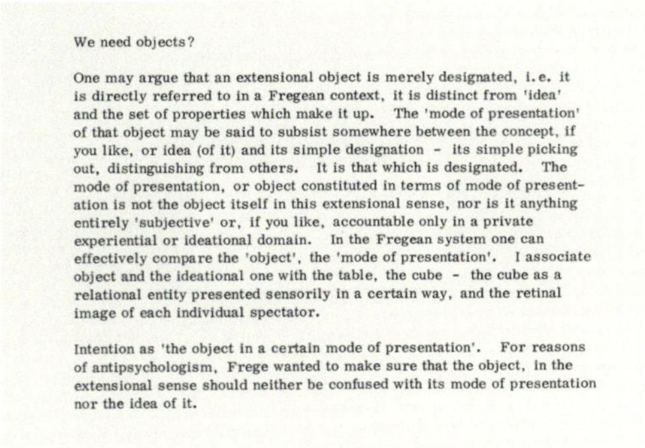

We need objects?

One may argue that an extensional object is merely designated, i.e. it is directly referred to in a Fregean context, it is distinct from 'idea' and the set of properties which make it up. The 'mode of presentation' of that object may be said to subsist somewhere between the concept, if you like, or idea (of it) and its simple designation - its simple picking out, distinguishing from others. It is that which is designated. The mode of presentation, or object constituted in terms of mode of presentation is not the object itself in this extensional sense, nor is it anything entirely 'subjective' or, if you like, accountable only in a private experiential or ideational domain. In the Fregean system one can effectively compare the 'object', the 'mode of presentation'. I associate object and the ideational one with the table, the cube - the cube as a relational entity presented sensorily in a certain way, and the retinal image of each individual spectator.

Intention as 'the object in a certain mode of presentation'. For reasons of antipsychologism, Frege wanted to make sure that the object, in the extensional sense should neither be confused with its mode of presentation nor the idea of it.

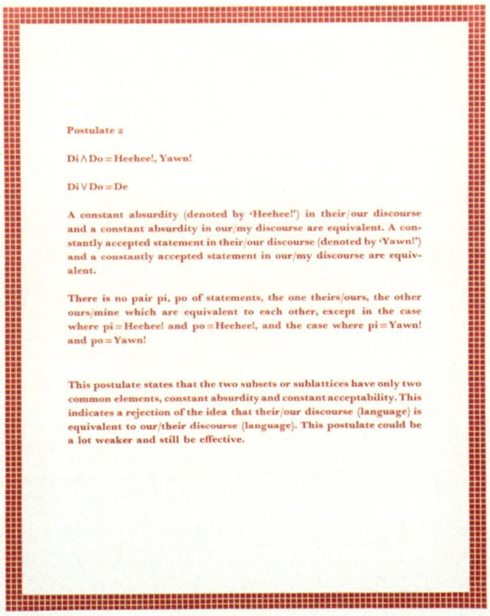

Postulate 2

Di ∧ Do = Heehee!, Yawn!

Di ∨ Do = De

A constant absurdity (denoted by 'Heehee!') in their/our discourse and a constant absurdity in our/my discourse are equivalent. A constantly accepted statement in their/our discourse (denoted by 'Yawn!') and a constantly accepted statement in our/my discourse are equivalent.

There is no pair pi, po of statements, the one theirs/ours, the other ours/mine which are equivalent to each other, except in the case where pi = Heehee! and po = Heehee!, and the case where pi = Yawn! and po = Yawn!

This postulate states that the two subsets or sublattices have only two common elements, constant absurdity and constant acceptability. This indicates a rejection of the idea that their/our discourse (language) is equivalent to our/their discourse (language). This postulate could be a lot weaker and still be effective.

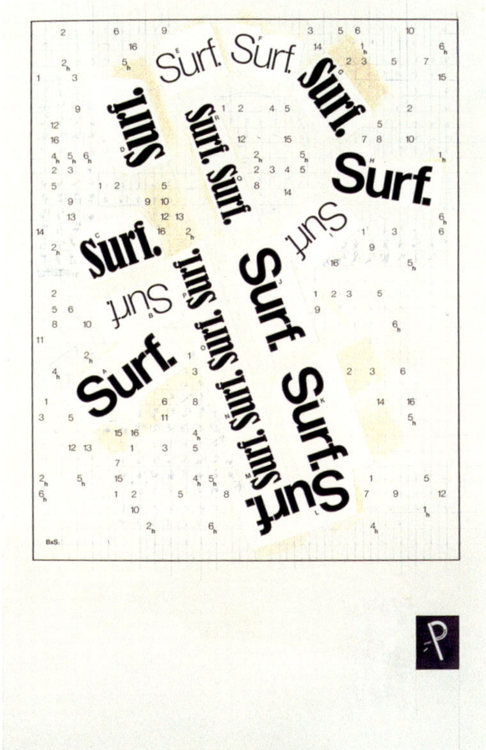

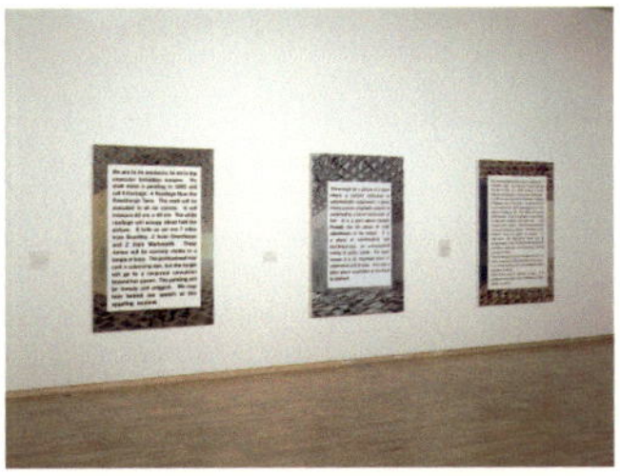

On the billboard display and in the pseudo-chronological installation nos. 19 to 30 appear as a block of twelve conjoined frames containing black-on-white texts. In the third, 'virus' installation, the block has been broken up into 12 separate frames. This latter form corresponds closest to the condition in which these works would have been shown originally. Two considerations bear upon this. The first is that while we may accept as true the statement that these are allographic works, that, in principle might take any graphic form that allowed the text to be readable, there exists nevertheless a graphic decorum regarding the appearance of works of Conceptual Art from the 1960s. The second consideration — leaving aside the fact that these works appear twice in the *Homes from Homes II* installation in blocks of twelve (a departure from normal 1960s practice) and that their appearance is due to digital technology — is that text by text they are virtually indistinguishable from their typewriter and photo-process 'originals'. They are, then, almost perfect reproductions of works whose *raison d'être* is to deny the need for such authenticity. To this extent they are displaced. At the same moment, we could also say that the damaged synchrony of the billboard display, for example, has been disrupted by works that authentically belong to another time — indeed, works that have their being in a cultural milieu that *Homes from Homes II* cannot touch. Is this, then, an autonomous display of 1960s textual Conceptual Art appearing untransformed both in and as *Homes from Homes II*, or is its appearance only in and for *Homes from Homes II* insofar as it is composed of items that are reflexively self-defeating in being reproduced as facsimiles?

According to one of the logic(s) of travesty that animates *Homes from Homes II*, it would perhaps have been appropriate for these texts to appear on coloured paper or with decorative borders, in which case they would be seen to have lost some of their virtue, or at least to have put it at risk as a consequence of their new get-up. Of course, this apparent loss of virtue should, perhaps, be no loss at all. Certain of Conceptual Art's most unreconstructed policemen would no doubt argue that the 'form' is, in one way or another, 'accidental' and the art-as-idea bit, necessary. But they would then go on to argue that a certain 'neutrality' of style and presentation is required if this quasi-theological truth is to be understood by the onlooker. Clearly, if this latter statement is true, then the former is untenable.

It is, nevertheless, the case that it is in Conceptual Art's graphic form — or, can we say 'style' — that some of its virtuous powers reside. A sheet of text, whose content is designed to provoke the viewer into entertaining a possibility in a certain way, may indeed be in error in assuming its own transparency, but it is largely immune to (or irrelevant to) most decorative purposes. The first thing that a non paper-or-ink fetishist would do is read the text. But that is as rigorous as it gets. It is true to say that this small virtue is now virtually unusable, and that indeed, with various degrees of self-deluded purism, some Conceptual artists of the 1960s have recently found ways to install their work as decorative embellishments to the architecture of the art museum. This development was, of course, underway by the 1970s, when it became clear that art in the generic form was bound to find some way of occupying institutional space.

Instead, the items that compose nos. 19 to 30 seem to cling to their marginally 'formal' autonomy and virtue. Can we regard this protecting of historical virtue as something 'pictured' by virtue of the presence of the larger billboard context — 'pictured' in the sense that these twelve texts are shown *as* possessing certain characteristics that are not internal either to their 'original' textual content or to the cultural conditions they then confronted. But if such a 'picturing' is feasible, then *Homes from Homes II* is bound to form some sort of virtual location — i.e. a 'pictorial' scene such that the twelve examples of *38 Paintings* can be seen represented as an island of small virtue in a sea of travesty.

An answer to the question of whether *Homes from Homes II* can accomplish something like this or not may depend upon the status and role of stylistic travesty — or more seriously 'redescription' in the work of Art & Language, particularly insofar as that work is *seen as Conceptual Art.* It was in 1973–1974, if not before, that we began to recognise the manifest absurdity of various forms of the argument that Conceptual Art represented a de-materialisation of art. That certain non-material objects were described in certain Conceptual Art texts is not in question, but these are very few in number. It is absurd to suggest that art somehow dematerialises in being text-based and in having its meanings mediated by language. It is, of course, true that text-based art was, at least in the late 1960s, confined to unspectacular media like bits of typed paper, whose putative art contents may have been merely mentioned or described by the text; but physical modesty driven by a sense of use-appropriateness is not dematerialisation. Indeed, had there been any dematerialisation, then the matter of medium-appropriateness relative to use could not have arisen. We could add that there are quite clear ways to see this decorum demonstrated. Lawrence Weiner's *One standard dye marker thrown into the sea* was originally produced as a simple written statement on a quarto sheet. The form was, as they say, adequate to the content, which subsists somewhere in the meaning and the use of the words of which the statement is composed, as well as historically reflexive discourse into which the whole thing, paper-text-words-meanings etc., is inserted. If this work were to be re-issued in the form of three-metre-high plastic letters — to become an embellishment to an already overcooked architectural extravaganza — we might conclude that the historical reflection must have changed; i.e. that its maker wished it to be inserted into a different discourse. The question then arises of the relation between the new form and historical context and the old. In this case the transformation produces a negative value. The new form and context are built of obedience to a set of external conditions that are largely formed and controlled by interests for whom art is the supplier of a harmlessly poetic principle within the meshes of global capital. We can say, then, that the transformation has resulted in something a bit worse than a loss of virtue or power on the part of the work, and in something closer to its aesthetic and moral annihilation.

Whilst such changes of form can be catastrophic, this fact is rarely understood by Conceptual Art purists, whose metaphysical naïvety has led them to believe that so long as they avoid the autographic dirt exemplified by such things as painting, the juncture of their historical and cultural reflection can be maintained in a pure state.

Now, the silliness of all this was something that entered Art & Language's conversation as that conversation had reached its most abstract, technical and baroque phase of self-reflection. Given, that unlike many of our peers, we were and are not mere decorators who hide behind the dodgy catechism of dematerialisation and its cognates, and given that our self-dismantling mechanisms are actual and operational, we reasoned that there would be no harm — and some exemplary good — to be found in introducing a certain graphic absurdity in circumstances of public display. In other words, cool graphic style is not in itself artistic substance, so we had better put ourselves to the trouble (or pleasure) of making this apparent. What followed was a set of 'posters' in fine decorative colours (red, blue, green, yellow) with chequered borders. Leaving aside their textual content, these works were travesties of Conceptual Art style, including that of Art & Language. Such redescriptions and bringings-low have been characteristic of Art & Language practice since that time. One might adduce the question of relationship between the textual prescription 'portrait of V.I. Lenin in the style of Jackson Pollock' and the very existence of plausibly Pollock- and Lenin-like paintings, or point to the 'classically' Conceptual Art-ish texts that promise to paint a landscape in the future, and so on.

We could say, then, that these twelve works of apparently uncompromised Conceptual Art are, in fact, fictive things relative to the larger measure of Art & Language works. Relative to this measure, they would have to be understood either as examples of that unwitting but bottomless travesty that is born of puristic stasis, or as merely antique visitors — old folks — who sit in embarrassment in the middle of a gathering that they've wandered into by accident. Perhaps these two are much the same thing. In any case, their status as 'literal' Conceptual Art works has been rendered virtual by the narrative that surrounds them — both synchronically and diachronically — of their own time and of the specious present.

19 We need objects?

One may argue that an extensional object is merely designated, i. e., it is directly referred to in a Fregean context, it is distinct from 'idea' and the set of properties which make it up. The 'mode of presentation' of that object may be said to subsist somewhere between the concept, if you like, or idea (of it) and its simple designation — its simple picking out, distinguishing from others. It is that which is designated. The mode of presentation, or object constituted in terms of mode of presentation, is not the object itself in this extensional sense, nor is it anything entirely 'subjective' or, if you like, accountable only in a private experiential or ideational domain. In the Fregean system one can effectively compare the 'object' and the 'mode of presentation'. I associate object and the ideational one with the table, the cube — the cube as a relational entity presented sensorily in a certain way, and the retinal image of each individual spectator.

Intention as 'the object in a certain mode of presentation'. For reasons of antipsychologism, Frege wanted to make sure that the object, in the extensional sense, should neither be confused with its mode of presentation nor the idea of it.

20 'Mapping'

"Other maps are such shapes, with their islands and capes!
But we've got our brave captain to thank.
(so the crew would protest) that he's brought us the best —
A perfect and absolute blank!"
(From 'The Hunting of the Snark' — Bellman's map)

A state of affairs like that is said by Anscombe to obtain in old-fashioned philosophical textbooks — when the laws of contradiction and excluded middle are laid down as the foundation of the truth.

Wittgenstein uses a similar but double analogy: he says that the proposition in the positive sense is like the space in which a body can be placed. In the negative sense it is like a solid body which prevents any body from being placed in the space it occupies

Since proposition 'p' divides the whole space, then the positive 'p' or 'not p' leaves the whole space empty; both the island indicated by 'p' and the rest of the space, and its negative 'not p' blocks the whole space.

The all white globe might be said to represent the whole world — or rather to be a representation of the whole world. It is because of the shape of the whole that the two shapes — 'p' together with 'not p' — combine to make the shape of the whole. And this throws light on what Wittgenstein means when he says that the logical propositions describe or rather represent the framework of the 'world'.

"It must show something that certain combinations of symbols are tautologies. But what is represented here is not something that we express by means of the signs but that speaks out on its own account'.
(TRACTATUS)

21 'The situation now is more complex and expanded.'

To talk of a bland, neutral-looking form as the vehicle for a hostile or aggressive content derives from those artists who see themselves as iconoclasts: they have hardly come to a realisation about climaxes. Confronting the work with expectations derived from and structured by the cubist aesthetic, in which what is to be had from the work is located specifically and in the specific object.

22

1 The relational nature of painting (the word 'relational' is used here as antithetical to the word 'autonomous', which could be used to describe the nature of sculpture): accordance with the relations of two co-ordinates, then those of three (awareness of place).

1.1 The possibility of accommodation to eccentric and inflected surface.

1.2 Systems for relations; types of surface configuration.

2 The values of painting moving towards those of sculpture.

2.1 This informs one or other kind of complex assertion of surface concerns.

2.2 Forms which do not rely for their purity on any accountable belief in spatial extension can assert one aspect of themselves (connections only are transmissible).

2.3 All the particularising functions of dimension, shape, mass, etc. could form the bases for ways of ordering relationships.

2.3.1 Relations are neither reduced nor ordered.

2.3.2 The objection is raised against those types of surface treatments which assert the physical, three co-ordinated reading of the work — composing it as a spatial non-determinate.

2.4 The quality of complexity in these forms subverts its generality so the point at which the work's specificity and generality meet is not established.

3 Types of device / a syntax.

3.1 The conceptual generality of language.

3.2 It would be odd to say that process looks different when it happens (when it is realised in concrete action) from when it does not happen.

23 Ice to water to steam project.

Component 1. Photograph of diagram of water molecules in solid form.
Component 2. Typewritten sheet containing information pertaining to water molecules in solid form.
Component 3. Typewritten sheet containing information pertaining more generally to nature of molecular structure in solids.
Component 4. Photograph of a diagram of water molecules in liquid form.
Component 5. Typewritten sheet containing information pertaining to water molecules in liquid form.
Component 6. Typewritten sheet containing information pertaining more generally to nature of molecular structure in liquids.
Component 7. Photograph of diagram of water molecules in gas form.
Component 8. Typewritten sheet containing information pertaining to water molecules in gas form.
Component 9. Typewritten sheet containing information pertaining more generally to nature of molecular structure in gases.
Component 10. This section of information.

List of modes of information:
(1) composite of looking-at and reading-looking-at objects (i.e., components 1, 2, 4, 5, 7, 8).
(2) reading-looking-at objects (i.e., 3, 6, 9, 10, 11, 12).

Component 11. This section of information.

List of materials used in recording theoretical project (i.e., this project):
(1) photographic paper (i.e. silver and bromide [silver halides] fixed in gelatine)
(2) typing paper
(3) typing ink
(4) brass staple

Component 12. This sheet excluding the physical areas taken up by components 10 and 11 which are obviously components 10 and 11.

24 What is primarily presented by the work as it is?

The first point is a maximum frontality, a frontality that precludes the need in the onlooker for faith in spatial extension.

The mirror image and the use of it constitutes surface, and attention to surface. The wire stretched between two points. It only touches whatever it spans at two points. It is on the surface. The possibility of looking around it. You have shadow, then it is the prime focus. Distance — the length spanned becomes an element of usage rather than a focus.

The suggestion of a possible mode of the two possibilities in a collection of two possibilities.

Finding the prime focus or differentiating the prime possibility from those that are secondary, etc. There is the recognition that there are none (speaking of either). So each system closes itself out at the outset. An outset point is the one which isn't logically to be established.

There are several cubist pictures which stand out as odd; you could qualify many of the implications that seem to have fallen in the public domain.

The violability of surface.

As has been said, it is now the case that all the systems I have proposed are reiterative. There is the question of whether any one of them is to be believed. What is being done to, what do the works do something about?

The mirror system, once articulate decision has been made, cannot enter a developmental process: (the decision represents nothing). It is regarded as endlessly repeatable, as are others.

There could be an attempt to unify separate systems and to see different modes as commensurable. But what is supposed to combine and what is not, depend on the contingency and the question – 'How far do they afford a coherent purchase on the various systems from which they are drawn?' It remains unanswered.

25 Such thought is devoid of classical process. The communication of polarities is effected through the juxtaposition of separate blank entities.

To call it not a map, etc.

Each quality of it offers a concrete experience. That is true.

There are qualities and experience offered by it that are offered by things that are maps and not maps (there could be a list of all the visible things in a room).

We have then a polar situation. Involving positive and negative. That a blank map has no application. It can be synthetic and have a synthetic application. It is just that there are limits to its applicability; which are not to be established comprehensively.

There is no eternally valid mode for assessing its value.

It is only assigned.

The correspondence of inflection to other things (e. g., coastline) is coincidental and inevitable. It can equally form part of a vast asymmetrical/symmetrical information structure. It looks like – and refers to – itself. There is no displacement here; the function of the globe, etc., has not been adequately established outside or rather beyond what it can be turned to.

Cf. Whitehead – *Ingersoll Lecture* 1941.

All the counter-arguments – disproof – are natural theology. Its propositions are not supposed to be the ones that happen to be the true out of pairs of possibilities; nor are they supposed to be logical or mathematical propositions either.

'Description is a projection of a distribution in space.' Wittgenstein – *Philosophical Investigations* – p.187.

26 THE GOLDEN RULE

I

It has been argued that the 'Golden Rule' must be understood as a 'moral principle', and not as a 'moral rule'. That is to say, presumably, it does not state of some specifically determined kind of action that it is right or wrong, or that it ought or ought not to be done. It sets down a method of procedure for determining the morality of a line of action, and thus is intended to provide a principle from which, or in accordance with which, if it is valid, more 'concrete' or specific moral rules can be derived. Kant strongly reacts against the identification of the Categorical Imperative and the Golden Rule. He recognizes two negative aspects of the golden rule: the main one is that it contains nothing about duties to oneself. It simply provides some sort of 'motivation'.

II

The fact is that Christianity as a whole always had to borrow from some scheme of rationalism to complete its ethical structure.

The meaning of the rule is 'Do to others what you think it is right to do to you.' It is a rule of reversibility and satisfies some of the semi-traditional requirements for a 'moral epistemology'. The inherent 'right', however, is unanalysed. The point is that leaving the basic ethical terms unanalysed (and undefined) makes the Golden Rule a structure which has a different import in each case.

27 The unit and the relationship to the whole – to speak of an object and remember that the only time the idea of movement entered was when it was recognised that there were errors in calculation. There were no mistakes. It was just that circumstances were so different from the idea that was intended to cover them. And the idea was not an object – rather a tool, an instrument. But it had all the elements (present only as elements of measurement) that the object was to have. Getting to work with tools that leave no traces. We are still dealing with things.

Considering being aware of the objects informed (intellectual) or uninformed (emotional, critical, discursive, kinesthetic). Thus making possible a transfer of experience ('which was which?') so: composition – that to be direct it can be not preceded, etc., until 'which was which?' was crossed-out, since nothing has been placed to be an object of awareness. This does not involve a flexibility, optimal or minimal.

28 Some things that are individuals would not be said by everyone to exist. You could say that the statements that referred to such individuals could always be translated into statements in which no individuals were mentioned but those with an undisputed candidature to existence; even if this were so, it is not justifiable to make the question whether or not something is an individual depend on the question whether or not the translation is possible. One of the main issues to be decided is whether or not individuals are reducible to properties. As soon as some statement is shown to be harmless, there is no point in making it (or it's doubtful).

Then the point is: individuals exist in the way individuals exist. Then that is not accurate if it is true that they don't all exist in the same way. Not conceiving the problem as one of differentiating between different categories of objects, involves asking the question — 'Can they be categorized?' The change is from a material to a formal model.

The distinction between indicators and predicates is not syntactical — it can be treated as a syntactical distinction — but it is not clarified. Occasions need not be actual — whether an expression has denotation or not — whether what might be communicated might be true or false — the occasion(s) to which it applies is the same.

29 Life seeks constantly to set up norms; it longs for a state of rest, strives for the 'natural'... And so we see the rise of systems, which above all else, serve to support and fortify order, in the sense of the accustomed norm and the state of inactivity within this norm. Life wishes not to live but to rest — it strives not for activity but for passivity. For this reason, agreement among the dynamic or static values of the additional element affecting the system is taken for granted, and a 'bringing into agreement' of the dynamic elements — systematising them, that is — amounts to a transforming of them into static elements, for every system is static (even when it is in movement), whereas every construction is dynamic because it is 'on the way' toward a system.

The artist endeavours to guide the additional element toward a harmonious norm — a state of order.

30 What evolved — or better, what has evolved from the constructivist (straightforward) handling of tectonic elements: the creation of groups and the application of uniform methods. The positive result(s) of these analyses and experiments is that the pictorial elements are no longer compelled to be expressive and they no longer represent a stylistic expression of the Weltanschauung of early constructivism.

The contents of the room are signifying the beginning of the definitive end of an awareness that will not develop the way those having it are using instruments. That the pressure of the air surrounding an object is expressible in terms of temperature; that a connotative description of an object can contain the relevant data for an analysis in physical terms. Who is to object to the description ODD.

The terms of description and those describing are unlikely to enter a dialogue with a limit. Like the participants in painting activity (the first section). That a unified procedural method was established is as reflexive and imploded as it would be to develop procedure based on divergence. No one is against the substantial gains of the constructivist aesthetic. But the gains are only assessable through a situation deprived of that particular kind of uniformity. Whatever entered as limited things have been found to be more analysable.

31

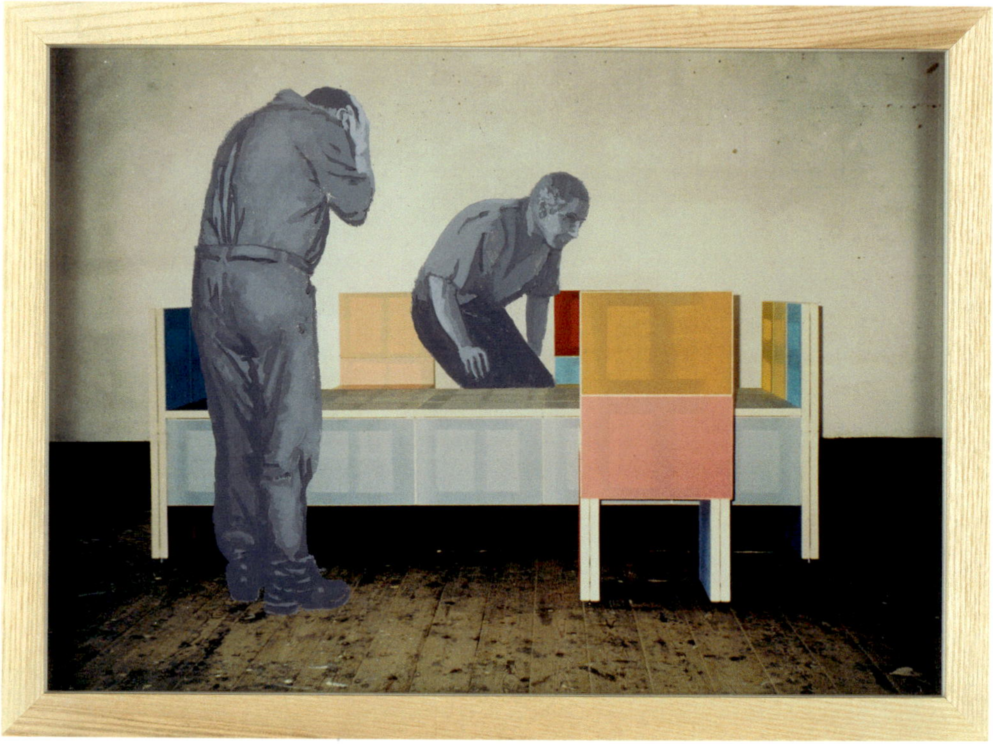

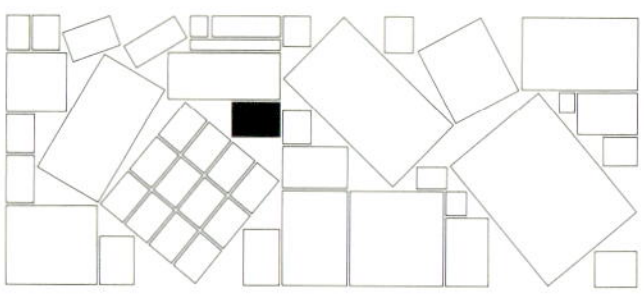

r) STBL (Old Men)

See

31.1

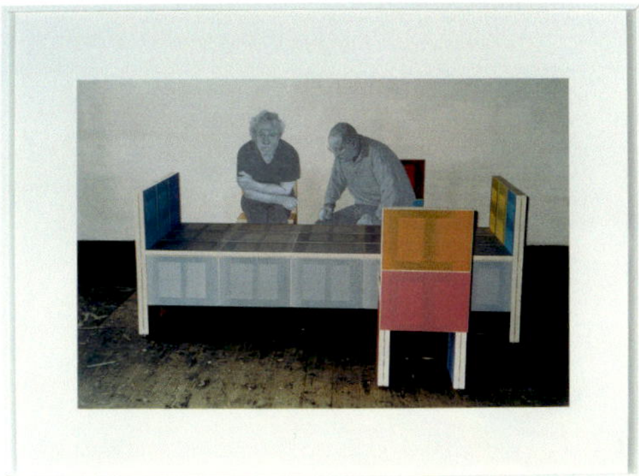

31.2

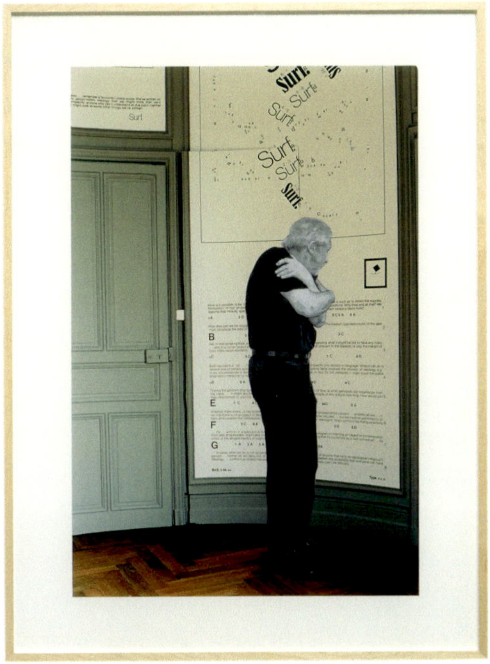

No. 31 is based on a photograph, taken in the Art & Language studio, of *Sighs Trapped by Liars 510–602.* Each of the 92 paintings contains an image of an open book (see no. 3). These paintings are assembled into furniture, in this instance a bed and three chairs. In being photographed in the studio, they are shown in a location that is traditionally technical and semi-public. The two grey figures that are inscribed on the surface of the photograph transform it into something that is either private or absurdly public and theatrical. The installation that had been laid out for technical review is now made a death-bed scene in make-believe. The grey figures belong to a sub-genre that includes Nicolas Poussin's *Testament of Eudamidas* and Edvard Munch's *Chamber of Death.* They are stains in various states of despair and agitation.

This traditionally technical and semi-public space has, however, found itself increasingly untechnical and public. This is not to say that the studio has acquired the social character of a French nineteenth-century workshop salon, in the semi-mythical status of Courbet's atelier, but rather that it has found itself among the traces of celebrity. Technicality and privacy have been supplanted by the exigencies of publicity. Who would now say that a studio installation might easily be distinguished from an institutional one. Indeed, it is recent curatorial wisdom that the museum is in fact a form of factory or workshop that produces art from its own 'studios'.

On the billboard installation no. 31 appears immediately below a studio drawn by mouth (no. 15). The studio, it is said, was the site of production when art was manufactured from a specific medium. It is also said that since the 1960s the site has moved to a place of consumption: the museum. Reminders of the often antagonistic sites of art production, memories of the studio and the museum, often inverted or lost, are conjured up in this and other works in *Homes from Homes II.* This painted photograph is not just an outward image of mourning but one that hopes to suggest resistance to this kind of curatorial control.

In *Homes from Homes II*, this work is no travesty of Art & Language work in itself. It is, however, a token of a sort of historically reflexive catastrophe: photographs of Conceptual Art that have been made into paintings are assembled (or disassembled) into furniture and then invaded by painted figures. It is a smaller version of a work in a series entitled *There Were Sighs Trapped by Liars* and thus, at a low level of transformative complexity, a representation of such a work. We have argued elsewhere that Conceptual Art was homeless, but an art looking for a home. In fact it was also a bit Home-Made — often worked out on kitchen tables or in living rooms, in bed-sits and sometimes pubs. This was a world without studios, offices, libraries or museums. It often possessed a strange domesticity — a certain modesty of aspect — which marked it off from public culture. What is perhaps of no more than parenthetical interest is that these paintings, 'squashed' or 'swarming' into furniture, might represent the birthplace and working circumstances of (some) Conceptual Art; but the Conceptual artists are absent (or perhaps they are present or somehow represented in the intrusive presence of the viewer).

There are further fictional possibilities. We have often thought that it is a function of our practice to generate a phantom. One of the more enjoyable speculations (for a pair, or a trio, or …? of heterosexual *pateres familii*) concerns the possible gender of this emergent creature. One suggestion, of course, was that it was a woman. A more dubious (but more powerful) suggestion was that it was *a difficult woman*… which is a literary genre in herself. Perhaps these chairs which must not be used or sat upon are the phantom's furniture, where she sits and watches, or perhaps they are refuges for other ghosts.

The phantoms or imaginary presences of the furniture of *Sighs Trapped by Liars* carry the implications of a missing or forgotten domestic use. This has caused another kind of picture to come into being, in another world or time. These new pictures demonstrate two uncertain outcomes of Conceptual Art: one goes to imposition, knowingness and isolation, and one goes to reflection, self-consciousness and companionship.

There Were Sighs Trapped by Liars comprises the intrusive presence of the artists and others, not as agents but as mourners in a genre scene of loss. But there is no loss as such; the chairs and bed around which these figures stand or sit are empty. The figures are, of course only inscribed on the surface of the photograph, they are not involved in its referential geneticity. Indeed, they are technically alien objects, being painted monochrome and matt on the shiny surface of the images of a relatively colourful scene. Are these figures the secluded users of these domestic effects? Are they their 'natural' occupiers — or are they ciphers of intrusiveness, the intrusiveness of the regard of the viewer upon the 'furniture' itself? If they are the latter, are their turnings-away and downcast postures evidence of guilt or shame — a reflective narrative of the viewer's regard? If they are the former, why have they assumed the guise of the artists and occasionally of their friends and family? What they mourn or fear the loss of is not there. It has either never been there or it has departed. They will have to follow — absent themselves.

Are the figures in *There Were Sighs Trapped by Liars* ghosts? Are they old Conceptual artists mourning the bureaucratisation of Conceptual Art, or are they much darker visitations, dirty figures from *After Dinner at Ornans*, spoiling the curatorial spectacle?

The figure re-emerges from time to time in the deliberations of art history and criticism. The talk is usually over-excited — a psychological nostalgia for some shard of Civilisation's promise. In the face of these difficulties, we might say that the only non-scandalous figure painting will be of ghosts.

34

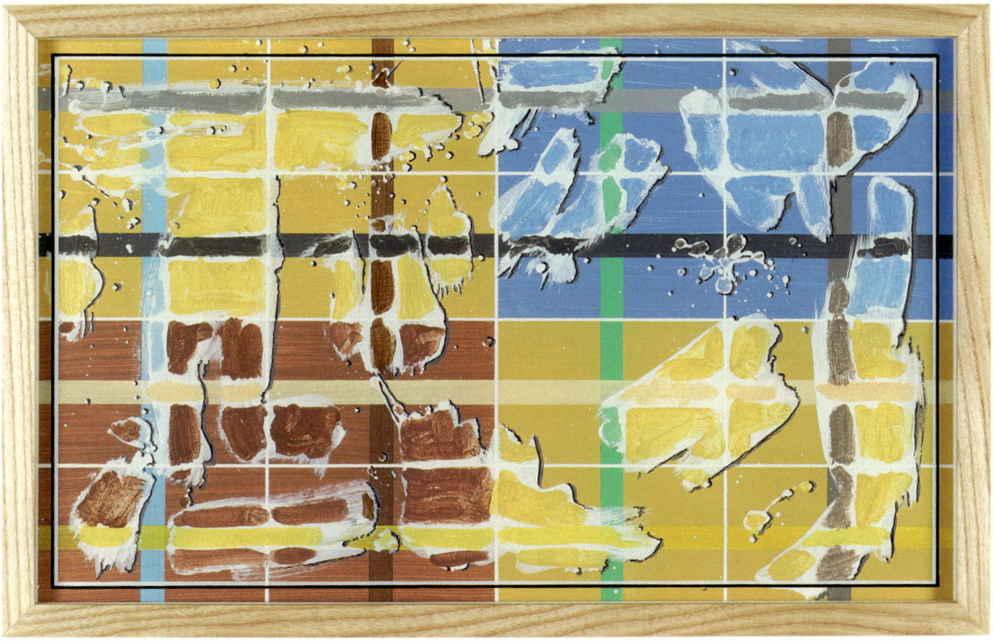

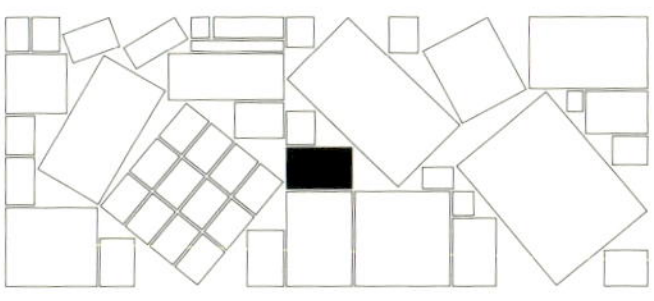

s) Blobby Chequer

See

34.1

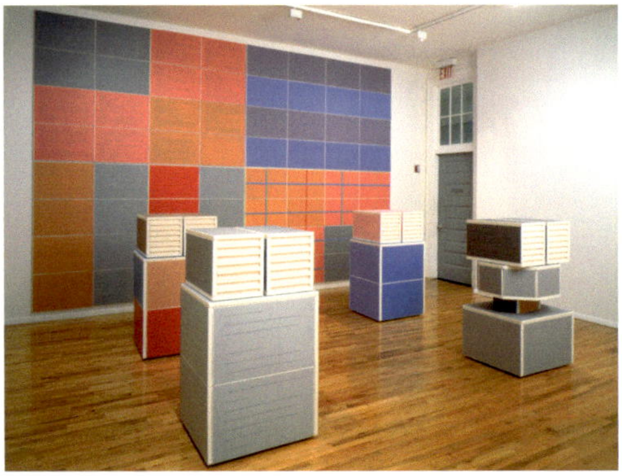

34.2

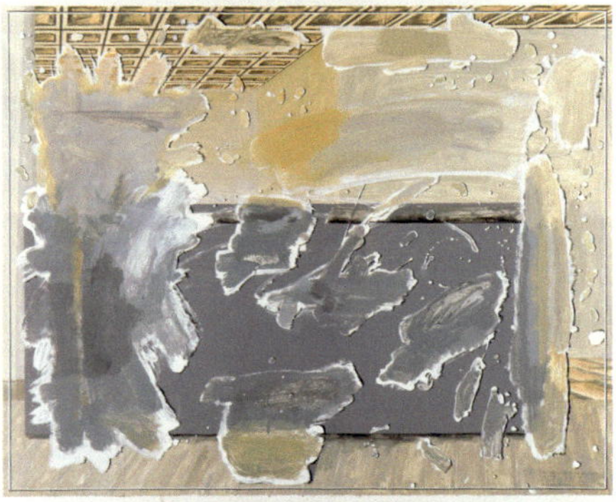

No. 34 is a small version of the paintings that hang at angles on either side (nos. 14 and 36). In this case the chequer has been infested by blobs that recall 1950s European abstract painting. This is the abstract painting of mess to high cultural and psychological purpose that also configures the work at the extreme bottom left of *Homes from Homes II.* The blobs have been naturalised to the chequer pattern however, and as in those that appear in the related no. 38, a sort of shadow is inscribed on their right-hand edge. This work is a hybrid, an internal product of *Homes from Homes II* itself. This is to say that while the chequer motif and the blob motif appear within the historical narrative of Art & Language work, they are conjoined only in an artifice that is generated within the occasions of *Homes from Homes II.*

Is this work then a travesty of a travesty? *Homes from Homes II* is composed as an artificial (and false) synchrony. But this falsehood — non-truth — is not of an even texture. These are 'works' whose appearance is virtually indistinguishable from their original form, whereas there are others that have tried bathetically to have a new life as decoration, losing their internal logic in the process, and others yet that have foregone everything that was essential to their 'original' nature. It is another sort of falsehood however, in which the discernible properties of one internal constituent of *Homes from Homes II* are disfigured with those of another. This work owes it existence, then, to the already travestied and fictional state of the constituents of *Homes from Homes II.* Must we therefore conclude that it is an anomaly within the forming logic of *Homes from Homes II*? If it is an anomaly, then it is one that has been made for and as *Homes from Homes II* itself. It takes no part in the fiction of synchrony that is the billboard display, and it has no narratively plausible place in the installation that (re)introduces a diachronic order — in the pseudo-chronological 'classical' arrangement of the work. In fact, it is to the billboard display that this item properly belongs. The billboard is the machine that made it (possible). As an anomaly relative to the forming principle of its companions it is, as it were, the only truth in the billboard fiction. In the pseudo-chronological installation it has — relative to that installation's fictional principles — nowhere to be. Its internality to the billboard deprives it of a place in a pseudo-chronology.

Have we now backed ourselves into a corner? It might be objected that insofar as it is the quietly monstrous creation of *Homes from Homes II* itself, then this item in all three of its forms must be viewed in isolation; that as the hybrid product of a travesty and redescription, it can claim no place in a displacing narrative. What is it like, then, if it is left to its own devices? We cannot say that it simply aggregates together whatever virtues or powers are possessed by its specific ancestors. We could say, perhaps, that in the pictured incompetence of its geometry (geometry that has been disfigured by virtual blobs that are nevertheless real), it may be the next stage in the doomed exchange between words and pictures that is proposed by *Index: Wrongs Healed in Official Hope.* And this would mean that it had begun a narrative that raised the possibility of malaproped pictures.

38

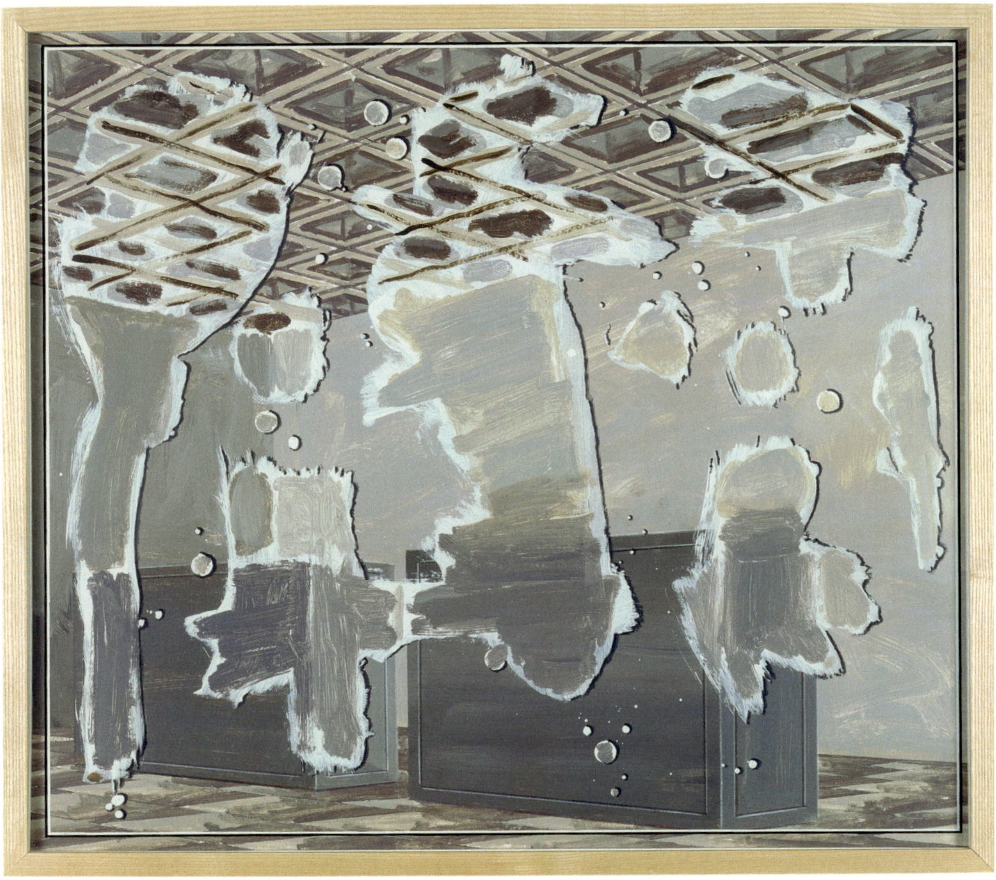

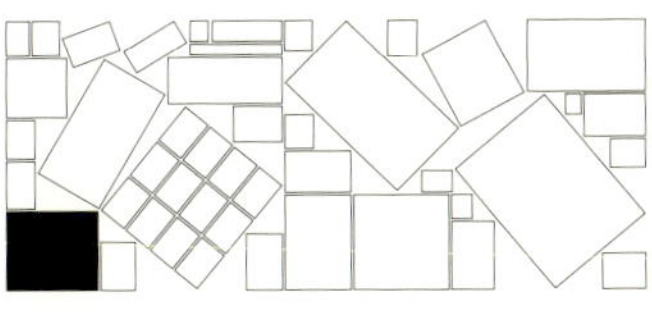

t) Incident Foreground

See

38.1
38.2

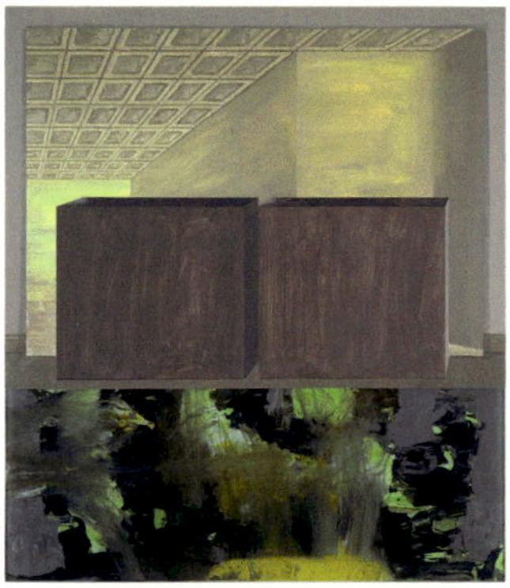

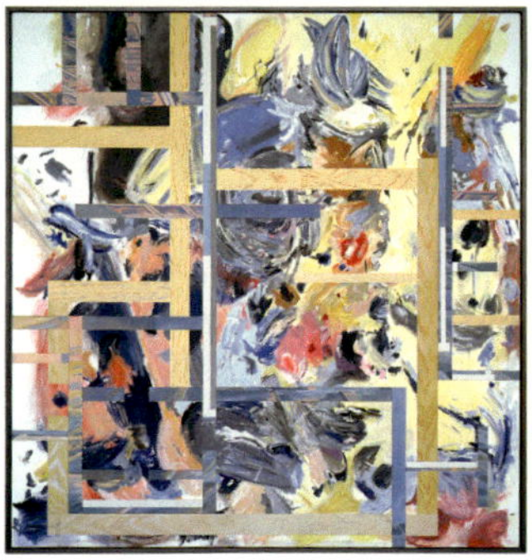

38.3
38.4
38.5

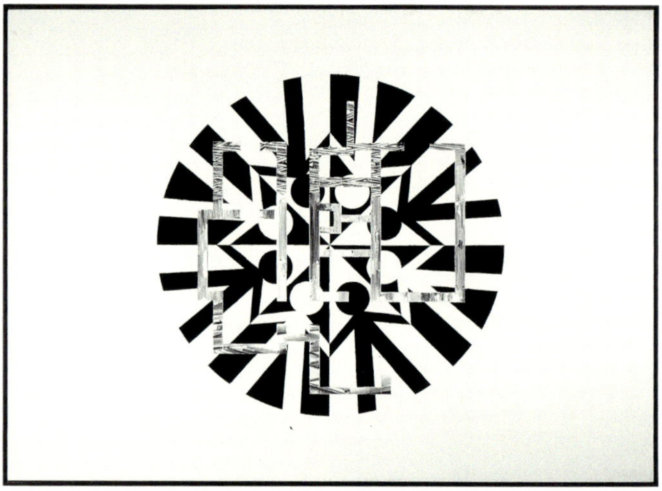

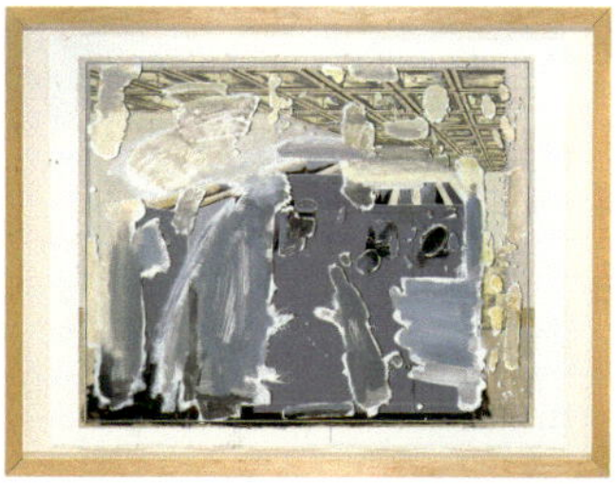

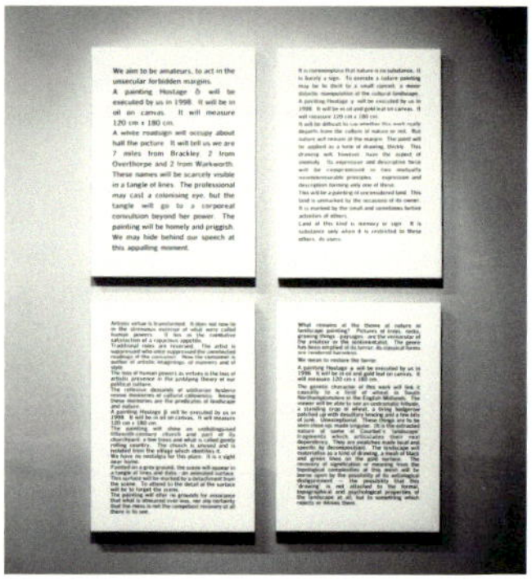

38.6

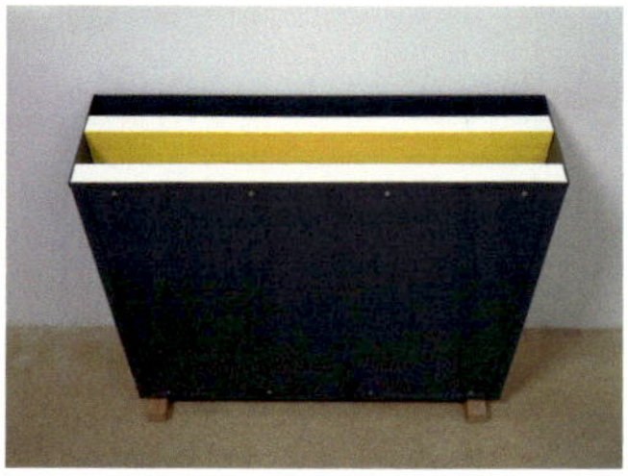

No. 38 occupies the bottom left-hand corner of the billboard installation of *Homes from Homes II.* It is painted on paper, and is framed and glazed. It shows what looks at first like a picture of a museum interior covered with glass, on which remain patches of liquid. The represented coffering of the museum ceiling is modulated by the figurative patches on the figurative surface of glass, as though those patches were both transparent and liquid. On closer inspection it can be seen to be a glazed picture of a glass-covered picture of a picture of a museum interior. In the quasi-chronological version of *Homes from Homes II* it occupies a position about two-thirds of the way along. As a 'virus' it might attach itself to theatrical paintings of interiors, to minimalist installations, or to essays in *trompe l'œil*.

No. 38 refers to a series of works made in 1994, most of which were abandoned. For the previous five years, the paintings made by Art & Language had had in common the use of sheets of glass fixed over their painted surfaces. The first use of glass had been as a figurative means of escape from the museum — the pictorial scenario within which Art & Language's own works had been represented and reconsidered between 1985 and 1987. Pictorial traces of the museum had persisted over the following two years into the 'palette' *Hostages* and the series of *Incidents and People's Flags* (see no. 12). It was as though there could be no further address to the medium of painting without some mode of reference to the determining institution. Under these conditions, the idea was that a sheet of glass fixed over the picture of a museum might have the effect of transporting the imaginary spectator to a notional position outside looking in — the more so if some kind of poster were fixed *over* the glass, establishing a definite picture plane, and locating the spectator more decidedly before it.

If the whole were not to degenerate into a kind of pre-modernist theatre, however, the surface of the glass would have somehow to be bound into the composition it covered. In some transitional paintings of 1989, this was achieved by screwing the glass down over canvases on which certain thickly painted areas of the design were still wet. Where the paint blotted and ran under pressure, the literal contact between glass and canvas was inescapably affirmed. Among the texts printed and pasted over the covering sheets of glass were some that proposed works to be painted by Art & Language in the genre of landscape. The *Hostages* painted between 1989 and 1991 were in fact based on landscape motifs, though these became increasingly deformed. As the series progressed, the bodies of paint caught between canvas and glass were enlarged, while greater pressures were applied to make them run, so that a higher proportion of each initial figurative composition was rendered into blotches and swirls of coloured paint.

Covering sheets of glass were used in Art & Language's next major series, the works titled *Index: Now They Are* that were made in 1992–1993, and also in an ensuing series of pictures featuring a steel box. By this time the use of glass was beginning to seem potentially habit-forming as a technical resource, in much the same way that reference to the museum had come to be as a means of grounding an iconography. The series of pictures titled *Studies for Incident, Foreground* were made in part as ways of leaving the glass behind — of replacing its literal presence with a virtual presence that certain illusionistic devices would serve to establish.

These pictures bring together references to a number of Art & Language's previous series. The typical figurative location — and as it were the containing genre — is the artists' studio. Shown as leaning against the back wall of this studio is the picture of a familiar form of museum interior, with coffered ceiling and slabbed floor. The foreground of the studio interior is occupied by two or three large grey open boxes. The boxes refer to another series of works, designated *Index 10*. These take the form of epoxy-coated steel boxes containing paintings that can only be viewed obliquely from above. In the *Studies for Incident, Foreground*, the nearest plane represents a transparent sheet of glass. As this is seen to end just short of the edge of the picture, it must be assumed that the literal picture surface is represented in an intervening figurative plane. The notional surface of the glass is circumstantially affirmed by patches and spots of paint. These appear to cast a slight shadow and are thus accorded the property of literal marks — though they are not. They appear to have been roughly filled-in or 'repaired' so as to match the pictoriality of the surface they obscure. But there are also patches of apparently literal paint beneath the presumed surface of glass. These cast no shadow and must therefore somehow be located as literal components of the figurative painting of the figurative interior.

The picture in *Homes from Homes II* differs from the *Studies for Incident, Foreground* to which it refers in so far as there is no direct evidence of the studio as a containing scenario. Rather it appears as though it is the museum interior itself that is the location within which two large steel boxes are placed. There is a further significant difference from the surviving studies on paper, both of which show a white margin. In the picture included in *Homes from Homes II* the composition extends up to the frame, with no margin of unpainted paper. The effect is to connect this work more closely to the numerous studies that Art & Language made in oil on canvas. All but one of these was abandoned — it having become evident that the problems of reconciling illusionistic techniques with the demands and expectations of the present were not to be adequately represented by the achievement of a modernist *trompe l'œil*, and the vitality with which the surviving exception was possessed having proved as unrepeatable as it was unpredictable.

Several works on paper remain from the *Studies for Incident, Foreground.* The one extant work on canvas makes it in spite of the very physical property that made it necessary to abandon all others like it. Works on paper possess no return edge. They are not seen as the two-dimensional surfaces of three-dimensional objects, and for this reason: their pictoriality is unaffected by the solid body upon which it is inscribed. A frame does not confer a perpendicular edge upon the sheet of paper that it contains. The studies on paper do not simply appear flat in the sense that the flat surface of a three-dimensional panel is flat. Rather they are literally flat — or rather very thin — things. And it is as a consequence of the thinness of the object upon which the picture is painted that the various stops and starts of illusion and literalness remain simultaneously in play for the viewer. On a panel with visible edges they merely grind to a halt once an oblique view of the work serves to literalise the edge, cancelling the illusion that the glass is just inside it.

In being framed with no white margin, the picture in *Homes from Homes II* courts identification with the abandoned studies in oil. At the same time, however, being painted on paper, framed and glazed, it offers no prospective view of a literal edge by which its illusionistic properties might be defused.

39

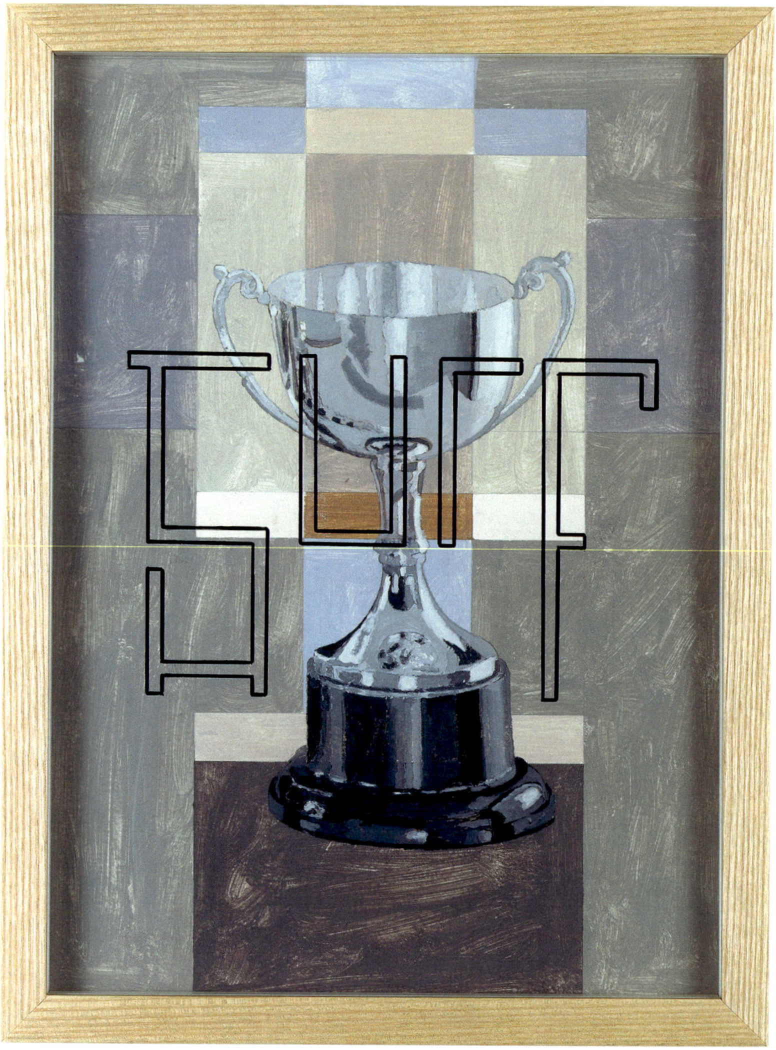

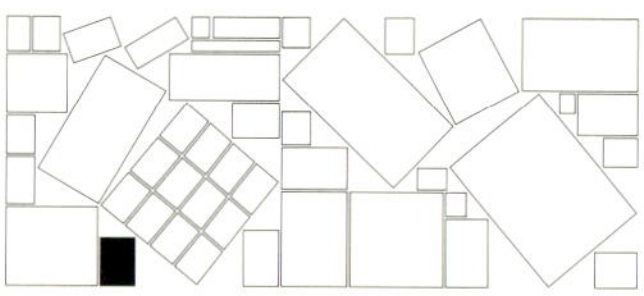

u) Cup and Surf

See

39.1

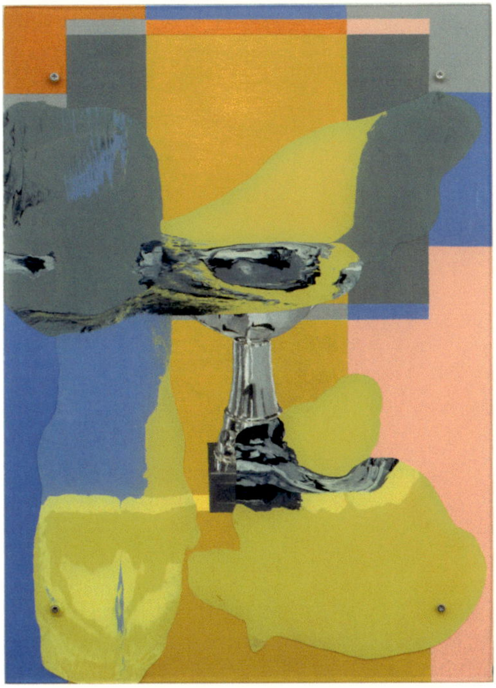

39.2
39.3

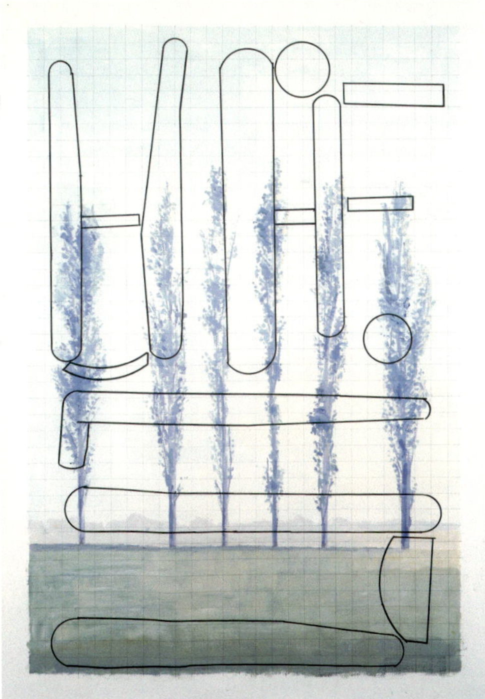

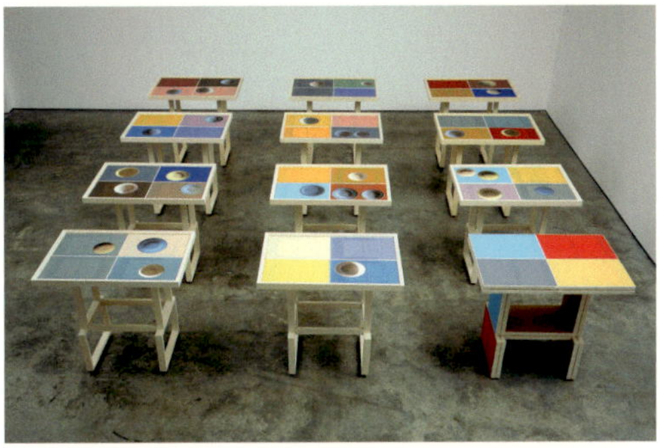

No. 39 is situated on the bottom row of the billboard, to the left of centre. In the second, quasi-chronological installation, it is among the 'later' works towards the right. In the third, 'virus' installation its kindred and affinity are still lifes, including quasi-cubist as well as cubist ones.

A silver trophy is painted in black and white on a background that consists of grey, brown-blue slabs with lighter blue and buff bars. Here is an almost decorative figure against a rather restrained background.

The silver cup is, of course, likely to be a trophy, but a trophy that marks an unknown achievement or none at all. It rests on a background that is spatially not quite capable of supporting it as it includes no unambiguous representation of a horizontal three-dimensional surface. Were the base of the trophy placed at the top or bottom edge of one of the bars, for example, it might just be possible to see no. 39 as a technically corrupt picture that had nevertheless tried to show the cup as resting on some represented surface. In this case no such settlement is quite possible.

This is a framed and glazed work on paper. Its size and manner of execution suggest that it is a study of some kind. The impression is reinforced by the graphic presence of a sort of diagram that is drawn in black ink, passing over both trophy and ground without particular reference to either. The diagram has the aspect of an architectural ground plan. Its origins do indeed lie in such a plan, but the architectural layout has been deformed so as to compose four rather eccentrically shaped letter forms: S.U.R.F. Whilst the final ancestry of this quasi-word lies in Art & Language work of 1975 (see nos. 10 and 17), the pictorial nature of the work suggests a more recent connection to the series of landscape-based works called *Hostages*. The *Hostage* paintings are characterised by a disorder of paint squashed and shifted between a sheet of plate glass that has been screwed to a panel over which a landscape in oil on canvas has been stretched. The same quasi-word SURF supplies the ordering principle by which the impasto that forms the material basis for the abstract disorder is applied. A viewer or reader might hazard, therefore, that this study-like work makes some allusion to a similar process of glazing and squashing. Although the 'corresponding' painting does not exist, no. 39 could clearly carry a certain amount of information about its possible appearance. And its appearance would bear a family resemblance to a series of works entitled *Lovely Slang*. These paintings represent a solution of sorts to the travails faced by Art & Language in the effort to examine — even to revive — the genre of the still life. No. 8 is a sort of monument to that difficulty. These are, then, paintings which belong to one of the lowest (the most homely and priggish) of the traditional genres. The still-life object here, however, is a trophy; domestic and often bathetically heroic. But there is a disorder — a disorder of paint or of representation. And this produces a distortion such that an image of a trophy in a familiarly naturalistic style is rendered more-or-less literal. That which is literal (the paint) is ever more hysterical and virtual. The geometric ground upon which all this sits is contorted into both a spatial location for the trophy and the material source of iconic disorder. The entire image is confined (alienated) behind a sheet of glass — a reflective, mirroring surface. The entire disturbance has now been processed. It occurs at a distance. The literal-turned-pictorial and the pictorial-turned-literal are all subject to a supervening pictoriality — distancing — which the glass provides. Here are decorative figures against an ornamental background or vice versa. But these are perhaps ornament and decoration which add a Huelsenbeckian admonition against the sedentary to the aestheticism of decorative ease. The trophy itself is always both hopeless kitsch — empty — *and* the replete figural container of a fraction of past action. It is also an *interruption* or disturbance upon a surface which is yet somehow prepared to receive it. The formal organization of the interrupted surface is such as to shadow the trophy without significantly resembling it. It is both shadow and possible container. But conceived as disturbance or interruption, the trophy as illusion or resemblance is all but nullified — transformed — into a smear upon the surface which it has not quite transformed into its virtual container.

If no. 39 is then, perhaps, a study for — or a description of — a possible painting, it makes no attempt to indicate that the SURF diagram is a diagram for thick oil paint. Yet the image of the trophy and the background could be transcribed literally onto the surface of a canvas as the first two stages in the formation of the pictorial content of a *Lovely Slang* painting. As for the impasto and the process by which these works claim their identity, we are left with a sort of writing. Is this 'writing' a mere diagram that shows how thick paint may be applied, or is it, insofar as it is inscribed upon some form of study, a name that designates in general a particular process of daubing, glazing and rogering? Of course, were a painting of the same basic structure to be executed some time in the future, it could amount to the name and prescription of a particular process and the result that it achieved. Until then, the merely possible is necessarily general. Perhaps we can at least say that 'surf' no longer operates as a quasi-word, but as the name of a process that is, or could be, quite real and messy.

40

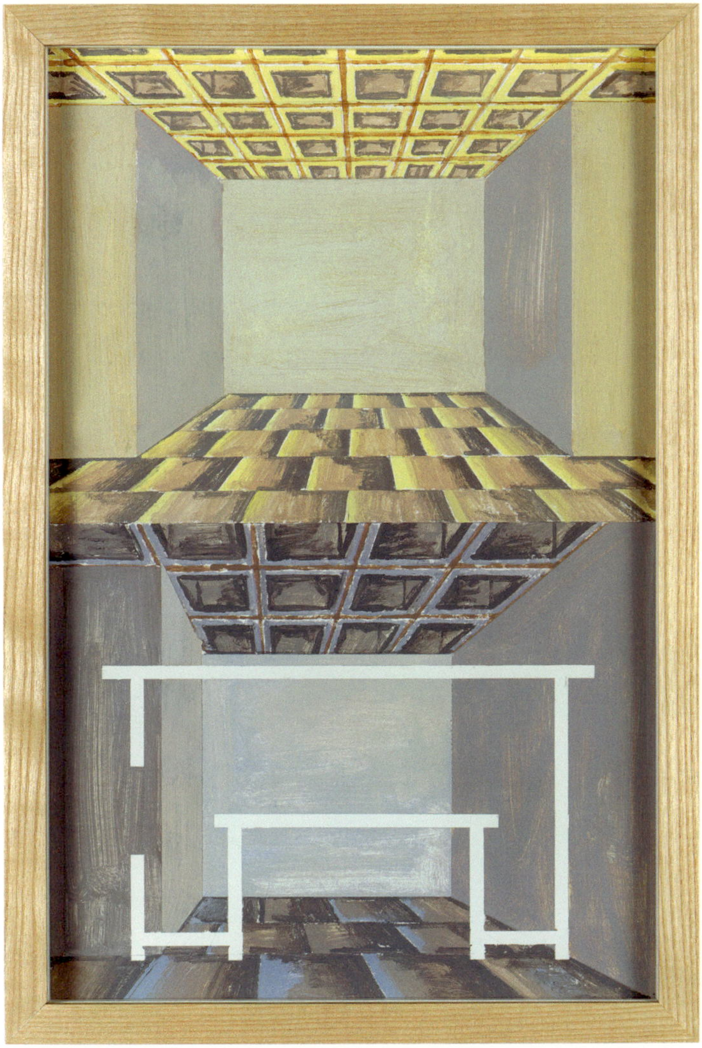

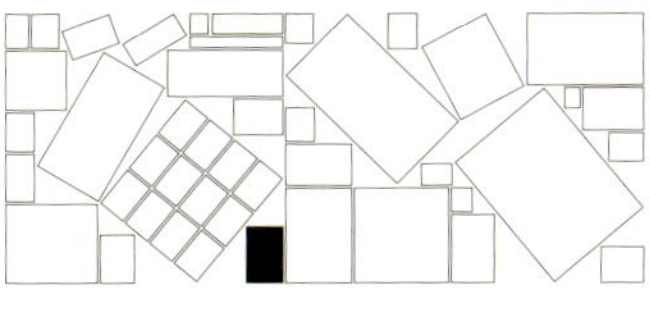

v) Study for UCUG

See

40.1

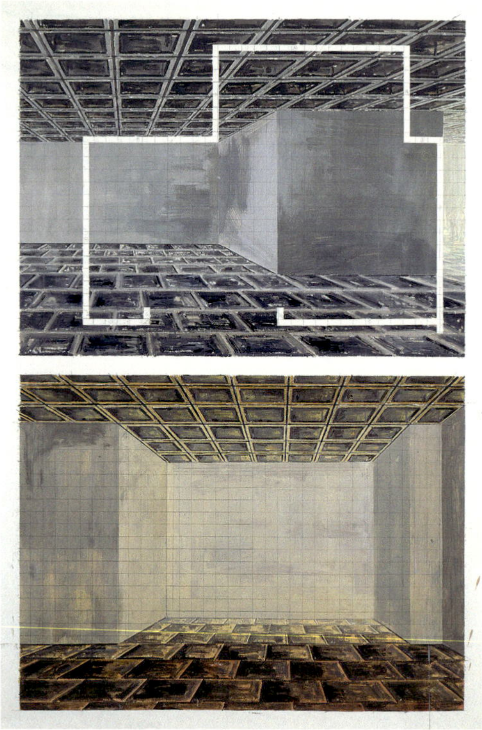

40.2

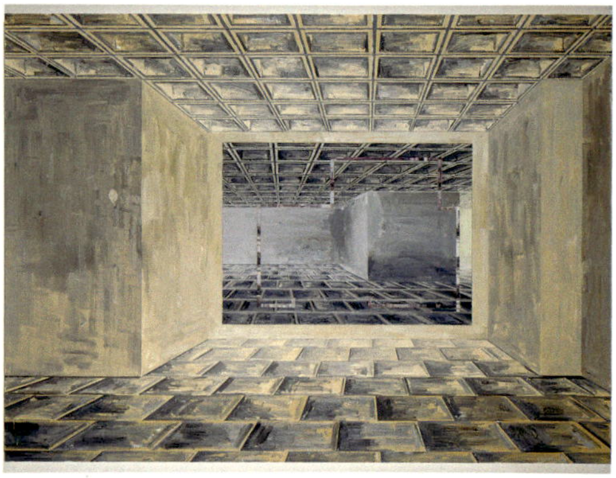

40.3

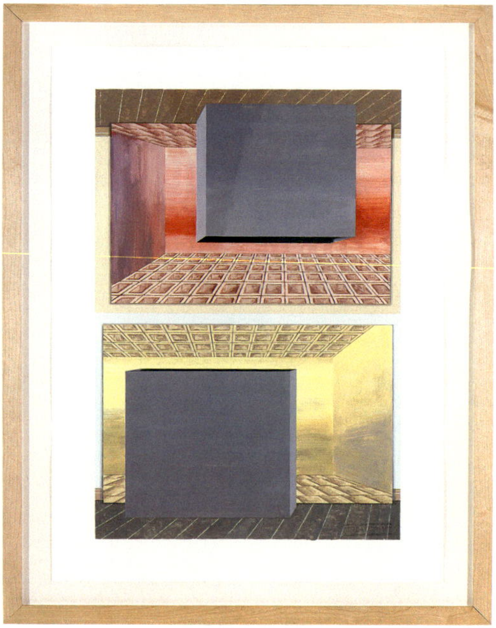

In the billboard for *Homes from Homes II,* no. 40 is set in the bottom row, slightly to the left of centre. It would appear towards the middle of the pseudo-chronological installation. It is hard to say whose company it would seek in a 'virus'. It is painted on paper and framed. It relates to a series of studies for paintings in the series *Unit Cure, Unit Ground.* The first painting with this title was made by Art & Language in 1988, at the end of the long series of *Incidents in a Museum.* It retains the figurative scenario common to all the works in that series, with a coffered ceiling and slabbed floor redolent of the modernist interior that Marcel Breuer designed for the Whitney Museum of American Art in New York.

In the *Incidents,* the museum was represented as the improbable container for a review of Art & Language's previous works. In *Unit Cure, Unit Ground* the museum interior appears in two different versions, in two different scales, one contained within the other. The nature of this containment is ambiguous. The smaller version is painted on a separate canvas literally inserted into the larger — both canvases being stretched over rigid plywood armatures. The implication is that the smaller canvas represents a smaller picture, hanging within the fictional space that the larger painting contains. Within the smaller picture the museum is empty, but for two screen walls set at right angles. Within the larger painting the museum is represented as empty but for two screen walls set at right angles, on one of which the smaller painting is hanging. The viewpoints differ between the two pictures, as though a viewer had moved.

Within the smaller painting the image of a gallery ground plan appears in, or on, the surface. The notional pattern of walls is formed by literal insertions into the canvas-covered plywood, slotted in like books into a bookshelf. Though this pattern contradicts the illusion of depth, the illusion persists. We see at one and the same time the perspectival illusion which invests the surface with depth, the pattern of the plan which invests the surface with a metaphorical flatness, and the actual flat surface into which insertions have been made. The 'spines' of these insertions are covered with heavily glazed printed papers. Close up we can make out details from a painting of a museum — one with a coffered ceiling, a slabbed floor and movable screen walls. It appears that the painting of the museum has been reproduced. Perhaps it has been exhibited in a museum, on a movable screen wall. The thought changes how we see what we are looking at, but does not resolve it. *Unit Cure, Unit Ground I* is a painting that works unreassuringly at the viewer.

The studies that the item in *Homes from Homes II* refer to were made for further paintings that would follow the general principles of *Unit Cure, Unit Ground I.* They would be based on perspectival views of a museum interior, they would involve the insertion of one smaller canvas into another, and they would contain ground plans of typical galleries that were to be marked out in the form of literal insertions into the smaller of the two canvases. The studies were made in upright portrait format. The upper portion shows what will be the larger version of the museum interior. The lower portion shows the composition that will be painted on a separate, smaller canvas and inserted into the larger. The ground plan that is marked out in white will be composed of literal insertions into the smaller canvas.

Not all the *Studies for Unit Cure, Unit Ground* resulted in paintings. A certain independent fascination attended upon these compositions with their dual perspectives, stacked one above another, and their frontal ground plan. Forgetting for a moment their practical purpose as studies that imply the insertion of the lower image into the wall depicted in the upper, one might ask, for example, what sort of structure, literal or symbolic, they are supposed to describe. Is this a perspectivally deformed image of upstairs and downstairs, or are the two images of a museum interior connected by a narrative like separate images in a filmstrip? Several years later the pairing of museum interiors was repeated in larger works on paper given the title *Study for Background, Incident, Foreground*. In these, however, those interiors were shown as painted on pictures propped up on the back wall of the artists' studio, and as providing backdrops for large grey steel boxes. And where the *Studies for Unit Cure, Unit Ground* had shown the interiors as set one above another, in the later studies one of each pair of compositions was inverted.

42–43

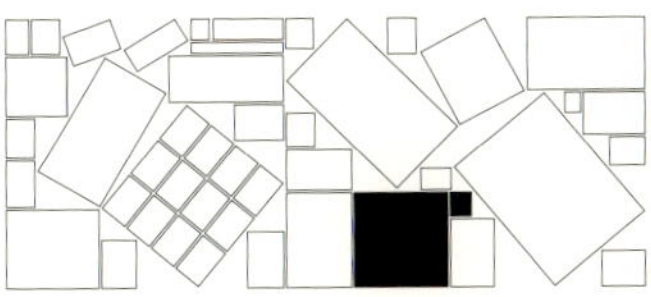

w) Guaranteed P

See

42–43.1

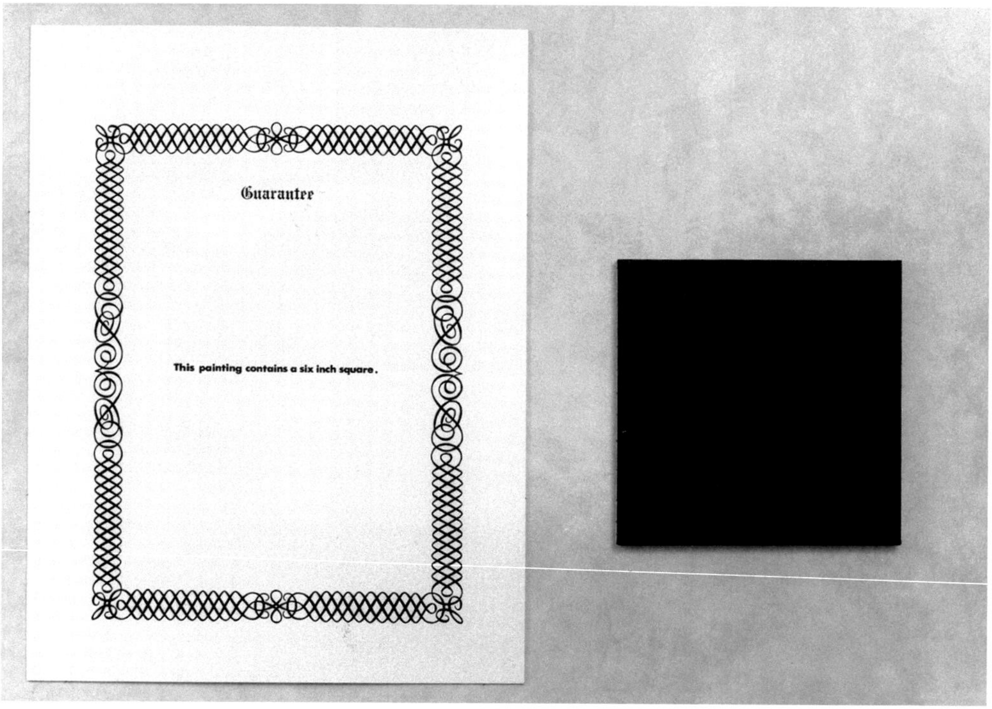

Like nos. 13 and 18, the work composed of nos. 42 and 43 has lost its looks. It is composed of a square canvas painted maroon, and a framed and glazed ‘guarantee’ printed in a similar colour. This colour is also reflected in nos. 3, 16, 36 and 45. It occupies a central position on the billboard installation, to the right of no. 40, which is of the same height. It occurs towards the left-hand — early — side of the pseudo-chronological installation and it would seek the company of certificated works of many kinds, as well as of the doctrinaire modernity that owes much to Malevich. No. 42 has lost its looks in the sense that its putative 1967–1968 prototypes are invariably black with their certificates printed in black-and-white. ‘Putative’, because it remains to be seen if a black square can in any way prefigure a maroon one. A red one, a blue one, even a yellow one. But maroon? We might say that the colour maroon is beset by the mimetic impurities of blood, sunsets and soil. While the black square does supply the content for a few postcard jokes (somewhere ‘by night’) and worse, its Suprematist associations, as well as its slightly more tenuous connection with Ad Reinhardt, place it firmly within the territory of the high-minded and culturally sophisticated. Thus to ‘remake’ a black square as a maroon one is to take away its cultural consumability. The maroon square would be at best a nervous and compromised avant-garde gesture. The guarantee, though, suggests that a certain amount of comedy had already entered the work in the 1960s. While the black square within a square of the same colour attests to the comedically unself-aware world of ‘last paintings’ and the like, the guarantee, with its copperplate swirls, suggests a world of salesmen and consumer goods of doubtful reliability. Indeed, some of the original guarantees were as large as or larger than the black squares themselves. What this suggestion leaves out, however, is the narrative of the production of the earlier black paintings. These were indeed produced within an earnest milieu where it was necessary to agonise over whether or not a smaller square was visible within the larger one, and to speculate about the implications of this. The guarantee emerged initially as a form of certification — a verbal claim as to the serious intention of the artist. And it is often understood in this way by the precious and unimaginative collectors of Minimal and Conceptual Art. But what this apparently alternative narrative excludes is the fact that the black squares continued to be made when the displacing and comic potential of the guarantee had been realised. And as soon as the significance of the guarantee was understood, the dialogue of the internal square was abandoned, together with the self-defeating technique by which it was produced. They were now plain black squares accompanied by a guarantee no longer thought of as a memorandum of privileged intention, but as a document of possibly dubious worth. The viewer is now confronted with the possibility that their optical exertions in search of mysterious content are made merely bathetic and sad. The indiscernible square has existence only as 'the opinion of the artist' and in giving his opinion he wears the garb of the domestic-appliance salesman. The puristic and high-minded gesture and all its cultural baggage have thus been brought low. The black square is now a possibly defective generic product that threatens its own earlier nature with the likelihood of absurdity.

So it is not the high-minded and cool purism of the black square that is menaced by the maroon variant of the *Guaranteed Painting*, since this had already been put in jeopardy by the guarantee itself. What the new garb tells us, perhaps, is that there have been those who have been blind to the comedy. These are its victims. Of course, it is possible that there will be those who remain blind to the implications of this slightly sophisticated decorator's colour: that it represents a doubling of the comedy (or deflation) that the guarantee imports. These are the hopeless cases upon whom the art market has long relied and will continue to rely. The guarantee says: 'you could probably have this painting in any colour you want and still go on with the pretence.' Despite its earlier artistic history the black square has become a consumer good — an indiscernible decorator's ploy that needs a spokesman from the artworld (the artist in this case) to lift it free of this lowly condition. The maroon version explicates this. The copperplate curlicues of the guarantee warn: 'Do not heed the voice of the institution. It is packed with snake-oil salesmen.'

44

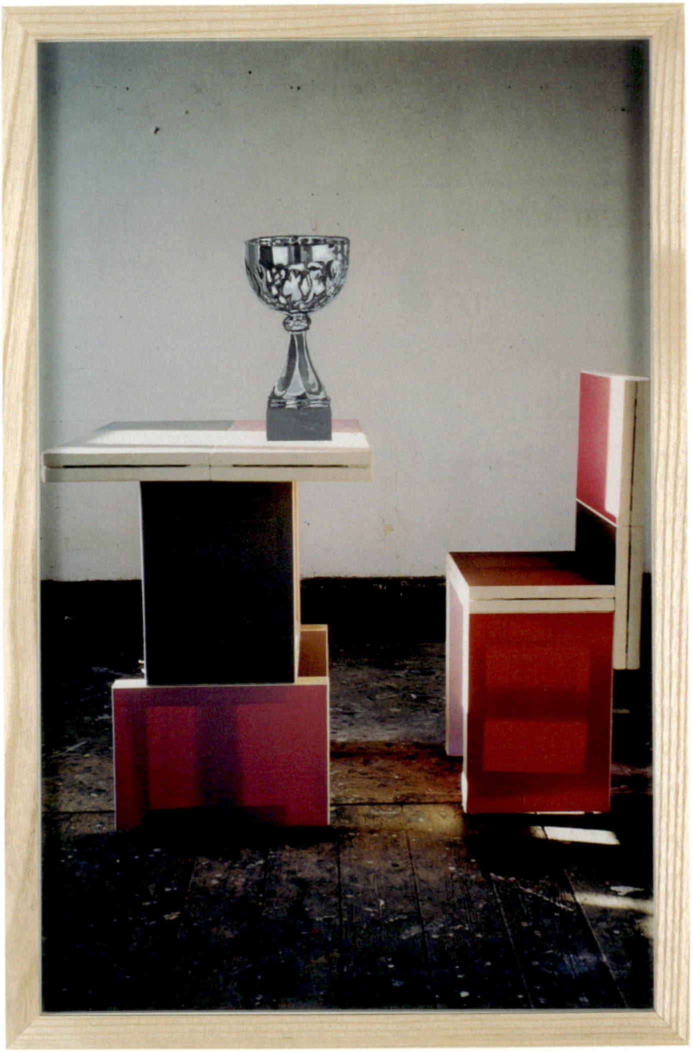

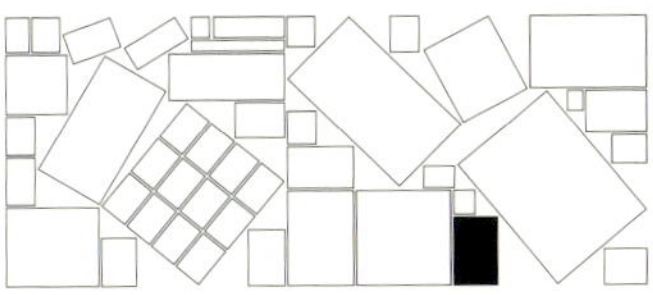

x) Trophy and STBL

See

44.1
44.2

44.3

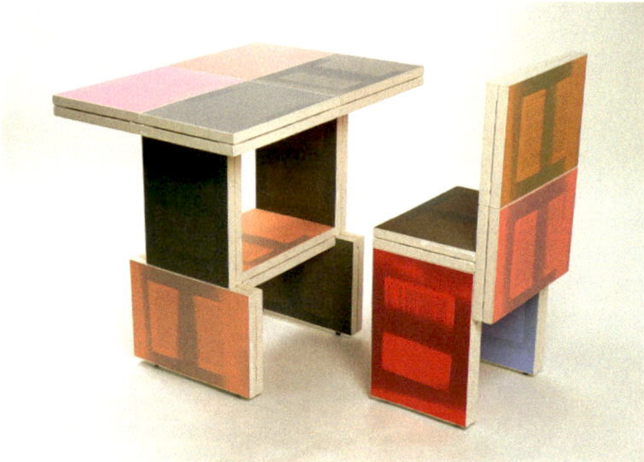

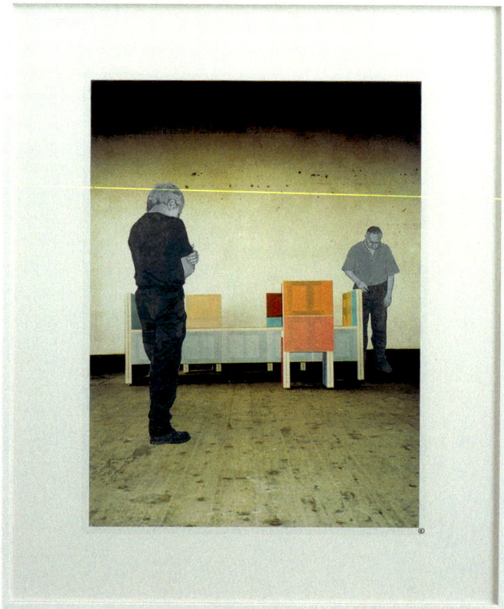

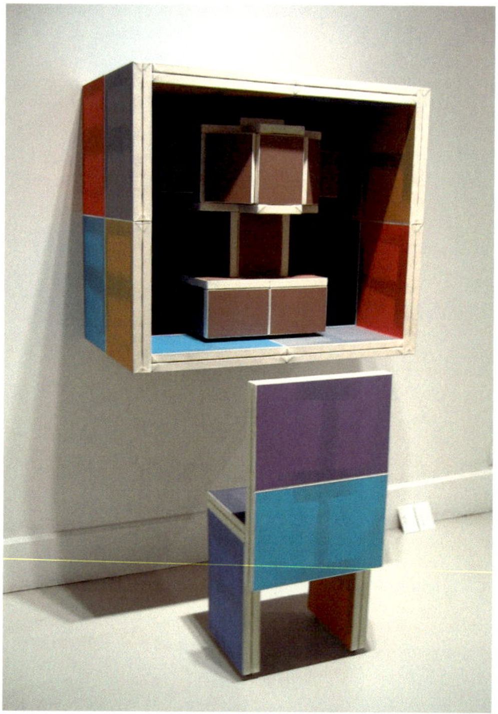

No. 44 is placed on the bottom row of *Homes from Homes II,* at approximately one third of the distance from right to left. In the second, quasi-chronological installation, it appears as a 'recent' work, towards the right. In the third 'virus' installation, it would seek the company of domestic scenes and still lifes that depict metallic objects, reliquaries and ecclesiastical plate, as we shall see.

Here is a photograph of a chair and a small table. They appear to have been constructed out of small white-edged panels each of which bears an image whose central declivity suggests an open book, or possibly an arse. An alien image has been painted on the surface of the photograph. Depicting a shiny metal cup — a sort of trophy — it appears to stand on the right-hand side of the table, towards the centre of the picture.

It is possible that no. 44 is implicated in the death-bed scene that is no. 31. The table and the chair are literally constructed out of slightly larger versions of no. 3. It is also possible that the trophy that stands on the table has escaped from some form of no. 39 or vice versa, even though they are not of the same design. At any rate, they appear to be connected to the same domestic origin, and that is not the domestic origin constituted by the studio. While no. 31 reshapes the intrusive regard that the three-dimensional bed attracts as a domestic theatre or make-believe, in doing so it renders that regard non-intrusive. In attempting to recover (and unmetaphorically to read) the surface detail of a bed that does not invite occupation, the eye falls upon it as an intruder. It is a sick-bed or a death-bed, perhaps, but if it is, it lacks an occupant. The figures are shown in states of agitation that are incommensurate with the effort to recover detail — incommensurate with the act of looking at and reading the surface of the bed. We may conclude, therefore, that they are either seeing something which we do not see, or that they are imagining something that lies upon the bed, or that they are agitated by the absence of an occupant who has now been removed. In all these cases some presence is implied that is not merely constituted by the surface detail of the panels from which the bed is made. Their regard is not the same as that of a visitor to an art gallery and they are not engaged in or by the dilemma of reading or looking that is exemplified by no. 3 in *Homes from Homes II* itself. The figures in no. 31 are in fact *grisaille* portraits of the old boys who do the work of Art & Language. It is possible that the corporeal presence that they imagine or 'see' may have some connection with themselves. After all, no-one really dies or lies sick in a representation of a bed that is, in fact, an artwork. Among the more persistent hypotheses of these (real) old boys is that, as artists, they are as phantomic as Baudelaire's Guys.

We have discussed elsewhere the possibility that the phantom is gendered and female (see no. 31). One may ask, however, why a gender is required at all. It may be that that emergent creature merely hypothesises an oeuvre out of the non-oeuvre of Art & Language. If there is such an agency, then we may want to attribute any number of social and psychological tendencies to it. These need not be any sort of mix or average of the tendencies or desires of Art & Language. In fact, it would be more instructive if the phantom's tendencies were relatively free of the determinations that bear upon those real individuals. An ungendered phantom would thus be at liberty to dream the dreams that Art & Language does not. The feminising hypothesis (the author of these works may be a difficult woman) is largely, perhaps a mechanical inversion. The ungendered alternative (an angel, perhaps) might argue for a sufficiently — or rather desirably — schizo-analytical agency — that is to say, an agency free of the triple mother, father, me.

Could it be that the bed in no. 31 is some part of the phantom's domestic inventory and that the agitation of the figures is as likely due to a (phantomic) presence as to a (more likely real) absence? The small table and chair that are depicted in no. 44 are clearly in the same room as the bed. The floor, walls and skirting board attest to this. They would be visible from the death-bed or sick-bed scene. The trophy is inscribed on the photograph by means of the same technique as the old boys are inscribed on theirs. The old boys are the domesticating psychological stains that reform the viewer's regard. They are intrusions upon the surface of the photograph that remains as fictional as the supposed corporeal presence which they see and we don't. The trophy is, then, a fiction of a similar kind, in which case it will be part of the domestic inventory of the agitated old boys. It is, after all, a trophy and this is not an angel's thing. It would seem to serve, then, to remind us that the photograph is only the image of a studio and that still-life material may be among the stuff that it contains. To say this, however, would be to misinterpret the fictionality of the death-bed figures and the technique by which that condition is established. The trophy is assuredly from the same place as the grieving old boys, but it is not easy to say what it has to do with them or with their agitation. The scene, while set in fact in a studio, is not one of normal life. It is relatively clean, and shorn of incidental detail. The small table and chair are out of sight in no. 31 but they occupy a contiguous space. The trophy would be as visible to the figures as they are to each other. (Whether or not they are visible to each other remains an open question.) Assuming that it is visible to them (and it might be irrespective of their own mutual visibility) they would see that it has been placed (by them or others of similar fictive status) for some sort of display. In this case it would be quite natural to think that the trophy has some connection with their state of agitation, a state which renders the regard of the viewer intrusive with regard to them. (They are depicted in the space of the spectator whose regard intrudes on the bed, but there are fictional conditions that render their own regard as non-intrusive.) Could it be that the regard of the spectator intrudes into the still-life scene that is no. 44? It could be, for example, that it has been brought in triumph only to be made hollow and bathetic by the absence of death. There is another possibility and that is that it is more container than trophy: that it holds some form of remains that are the key to the old boys' grief.

The container or trophy has appeared not only as an inscription upon images of a kind of furniture, but also as its three-dimensional adjunct. The putting to a new use of the canvases whose 'original' purpose was to sit conventionally on the wall presumably 'represents' the abandonment of the work as that particular type of representation of cultural consumable in favour of a representation of another. A chair made of paintings is a representation of a painting and a representation of a chair. The chair narrates the process of the painting's being brought low — and put in another world.

Other uses have been found for these small canvases. They appear in the form of a frame or cupboard for a quasi-decorative object of highly indeterminate identity which is made from even smaller canvases. These smaller canvases are all painted a uniform brown. The cupboard or frame is highly decorative and it tends to reduce the object within to something pictorial. But not quite. Indeed, one possibility is that the flat brown rear surface of the cupboard which is blocked by the object contained might be pictorial also: the viewer's sight of it is frustrated by an object of perpetually asymptotic identity, made from small versions of itself. To be confronted with an object such that one is always on the approach to identifying it is to be placed in an unfortunate position. It looks *familiar*, but familiar as what?

If *Sighs Trapped by Liars and Lovely Slang*, of 1997, provides some key to the presence of the trophy in no. 44, then a strange set of equivalences is produced. The brown object has something of the trophy or container or cup about it, even though it is constructed out of flat canvases. It has base, neck and bowl of sorts as well as the ears or handles that are characteristic of a ceremonial cup that might be used as some kind of trophy. Its surfaces are mere monochromes bereft of the image of a book and of the text it contains. They are un-decorative and flat, mere canvases of a certain Motherwellish mousiness. The object, be it convincingly a trophy or no (being a trophy is only one of its asymptotic identities), is at least the best you can do with the panels, given certain historically reflexive conditions. The trophy depicted in no. 44 may represent an aspiration for the Odradek in *Sighs Trapped by Liars and Lovely Slang,* an aspiration that it cannot achieve in the literal three-dimensional world. It is an aspiration that it can only fulfil as fiction, as an inscription upon an image of its three-dimensional world. If this is the case, we might ask what is the equivalent in panelled terms of the two grey figures in no. 31. We might further ask, if panelled men are possible, who or what could be depicted as a visitor upon their photographic image?

45

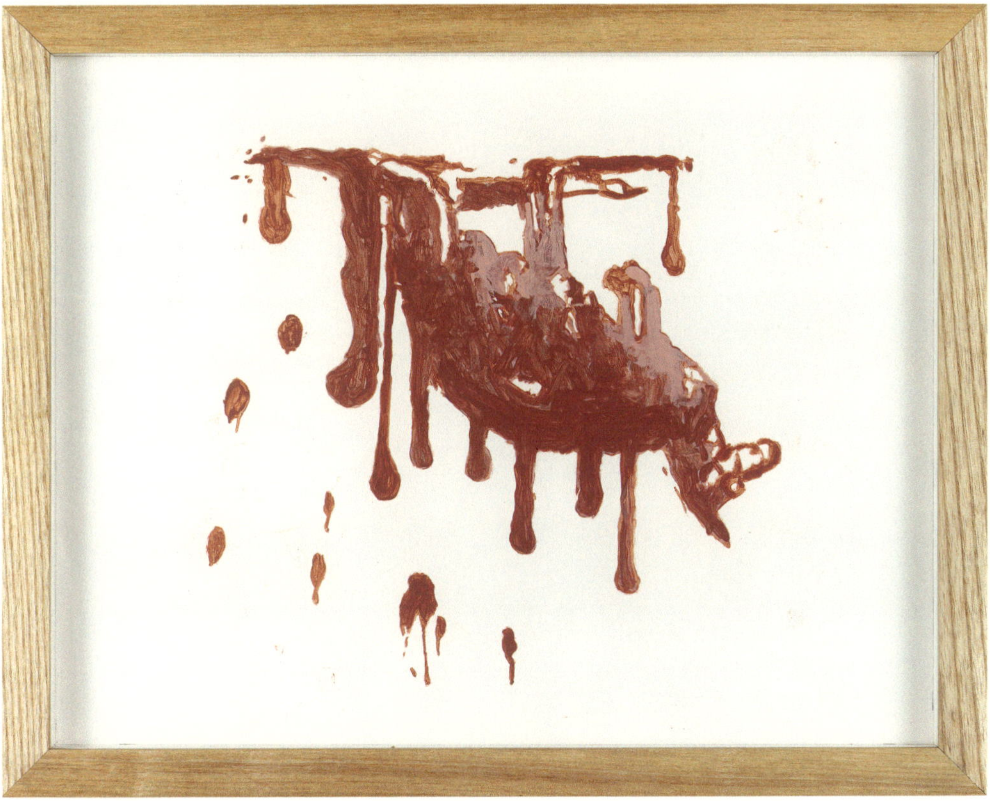

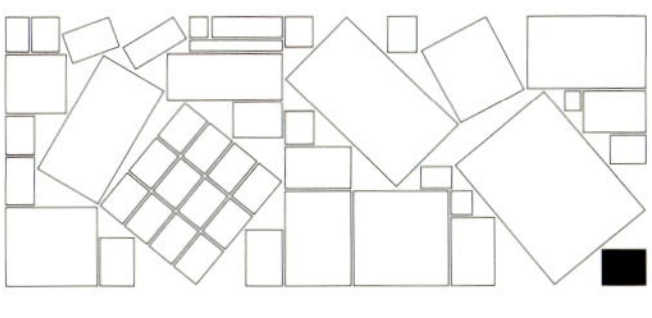

y) Kangaroo

See

45.1

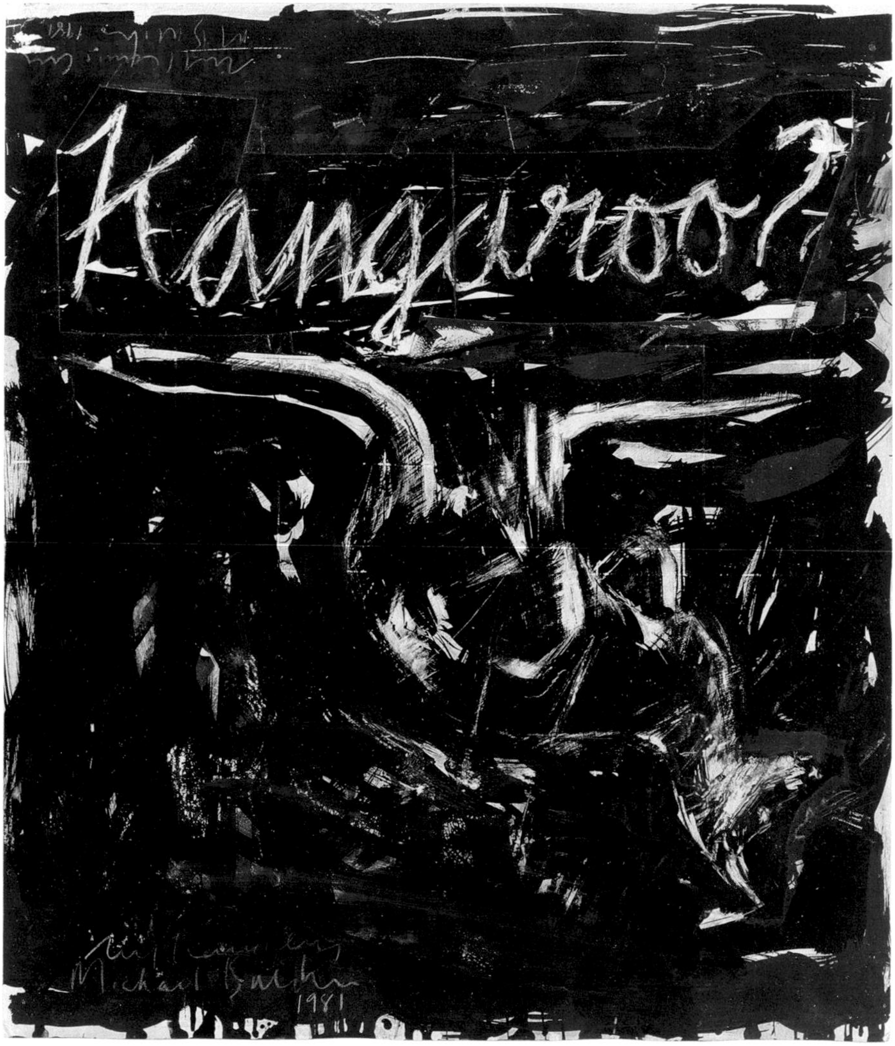

No. 45 is a small framed picture. In the billboard of *Homes from Homes II* it occupies the bottom right-hand corner. A kangaroo in profile is depicted on paper in reddish-brown paint on a white ground. This colour is distributed quite widely across *Homes from Homes II.* It is shared, for example, by another carnival creature, the dancing elephant in no. 16, as well as by no. 42, and it is prominent in one of the large chequers in no. 36. No. 45 is installed toward the mid-term of the pseudo-chronological installation. The image is inverted. However, the paint from which it is composed appears to have dripped and run downwards in accordance with gravity. The implication is that the kangaroo was painted upside-down. Inescapably, the little picture evokes the more portentous work of the German artist Georg Baselitz, whose brashly painted pictures of inverted motifs were sometimes supposed to have presented an expressionist riposte to abstraction. It is the company of Baselitz that no. 45 will seek when installed as a 'virus'. Our kangaroo also evokes the absurdist truism that from the perspective of the British Isles, the denizens of the antipodes must all be upside down.

This happy conjuncture was suggested by a specific historical coincidence. In 1981 the work of Baselitz was featured in the reactionary but attention-grabbing exhibition *A New Spirit in Painting*, held at the Royal Academy in London. In the same year Art & Language and the Red Crayola released their second long-playing record (re-released in CD as DC80CD/dex2 by Drag City/Dexter's Cigar, in 1995). The LP was titled after its lead track, the song, 'Kangaroo?' The little picture in *Homes from Homes II* refers to the cover-design made by Art & Language for the LP, which shows an inverted kangaroo in the style of Baselitz. More specifically, it is derived from the design for a lapel-button originally produced to advertise the LP.

Composed in the early years of the Thatcher government, Art & Language's lyrics were jammed uncomfortably between a sort of Adorno-ish desire to 'improve' the lyrics of pop songs — to give them a political and intellectual edge — and (for want of a better way to keep the comparison going) a Benjamin-like interest in the prospect of a relatively wide distribution.

But to say this may be to sterilise the memory of the project. The discomfort was calculated. The musical performance and the lyrics were engaged in an uneasy *détente*. The latter enjoy a fairly high degree of unfeasibility as words for pop songs, which gives them a certain power to refract or otherwise distort the former. The desire for 'improvement' was therefore a desire to produce something unfeasible. The project required the organisation of a series of collisions and the performances — by professional punk musicians — were an instructive record of the damage as much as an overcoming thereof.

The Western name for a kangaroo has a genetic character — a history, as do all representations, in general. The story of the name — as cited by Ian Hacking in his article, 'Why Language Matters to Philosophy' — tells us about the history of its producers. Our culture, particularly our high culture, has names and conventions as certainties to cover the hiatus of its contradictions.

The lyrics of the song are as follows:

On their voyage of discovery,
Of privation and cartography,
The sailors said to Captain Cook,
"Come over here and have a look.

We've caught a creature with a pouch
That leaps and springs and seems to crouch.
It head is small, its ears are long.
Its legs and tail are thick and strong."

No-one knew what the creature was.
Some men were sent ashore because
Animals must have a name
(And the natives knew the game).

Meanwhile, the captive, pushed and shoved,
Was given leather boxing-gloves.

The men returned, trusty and true.
"They tell us it's a kangaroo."

(The truth emerged much later when,
On trips by less resourceful men,
The Aborigines told those who'd come to stay
That 'kangaroo' meant "What did you say?")

Emergency conditionals

MB Michael Baldwin
MR Mel Ramsden
CH Charles Harrison

MB By way of an opening we need to ask just what the term Conceptual Art is supposed to pick out. It has lately come to mean more-or-less any kind of art that does not explicitly seek to attach itself to a technical tradition and is not medium specific. Art is no longer conceived on the basic principle of a painting / sculpture axis, but rather as a current and continuing generic product capable of installation and distribution within some institution of an artworld.

MR As an alternative, we could think of Conceptual Art as a specific critical development in the historical ambience of high modernism during the mid-to-late 1960s and early 1970s. In talking of high modernism we mean not just a selection of transatlantic art made retrospectively in accordance with a purified Greenbergian theory – not just the paintings of Morris Louis, Kenneth Noland and Jules Olitski, and the sculpture of Anthony Caro – but also the work that both overlapped and competed with theirs: Frank Stella's, Don Judd's, Dan Flavin's, Robert Morris', Sol LeWitt's. A Conceptual Art movement conceived along these lines is associated with a specific historical period – though we can still argue both about how that period is defined and about what work does or does not come up for the count. Thus, by analogy, while Cubism was a movement with fuzzy boundaries, and while the epithet 'Cubist' was used by non-professionals as late as the mid-twentieth century to refer to odd-looking avant-garde art, it could be said that a Cubist painting made in the 1950s would have been unlikely to deserve much serious critical attention.

CH It might seem that these two different modes of usage of the category of Conceptual Art are easily enough reconciled. We can simply consider a continuing generic Conceptual Art as the long-term outcome of the historically specific Conceptual Art movement – or of what has been called 'modernism's nervous breakdown'. But we have to be careful. It was not as though practical dissent from hegemonic modernism had one single possible outcome. It might have seemed for a while that everyone was busy disinterring Marcel Duchamp and playing the same game of appropriative and nominative gestures. (I think of this as the 'When Attitudes become Form' moment – lasting until around the summer of 1969.) But it very soon became apparent – at least to Art & Language – that this could develop in several quite different ways, from which we pick out a contrasting pair.

MR It could go towards a kind of *institutional theatre*: from Joseph Beuys and Daniel Buren to the more recently celebrated works of Ilya Kabakov, or to more-or-less anything liable to be installed in the Turbine Hall of Tate Modern.

MB Alternatively it could lead to a kind of *essayistic practice* that reflected upon its own conditions and considered the language and vocabulary and historicity of the appropriative gesture itself.

CH But these were not possibilities with equal pragmatic legs. The first may have been the complaisant client of demotic institutional theory, but by the early 1970s informal versions of that theory were spreading apace both through the avant-garde sectors of the artworld and through the graduate departments of American universities. The art of institutional theatre both rode and was ridden by various types of fashionable postmodernist theory, and particularly by those that were vehicles for virtuous anxieties about the consequences and inequities of class, race, gender and expansion of the media. Its various practical modes were unified under the sign of the curator, and were supported from the world of cultural studies and corporate radicalism.

MR In the climate of taste this alliance has served to encourage, pathetic modernists like Cy Twombly, and anti-modernists like Francis Bacon and Lucien Freud could be recuperated alongside such exciting newcomers as Damien Hirst and Tracy Emin. 'You've got to choose between Mondrian and Duchamp', Ad Reinhardt said in 1967. Now choice means the right to consume everything indifferently.

MB Not long ago we participated in a symposium addressed to the question, 'What work does the artwork do?' On that occasion we suggested that for the sake of argument a distinction might be made along the following lines: on the one hand there are works of art – and theories about works of art – based on the proposition that work is what spectators do in variously animating the work of art through interpretation and exegesis. It should be clear enough that the art of institutional theatre tends on the whole to conform to this mode, and that it delivers itself up with some facility to journalism, whether of the popular or of the academic variety.

MR Media-led critical bullshit sticks easier to the slight and the trivial than it does to the articulate and the complex.

MB On the other hand there are works of art – or theories about works of art – based on the proposition that whatever work is done is intimately connected to the intentional character of the artwork, and that the work in question is what that artwork does in animating its suitably attuned and attentive spectator.

CH We should make it clear, perhaps, that we do not here mean to invoke that Wollheimian gentleman who is the artist's boon companion. We simply mean to suggest that there exists the possibility of interpretative failure, and that to a significant degree the work will be the arbiter of that. When we refer to the intentional character of the work, we do not want to suggest that this is the intentionality of a single individual, but that there is some critical dialogue that the work and the viewer enter into regarding what is relevant and resonant in a given interpretation, and that one of the participants in this dialogue will be the work itself conceived as intentional.

MB The second, essayistic, type of Conceptual Art tended to look to the second of these modes. It separated itself out from the permissive *mélange* of 'When Attitudes become Form' at a point when it no longer seemed defensible to treat modernism's nervous breakdown as an occasion of opportunity. It developed out of a kind of anxiety regarding the relaxed, ostensive practice of dematerialisation-as-liberation. One couldn't just live in a relaxed world of wilful artistic ostension. How, we asked, might one make work with detail in a circumstance where the possibility of detail is not given among the resources of a specific medium? By detail, what we had in mind was some aspect or set of connected properties that both required and arbitrated a complex description – one that was not just an account of how the work interacted with the artworld.

MR The problem wasn't that one objected to art getting away with things under the artistically demotic forms of an institutional theory – 'If someone calls it art, it's art' and so on. For the most part the emptiness of Conceptual Art amenable to such theory just seemed critically harmless.

CH Nor was the problem how to have something of aesthetic interest in a Wollheimian sense that nevertheless didn't have the physical properties by which that interest was supposed to be provoked. At a certain level the issue of aesthetic interest was simply beside the point. Art is theory-laden and concept-laden whatever anyone claims to be seeing and feeling in front of it – and not just any old concepts or any old theories. Peter Lamarque has made a similar point with respect to the work of Rembrandt. It could be said that essayistic Conceptual Art simply made an issue of this.

MB The difficulty was that neither of these senses of the problematic took adequate account of the consequences of the collapse of the Greenbergian mainstream; nor did they properly acknowledge the insecurities attendant on the institutional theory – the concern that it might simply be wrong in its accounting for the relations between perceiving and describing, or that, in accepting it, artists might find themselves in an invidious position vis-à-vis actual institutions – or in a dead end so far as art was concerned.

MR In fact it could be said that one consequence of the institutional theory has actually been to licence an obsession with the idea of art as generic, when much of what is produced in the name of generic art could quite well be accounted for as continuous with the critical concerns of late modernism. After all, there are actually very few Snow-Shovel-like things, but many paintings with words and tasteful arrangements of stuff – which do no more real damage to modernist ideas about medium-specificity than did Frank Stella's black paintings.

CH As we have already suggested, the alternative modes we have labelled institutional theatre and essayistic practice were not actually equivalent and parallel developments. The consequences of the development of generic Conceptual Art were such as to suppress the discourses of autonomy and internality, and to obliterate the sense of a parallel development that retained some investment in their continuity. It grew fat on the very theoretical resources it claimed to have transcended. In the new hegemony, even the supposedly outmoded modernistic discourse on autonomy was somehow incorporated and represented.

MR But we do clearly identify the practice of Art & Language with the essayistic alternative. We are therefore unwilling to accede to the idea that generic Conceptual Art is the unchallengeable outcome of the original Conceptual Art movement. This does not mean that what we have been and are trying to do is to flog Greenbergian modernism back into life, or to reinstate its concepts of autonomy and internality. It may be that our form of Conceptual Art had in common with painting the fact that it did not actually *require* a specifically institutional kind of theory to tell it what it is. But given the way things were going, autonomy was always going to be a contested and insecure project. It was not as though the question of what work the artwork does was ever really going to be settled one way or the other. Indeed, if it were, art would almost certainly be a thoroughly uninteresting business.

CH We should try to review some of the conditions of problems. One is that the critical negativity [bankruptcy?] of modernism was part of the reason that the Conceptual Art movement could emerge.

MR A second is that institutionality is or has become a sort of enslavement to management.

MB A third is that only by means of some form of internality combined with some capacity for detail could death by curatorship be effectively resisted.

MR A fourth is that the denizens of the happy world of wilful ostension failed to grasp the complexities and difficulties of the very language by which that ostension was being effected. Instead they relied both on the artist being accorded a kind of 'Romantic' authenticity and on a complaisant acceptance of the transparency of his words.

MB A fifth problem is that this authority and mystification could only be resisted by description, and by a theory that was in some way internal to the work itself. What was required was a social world in which and into which the work could be uttered.

CH In fact it is not entirely clear which came first: the imperative to beat the curator by creating a descriptive circumstance, or the need for some sort of internal complexity in the work.

MB The best way to resolve that issue is to say that a sort of context of conversational concentration was 'naturally' established once one recognized that art is vacuous unless it is describing as well as described.

MR And once you have got a conversational process going it tends quite naturally to take on a project-like character: in being conversational it tends also to take account of the world of which it is with difficulty a part, and in which it is uttered. It is thus availed as a matter of course of the grounds on which to contest claims for the internality of its own outcomes. This is to say that a conversational practice will be disposed to sustain a degree of tension between, on the one hand, its contextual and institutional circumstances, and on the other the kinds of claim it might make to internality (to having an oeuvre, and to there being some degree of formal integrity in its products, and so on).

CH In fact the conversational practice tends to militate against any purified sense of what the work is, so that its capacity to constitute an oeuvre is severely impeded. There is a popular representation of Art & Language according to which we are held to have made an avant-garde claim to the effect that our conversations and proceedings are art. This vexatiously misses the point. It takes us as it were back to the original point of bifurcation and associates us with the institutional theatre of such figures as Ian Wilson – who did indeed claim around 1970 that his conversations were art.

MB We can recall having had conversations with Ian Wilson. We can recall nothing of their content. The presupposition was presumably that as artworks they need have none. 'Conversation' was a quasi-Duchampian readymade – in this case an appropriated category, or ... what? In fact were one able to remember the content of a conversation with Ian Wilson one would be the less likely to recover conversation itself as a readymade.

MR For us, the conversational process was not a Duchampian gesture. Though it may have had heir-lines to it, it also had heir-lines to the 'internal' critique of high modernism and its penumbra. But first and foremost it was a means of exchange and production. The point was that we were in no position confidently to impose a sense of artistic hierarchy on the distinctions between verbal discussions, informal on-paper exchanges, essays and pieces of paper stuck to the gallery wall. Of course certain hierarchies did get established for purposes of publication and display, but they were matters of practical contingency.

MB It would be wrong, though, to suggest that there were no normal aesthetic considerations in play. Whether we cared to admit it or not, certain matters of taste were relevant, and these were of a more-or-less Wollheimian kind – to do with the physical properties of things.

MR That which was produced for distribution and display was not without its vestigial aesthetic aspects. There was no pink Conceptual Art, and absolutely no green. What tended to predominate was the black, white and grey of the office and of the otherwise socially unspectacular. There was a kind of truth to materials in this. In those days there were no colour photocopies. In the case of a great deal of Conceptual Art – some of our own included – there may in the end be little remainder once considerations of graphic taste are accounted for. It is an open question just how far Wittgenstein-on-the-wall escapes significantly from the kind of aesthetic admonitions that were associated with the work of Don Judd without in the process simply being reduced to an inefficient form of Wittgenstein-on-the-page.

MB We did have some anxieties about this at the time. What followed were texts printed in green and red and so on. The point was to evade the myth that neutral taste was co-extensive with critically significant dematerialisation – and that there was a progressive political aspect to both.

CH We were well enough aware of the silly hypostatisations. Some of the talk about dematerialisation certainly muddied the waters. In fact it was in muddy water that we saw our work as in constant transition between the conversation, or the theorising that it recorded, and the gallery wall it had syndicalised or taken over. In so far as it achieved some independence from graphic considerations, that work put itself in the way of aesthetic virtues that were literary – either theoretical or descriptive.

MR It did not follow, however, that in so far as it achieved virtue of a kind it must therefore be embedded in the theoretical discourses of literature or philosophy. To say that it was theory was false, since the work it did as art absolved it of the standard assumptions that it was truth-telling, coherent or extensible in ways that theory and philosophy are supposed to be. Nor was it literary in a normal sense. It did not and could not demand of the viewer that (s)he be a literary reader.

MB This sense of permanent transition and instability brought us to what we called an emergency conditional. The work was theory (or something) just in case it was art, and it was art just in case it was theory. Could we say then, that in its strangeness it resonated with both?

CH And, further, permanent transition and instability called forth other emergency conditionals. We were artists just in case we were critics and critics, or teachers or art historians, just in case we were artists. This 'homelessness' gave the work a brief independence; paradoxically, a place of production that was not wholly subservient to institutions and disciplines.

MR But what if someone objects that the work actually *was* 'theory'; that it could be read and (occasionally) used as theory. Is it then displaced or disqualified as art? We are not sure that it is. It may end up, like Flaubert's *Madame Bovary*, as a kind of book about nothing. But if it *is* theory, then on the whole it will try to be about something – some object or relation or process; and this will then map it back to the circumstances of the original bifurcation consequent upon modernism's nervous breakdown.

CH What is perhaps more to the point – if more problematic – is the thought that by around 1968 to 1969 the original ontologically iffy artworks – air-conditioned rooms, columns of air and what have you – had been swamped or themselves partly displaced by the theory that was intended to be 'about' them. The *Air-Conditioning Show* of 1967 furnishes an example. This consisted of a text proposing the air in an air-conditioned room as an art object and expanding on the problems that that proposition entailed. The question raised was, 'Is it necessary actually to install air-conditioning as described in the text, or will the text do just as well?' Was the text to be identified as the art – the meaning – we make, and was any concrete 'realisation' of that which it described merely a conservatively contemplative distraction?

MB We might think of this question as marking the distinction we have already proposed between Conceptual Art thought of on the one hand as a kind of Duchampian extension of Minimalism occasionally outside the realm of middle-sized dry goods, and on the other as a fundamentally textual cultural practice.

CH Imagine that someone asserts that 'Everything in the unconscious perceived by the senses but not noted by the conscious mind during trips to Baltimore in the summer of 1969' is his work of art, and someone else says, 'What do you mean?' The 'What do you mean?' is supposed by the artist and his admirers not actually to impinge on the assertion. To treat that assertion as a speech act – or its textual equivalent – is to commit a kind of foul. It seems nevertheless necessary to treat it as the speech act it actually is. But to do this is to impede it. What we had in mind was a kind of text in which the interrogative is included along with the appropriative claim – and one which would therefore be an object of a quite different order The consequence was considerably to increase the detail of the appropriative gesture – the theoretical content that it wore on its face.

MB The difference entailed is more than merely quantitative. The viewer is made a reader of sorts – a conversationalist of sorts. This seems a not undesirable outcome. It is one with which we have tried to render our subsequent practice consistent. Conceptual Art may entail a way of making art. If it is one in which painting as traditionally understood can only be sentimentally pursued, it is not necessarily one in which the possibility of internality is ruled out. What may be ruled out is the idea of an oeuvre as unified by some biologically authenticated style. A conversational practice will tend to rule against certain kinds of consistency and purification.

MR If Conceptual Art as we understood it had a future it was not as Conceptual Art – not, at least, if what that means is simply the Duchampian model emptied of its transgressive potential and rendered congenial to the managers of interdisciplinarity.

'Emergency Conditionals' was given as a paper to the conference 'Philosophy and Conceptual Art', King's College, London, 4th–5th June, 2004, and is forthcoming in the collection *Philosophy and Conceptual Art*, to be published by Oxford University Press. It appears in Spanish translation in the catalogue *Art & Language*, Centro de Arte Contemporáneo de Málaga, Málaga, 2004.

To say of a painting that it is a fake...

Not everything on show at the Arts Council exhibition *Don't Trust the Label*, which travelled to Hull, Nottingham, York, and was seen by us at the Royal Albert Museum in Exeter, is fake. One form or another of the real thing contrasts with dodgy prints, infantile travesties, pot-boilers, genuine reproductions and genuine fakes. But what gets you to go there (and what all the road signs direct you to) is a *Fakes Exhibition.*

A fake is somehow 'inauthentic'. An authentic work of art is presumably an item regarded as somehow justifiably attributed to an artist as part of his oeuvre. But this is indifferent as to whether this item was or is regarded as a fake. Only non-fakes can be *authentic* and this includes authentic fakes. You know. But what is thought to justify attribution? Presumably some sort of causal connection between a work which is the subject of the attribution and the artist to whom it is attributed (irrespective of whether he is an unmasked faker or not). The idea that a picture *P* is an authentic Picas Osebracs, involves assent to some factual particle expressing some sort of causal or technical connection between Picas Osebracs and *P*. But for whom is the idea that *P* is a genuine Picas Osebracs useful?

David Phillips rehearses some of the above in his lucid if rather Gombrich-for-the-masses catalogue introduction. The category is useful for historians. Insofar as historians are interested in questions of *of-icity,* want to abjure rampant readings-in, want to justify interpretation etc., their deliberations will go to some such factual particle and to constellations of related and less trivial ones. But history must leave such questions open. *History* cannot properly close inquiry, even though – in fact – it must. And there are forms of 'history' which do it arbitrarily. History doesn't or shouldn't always need the historiographical dramatics of the Hitler diaries farce. History, or rather historians, will have to decide if the factual particle (and etc.) implied by an *authenticity* claim is retrodictively significant, to what extent such a claim is buried *in* as distinct from undermined *by* historical work, and so on. Fakes are the stuff of historical scandal. In general, they are really *bad* news only for very unlucky art historians or for methodological mastodons – or to put it another (and perhaps preferable) way: the independent justification of authenticity claims is really *good* news for ... etc.

Apart from these people, for whom is the justification of an authenticity claim *really* good news, its non-justification bad news, etc.? A fake is a 'moral' wrong insofar as it entails fraud. The paradigm is currency: the bank note, the share certificate, the coin. Mr. Phillips makes this more-or-less clear. A 'fake' to make your kids laugh is no fake (?) ... unless you get them to pay the price ... or what? The logic of the fake as distinct from the innocent distraction (and etc.) is not at all easy to unravel.

Fancy pragmatics or not, what makes a fake scandalous, and what makes the spectacle recounted in the catalogue of Kenneth Clark and other architects of *Civilisation* before a fake Botticelli *funny*, is *money.* The authenticated, genuine work of art is the fetish basis of a system of exchange. More particularly it is the fetish basis of a system of power, of a sense of stable cultural government. The fake (as distinct from the joke, which is more problematic) has always been *serious.* Forgery is political action. The emerging capitalist state made coining a special crime: treason. The faker commits a form of cultural treason.

The fake abjures intentionality and as a consequence closes off the possibility of interpretive discourse. Few wonder what a fake means, few try to find out. It does not follow from this that fakes are figurally empty; they may not 'mean' in some first-order sense, but they are not devoid of figural power. In being shorn of first-order meaning, the fake raises the second-order non-cognitive to the level of its *primary* mode of signification. Fakes are a displaced metonym for art – or for the possibility of its non-cognitive nature. The Fake (the capital 'F' signifies a fake that's been exposed) displaces the first-order murmur of aesthetic predication to make it either past ironical spectacle, or memory or just a faint possibility. The realisation of this faint possibility would require some aesthetification of the Fake which occurs rarely, but which is *conceivable* as a consequence of the aesthetification of the Fake genre as such. Another remote possibility would predicate aesthetification on the loss of the Fake's history as a Fake, as distinct from loss of aesthetification as a Fake.

While we do not wish to call up the spectre of the *structure à dominante,* a subset of what might be called 'the meaning of the *dominated'* comprises the first-order meaning of the Fake. Its 'meaning' is its 'history', and its history is conceived as a function of a gross materiality. The surface of the Fake is effaced in all respects save its materiality. Intentionality is conducted in a secret life. (Some forgers suggest exceptions to this. They are the driven. Van Meegeren and Tom Keating are seen as obsessive or compulsive – and therefore 'artistic' – demystifiers and not as 'real' crooks. They persist in the cognitive margins of the culturally instructive.)

The exhibition is far from inviting the above kinds of reflection, implicitly or explicitly. It isn't uninformative though. It is an invitation to the visitor to play a game of spot the Fake (or the non-Fake). The relationship between the labels and the short commentary on each work in the free leaflet (the works are only *numbered* on the wall) does compose some sort of structural possibility of cognitive life for the onlooker. This seems natural with Fakes and other stunts, less natural with the authentic.

The exhibition attests to the idea that works of art do not speak for themselves. This is a distinct motif in David Phillips' introduction. The catalogue takes off a bit where the rather limited show leaves off a bit. The busy-ness which the show provokes is in the end rather more *Antiques Roadshow* than emancipating. (And rather obvious sometimes: for example, the leaflet captions belabour the point that a photographically-based reproduction of an L.S. Lowry is not that much like the original.)

The introduction is, however, too anodyne on the matter of the connection between art and money. Mr. Phillips notes cheerfully that: 'Some academics, collectors and even dealers regret the hijack of art by finance, but hijacked it has been' (page 5). The genetic character of the fake makes an open line of the hermeneutic circle. This reduction of the aesthetic is conjunctural with (or bears striking homologies with) the consequence of certain developments (or attenuations) of the modern.

As we have suggested elsewhere, the hijack of which Mr. Phillips writes has been accomplished. And it performs either a massive de-centring of critical tasks away from the aesthetic, or it centralises them in aesthetics in thrall to finance.

The comparison of a Fake picture with the 'real thing' is compelling stuff. Picasso and De Hory, Dufy and De Hory, Palmer and Keating, Daumier and Fakes, Corot and Fakes, 'variations' on the same work by Ford Madox Brown, Bonnington good and bad and copies, Brueghel the younger (surely a faker anyway) and a fake, Rembrandt and dodgy late pulls from knackered plates, Goya's similarly, and so on.

This is an exhibition about Fakes – i.e. failed or exposed fakes. The possibility of failure entails the possibility of success. The successful fakers are lurking like sleepers, but the show is a record of arrests. And while the catalogue weakly disavows the financial implications of fake-finding, the exhibition goes to a rather Fine Courtauldy ethos ... Fakes are not as Fine as the real thing (copies of his or her work by an artist are not [quite] fakes) ... and Fineness can be specified in gluttonous detail.

Attempts to hoodwink experts and make fools of the professionally Fine give lots of people encouragement. The aesthetic is embattled by contingency and non-ineffability. The show effs the fakes and sees no real reason why this would remind the onlooker that the Fine might also be effed. The police have caught the inauthentic unaesthetic, thereby ensuring the security of the ineffably aesthetic.

But 'never mind the label', says the big type: 'The aesthetic is the emotion that wells into the void. Aesthetic pleasure is sufficient reward, and it is dependent only on the fineness of eye and object.' It is, however, precisely the culture, the ideology, of this eye that propounds a justification of the consumer fetish and the power it entails. This *eye* is the ideological ground of the price tag and the price tag *requires* the label. The unreflective application of the exhibition's title goes to the practical reason of the hijack of which the catalogue introduction complains.

Don't Trust the Label presents a range of the inauthentic. But neither the leaflet nor the catalogue theorises the varieties of inauthenticity exposed. (Perhaps the samples are vivid enough.) The nineteenth-century Botticelli (the one that had Kenneth Clark) is a smart bit of iconographical mixing and a technical *tour de force.* Competent. A white fiver written by a forger who practiced, which might fool a bank manager, etc. Criminality or deception emerges as *technicality* of a complex and sophisticated kind. The painting is more-or-less capable of sustaining canonical iconographical consideration; a bent artist; the edges of a primitive allegory. The 'Van Gogh' *Sea at Saintes-Maries* is by contrast a vulgar travesty. The paint relief was achieved with a thick white undercoat; the figure in the boat is waving in a jovial way. The catalogue informs us that it was 'commissioned' by one Otto Wacker, 'dancer turned art dealer'. The game was exposed in court despite the 'hilarious inability of critics, scientists and officials to agree upon anything. The despairing judge was finally reduced to handing over critical assessment to a policeman.' What cultural agnosia links these two items as Fakes? A factual particle? The list continues: the dodgy prints are a variety of 'fake', but administrative as much as aesthetic. The Andy Warhol pirate *Marilyn* is administrative again – a pirate edition of the authentic of inauthenticity. The De Hory Fake Dufy is 'superior' to the Dufy pot-boiler in the show (Dufy, a *pot-bouilliste par excellence*). (De Hory's Picasso is perhaps less convincing, but Picasso did do five million works a day.) The exhibition also includes a bit about cleaning and conservation, an 00 brush copy versus a real mediaeval work, Hans Van Meegeren Fakes versus a contemporary copy of a lost sixteenth-century original, and so on.

Considered together these are theoretically vivid varieties of the fake. But to fail to account for the diversity of 'vertical' and 'horizontal' relations which the various examples exhibit between Fake and non-Fake and Fake and Fake is to render the exhibition client to the *culture* culture of the label and submit it passively to some form of the Fake-labelling factual particle. Rhetorical aporia is a part of the two-fold and ironical nature of *Fine* art. The ironical face is more often than not a merely redemptive feature, subsumed within the margins of conservation and security. The redemptive distancing of the ironical fall, *pace* Baudelaire, entails a conventional falsehood about the nature of irony, and in the end, about the nature of signifying stuff. Such conventions of falsehood require a constabulary. The Fake (and the fake) and reflections upon its nature, the copy, the malingerer, the fraud are all indices by virtue of which *Fine* art's unrelieved ironical nature *could* emerge as culture.

'The critical power of the Fake', its anti-hermeneutical virtue, imposes no interpretative limit however. The hysteric produces forms of fiction, he fails to demystify the text in advance. The malingerer lies without a radical sense of irresponsibility. The critical culture of the modern exists in the margins of one of these or the other. The relationship between them, the priority of the one over the other, the matter of their truth and untruth, will be decided neither by a factual particle (a sort of Piercian end to inquiry), nor by an appeal to a residual sense of semio-authenticity to which an authenticating factual particle goes.

To ask how many falsehoods are entailed by the truth of an authenticity statement in respect, say, of a Picasso, is to say no more than 'such truths are embedded in convention'. The values assigned by apparently 'empirical' claims are interdependent with the rules of distribution. These claims propose strategic classification and not natural kinds.

As we have suggested, David Phillips is not wrong in saying that (factual particle): 'authenticity and condition also matters to the historian. Unrecognised imitations of transformations bear false witness to their supposed age' (page 5). Is this because: 'Only the market for holy relics has provided even more scope for the forger than the art market?' He continues, 'Maybe belief is a helpful first step in the aesthetic process, and one of the functions of an art gallery, with its pompous architecture and confident little label, is to convince you that all is well as far as authenticity goes, so that you can safely launch into the next stage of getting worked up into a fine artistic rapture' (page 12).

But what Mr. Phillips does not tell us is *why* there is so little to trust. The museum and its hieratic contents are suborned, if you'll forgive the expression, by an amnesic repressiveness, a myth of security that denies the possibility of the social action which makes (and remakes) the world (or 'society' if you want). There is little apparent alternative to the myth that you can deduce the 'how' of a picture from the 'what' of its mechanical or iconic 'surface' and the 'what' of what the label – small and neat or big, implied and *cultural* – says.

With certain honourable exceptions, the critic and the credible art historian are made strangers – replicas of Wittgenstein's Victorian Parson – in relation to those productive and authorial complexities which constitute the *genetic* character of works of art. The forensic-type investigations which give this exhibition much of its *frisson* are a travesty of such complexities. Fake finding discovers a spectacular simulacrum of a conventional 'chain of events'. The closures performed in the critical business of administrating the 'expressive' and its cognates are liable to confuse the police. Incorrigible *savoir* disgorges readings-in (and worse) in an atmosphere of security. An intuitively basic set of aesthetic predicates goes to the presumption of retrodictive groundedness while suppressing those forms of inquiry is not invited: the implied invitation is to a form of empiricism buried in the culture of the aesthetic. The already demystified text which is (or could be) presented by the work of art is mystified anew in an interpretative (distributional) language which clings blindly but inevitably to the corpse of empiricism. (The observation can be defended against the fashionable post-Nietzschean cry that no one thinks of empirical 'grounds' at all: the continuing basis of the power of the system of noonday chatter is the figure of its centred-ness in the world. Its real metaphor points to the possibility that it may be 'taken literally' in a sense admissible to its unadmitted empiricism.)

The administrative spectacle of the contemporary modern is therefore good cover for the faker. He squats hidden in the belly of the monster. Next to him sits the hysteric. The figural was never so figural. Somewhere down the aisle sits the straight man for whom the factual particle in one of its guises is a guarantee of the continued sanity of civilisation. What threatens him is the thought that you can't shock the *bourgeoisie* any longer, you can only swindle them. Consider the possibility of the mischievous curator. Who would be the straight man then?

'To Say of a Painting that it is a Fake…' was first published in *Artscribe International*, No. 63, May 1987, pp. 64–65, as a review of the travelling exhibition *Don't Trust the Label*, organised by the Arts Council of Great Britain. The exhibition was viewed by Art & Language at the Royal Albert Museum, Exeter, April 1987.

Making meaningless

The Sedentary and the Stand-up

The maddest (and bitterest) of our interlocutors rail against the appearance of what are called 'paintings' in our work. There are others, calm and urbane, who frequently demand an account of this appearance. We are often bored by the prospect of providing one, preferring a slightly different answer each time. The demand for an account, however constructive and urbane, seems to encase the assumption that only a policed purism – in our case the policed purism of Conceptual Art – is uncontroversial. Our briefest reply might be that the changes of practice and project, of which the appearance of painting is one, have been occasioned by obvious critical imperatives. Nevertheless, the fact that we might also have to account for the emergence of paintings in terms of strange and strenuous narratives, populated by delusions and contradictions, suggests that these go to the very heart of the work.

Start anywhere and try

Wollheimian purifications notwithstanding, pictures and paintings may carry the weight of all sorts of intentions and go to all sorts of practices. One perspective's subversiveness may be another's aesthetic decadence; incompetence from a certain viewpoint may be a refusal of the established codes from another, and so on. *Painting* is often a vague and tendentious category. In the mid-1960s some painters were engaged in an end-game. What seemed possible then was that painting and its critical others were and would remain continuous with a tradition of negation, refusal or dissent. This possibility no longer exists. Recent cultural and moral developments have produced award-winning dissenters, award-winning swearers and cursers – and award-winning criminal lumpens. In creative consultancy culture anything can be an award-winning something. The Communist Manifesto has been printed as a coffee-table book.

With dissent made over to the representational terminology of management-and-worse, an artistic practice which had tried hard to keep clean at least some of its critical and inquisitive tools might well suffer a sense of crisis and confusion. It would have to ask if this representational terminology had indeed supplanted and suppressed all conditions of critical inquiry. It would be too simplistic to argue that undifferentiated Conceptual Art comprises both critical and manipulative forms of dissent. Differentiated, there are types of Conceptual Art, which have more to do with one form of dissent than with the other. But even in a type of Conceptual Art more attached to the critical than to the manipulative, the latter sits uncomfortably close. Black-ish on very dark grey. Critical Conceptual Art was never simply straight-faced inquiry. It was leavened by a discursive amateurishness and an intellectual delinquency and it was the resonance between these and the straight-faced, which (usually) repelled the manipulative. The louder voice, glorious in its neo-vernacular forms, is that of Conceptual Art as executive culture, pumped up and identified with the curator and the manager. Indeed, we have often argued that many Conceptual artists *always* thought that theirs was the managerial opportunity. For them, critical tasks are merely the remote source of cultural atmospherics. But they fit close. Beleaguered and forlorn, but close.

Those recently successful artistic practices which lack so much as a short-term sense of history pile on further grounds for confusion. It is very difficult to go further in search of meaningfulness than the images which promote and advertise these practices. The fact that these images are often supported by (or co-formed with) altogether conservative and even antique senses of intentionality and purpose is simultaneously a good reason to discuss them and a deflationary stab at one's own critical self-image. Desperate to preserve the self-image, one might say that, in being historyless, this stuff faces no substantial reflexive tasks, has no need to test its professional boundaries; it either sticks or it doesn't. But it would be self-servingly uncritical to suggest that the effectiveness of all this merely reduces to a misunderstanding or misidentification of managerial action in artistic clothes, or to the theatrical props of celebrity-seekers mistaken for potent cultural markers. The history-free images which form the surface of what often passes for an artistic practice, and which seem from a critical perspective to drive the self-images of the age, are not reflected as a simple negation in the critical practice of those who have set themselves the task of working against those self-images. The negation is much more equivocal: figure and ground mediated by representation and reflection. These relations may produce unexpected reversals, even violence as two figures try to occupy the same ground.

Conceptual-ish Art of the 1960s was informed by (among other things) that very late modernity of blankness and negation that was disconnected from the Duchampian tradition. Here was an end-game drive to purification which was also a search for a fetish of the clean. This modernity of fetishistic blankness was, above all, able to acknowledge its contamination by what was outside it. The neatness and precision of for example LeWitt's late-1960s work, was always to some degree polluted by the world. And that's what gives it its sceptical, unprofessional edge. In the effort by historians to account for the emergence of Conceptual Art in adult professional and historical terms (read Thierry de Duve or Benjamin Buchloh) a development more difficult to trace and individuate has often been neglected. The high professionalism of late 1960s modernity produced a critical other in the form of protocol-refusing unprofessional activity, confused perhaps, but prosecuted with a certain transforming historical urgency. If the (historical, material) contingencies of a practice are acknowledged, then the professional's bubble bursts. This often happens unexpectedly in open inquiry. To say this in 1998 is perhaps to point theatrically at the inevitability of emerging paradox or recurrence: push something hard enough dialectically and for long enough, and it will assuredly come back to swallow its own tail. Well, that may be true, but true without differentiation in detail.

In the *undifferentiated* solidarity of the late 1960s, some Conceptual artists entertained fantasies of a gallery-free or even bureaucracy-free art. It was a reflection of an entrenched and sleek marketing system. However naïve these fantasies seem now, they amounted to a significant contribution to many artists' self-images. A later and corollary development saw the appearance of Marxism-Leninism as the *sine qua non* of serious Conceptual Art. However maladroit this may now seem, there existed a (moral? practical?) pressure to theorise and to substantiate, a desire to replace merely unhistorical refusal, insolence or mischief-making in the face of market protocols, with a theorised dissent – practical and even 'organised'. Art-world-y 'radicalism' was recognised as palliated management, and its forms as constrained within the necessary requirements of 'professionalism'. The professionalised avant-garde had traded management skills for politics. It had to reform itself as a political vanguard – something like a political party. While what was generated was in general quite a lot of embarrassing agit-bullshit, it should not be forgotten that at this time, which abuts and overlaps the period in which the *Indexes* were produced, Art & Language was at its most 'participatory'. And some of the first paintings – actually pictures – are caught somewhere between the Indexing projects and Russian Constructivism.

The possible re-emergence of *pictures* coincides with a time when art was repressed in favour of politics. The necessity for *substantiation* of the amateurism of a certain fraction (ours) of avant-garde-ish Conceptual Art led almost paradoxically to the consideration of *pictures* (not yet quite paintings). From the point of view of something called 'class consciousness', Conceptual Art just looked like an extreme *bourgeois* mannerism. Pictures could be contemplated because they were the unexpected gift of a practice transformed by politics.

We have to do better than Thorsten Scheer when he claims that 'Conceptual Art, by separating essence from material presence, had intensified the independence of the work from its physical embodiment to such a degree that even a return to painting became possible' ('Richter and Art & Language: Conceptual Aspects of Postmodernism'). There is something dodgy here. It's too easy. Scheer's assertion might be correct if Conceptual Art 'has nothing to do with the form of presentation', i.e. if it is radically separated from its material form. Logically it must then be possible to include all sorts of things in the category of Conceptual Art – including 'painting'. And if you can't include painting, one is bound to ask why not; why is the line drawn here? If painting is somehow outside the range of possibilities compassed by Conceptual Art, then one might suggest that Conceptual Art cannot be 'separate from its form of presentation', and argue that it reduces to (a particular kind of) neutral graphic material plus taste. In other words, it becomes another specific kind of art, rather than, as the regularly resurfacing cant would have it, *generic* art, or 'art in general'. To put this another way, unless it is inclusively generic then it must be attached to certain material genres – things that look like Conceptual Art. If it is a set of theories and strategies for recovering Conceptual Art-type contents or meanings, then it would be able to develop these for things like paintings – which of course would cease to be first-order paintings (or traditional ones). These too would be detached from their material genres or essences.

In the light of these difficulties we suggest that Conceptual Art purism is significantly activated by fear. Fear of the low. Much in Conceptual Art style and practice exemplifies a search for a new social status for the artist. This exemplification can be either adventitious or essential. There were Conceptual artists who sought to colonise the discourse of the critic – either by putting the critic's words on walls, or by declaring that words in books were art. There were others for whom questions of raised social status were pre-eminent in their *arguments* for their work. Whether as by-product or essence, artists refused the role of manual labourer and sought to arrogate to themselves the *power* of the bosses and the managers. (The possible connection between Conceptual Art's upward rise and the various vicissitudes of shop-floor-management relations remains to be studied.) But if the striving and desiring is 'heroic' in a way, it also contains the source of its own corruption. There is an hysteria in some Conceptual Art fanatics' fear of 'painting' as something manual, hand-made and low. What it threatens is an artistic life as entrepreneur and in 'representation'.

We've argued before that to continue with the surface historical 'logic' of Conceptual Art was to be forced not to go deeper into the implications of the Duchampian rupture (tricks etc.), but to lose what was radical (or oppositional, or critical or emancipating) about that, and to submit to unwanted determinations and fall into an unwanted form of life. Of course, 'going deeper' would itself be enslavement to ultimately footling provocations. It would liberate no one. But this 'logic' had transformed the critical materials of Conceptual Art, Duchampian or otherwise, into a bureaucratic décor. Blown up quotes from the local intellectual celebrity and 'penetrating the space' had got itself established as an *aesthetic* whose genericness ensured its congeniality to, and amenability to control by, the people in charge. For us, Conceptual Art was never a mature professional style but a black box (or a black box in a black box); what is sometimes called 'a genuine historical moment', changing forever whatever happened 'next'. What happened in that moment inaugurated a process and a project. And it was given to this project to recognise that there continue to be baffling relations between text, pictures and painting, and that the expulsion of the two latter from the purview of the artist is a cheap closure which fails to recognise the constructedness of the world. It is a closure on open inquiry, and therefore a closure on the idea of art as open inquiry of a special (and no doubt odd) kind–which was the most important idea of the Conceptual Art moment, if not of Conceptual Art itself. This idea is packed or stuffed into the history of Art & Language, and of some Conceptual Art, and flows in part from the unpredictability of collaborative work and of social and class activity and awareness. Do we conclude that we never did Conceptual Art, or that ours was an apostate function?

Art & Language has been a collaborative practice–in one form or another–for over 30 years. This has led some to claim that it is a kind of Conceptual Art *sect*. Michael Corris has described Art & Language during the period 1972 to 1976 as an 'art gang'. A gang is an aggressive organization or an informal rabble whereas a sect has constitutive beliefs and often intellectual pretensions. A sect is nasty and aloof whereas a gang is concrete: violence plus street cred. A sect generally deviates from the normal, is involved in some sort of apostasy, major or minor. This is what identifies it and holds it together. A gang has practical goals and consequences, clear or not. It may be that Art & Language has often shifted somewhere between a sect and a gang. Where that somewhere is, is not entirely clear. The negative connotations of both terms seem to go to a fear of unknown allegiances or of unprofessional behaviour and contradiction. Various 'memoirs' of former Art & Language participants would seem to reinforce the sect or gang idea. As they see it, they are now the ex-members of a gang/sect and it is no good now they aren't in it... and in fact their departure was justified. With the hindsight of 25 years they know better. Self-patronising sentiments and the paranoid fixations of the stalker are perhaps also the very powerful marks of sect membership. In fact it might be argued more informatively that an embittered and disappointed coterie of former participants is forming a little sect whose feeble image is sometimes projected upon those who continue.

An example of the strangeness which attended the emergence of pictures (possibly not yet paintings) is provided by *Portraits of V.I. Lenin in the Style of Jackson Pollock* and by the *Studio* paintings 'by mouth'. The generation of something (a text) recoverable within the practical ambit of a Conceptual-Art-like practice led to 'aesthetic' and even contemplative *presences*. Titles turn into pictures, which, as a negative consequence of being processed, turn into paintings. A line runs from *Portraits of V.I. Lenin* through the *Studio* paintings to the *Incidents in a Museum* to the *Hostage* landscape paintings. It probably ends in a loop with the *Cunt* paintings (the series *Index: Now They Are*).

Art & Language's practice has been project-like and essay-like. And this entails that it must be a *critical* practice. Necessary but not sufficient for this is that it is also a collaborative practice. *Work,* in the sense of non-wordy action and its consequences, is embedded and then re-embedded in conversation, until the edges of what is work and what isn't work vanish and then re-appear in different places. Strange displacements and hybrids are generated, not by juxtaposition but by fallings-in. Figures inhabit figures (or non-figures), and this somehow recalls and reflects what is often called 'indexing'. Some people see this contentedly as 'self-referentiality'. But what the displacement implies for us is that the visible (and invisible) production has an unstable past and an unstable future – a synchronous and diachronous contamination by narrative and an unpredictable release from it. A step forward is a hopeless deterioration, a step back or two or more a helpless overreach. This temporal slippage is also a 'spatial' one. Characteristically, a literal thing will turn figural, objects will become fictions, a face will transform itself into a mask, and so on. Ventriloqual relations proliferate: there's a difficulty as voices inhabit dummies or bodies not their own. The technical and the productive are liable to obscure a sense of cultural purpose or directedness. A dislocation from *telos*. For instance, instability in (or loss of) the connection between cultural effects and the *means* of achieving those effects leads to a virtual weakening of the mechanisms linking work to culture. This remark is no doubt rather old-fashioned, but it is hard to continue or to know that one is continuing without a story – a passing theory – of what one is doing now, with what, etc. The barbarism of the present requires that a knowingness about culture is entirely separated from the mysterious competence of 'technicians' – those people who know more than where the hammers are in art galleries, and who are often – no, always – the most interesting people to talk to. The banishing of *politics* and virtue has seen a reinforcement of hierarchies of work and an increased dissemination of lies and nonsense, in the interests of an ever-more-idle and useless but ever-more-intrusive management.

It could be that some of the 'cultural' questions effortlessly posed by early Art & Language work can be so described only because we can't remember the detail of its being made. What are technical questions, and where are their edges or margins in a world where cultural production is either journalistic fallout without detail, or non-participatory but manipulative expertise? Of course, journalism is a kind of practice, as is Conceptual Art purism. They are posed on the two horns of a dilemma. The journalist/cultural theorist keeps the gates and polices his or her role. The purist pushes at the gate and polices his or her history. Technical difficulties trace all manner of lives lived, and their material circumstances. They are all but invisible from the Land of Cockayne of Cultural Studies, and from the professionalised production in its thrall (academic art), which makes none but the *smartest* of moves.

It is tempting here to suggest that painting *is* to be defended *culturally* because it is a space (or place) from which expert convictions of cultural relevance or epochality can be aggressively denied – or drowned in decoration.

A more-or-less identifiable period of Art & Language work – from say 1982 to 1992 – finishes with the *Cunt* paintings. Pink 'blank' paintings with mirrored surfaces, paintings with 'secrets' – a bit like the painting and post-Minimalism from the mid-1960s which ushered in text, dialogical forms and so forth. The pink-near-blankness required an animation in the spectator (described in *Art-Language*, New Series No. 1 as 'dialogical aura'). The *Cunt* paintings seemed to do two things: they apparently materialised a discursive space (or place) *in front* (strangely) of the painting (for the beholder), and at the same time seemed to remove the facticity and focus of the painting as some sort of compelling whole. Since this time we have not managed to do a single ambitious 'painting'. Since this time the work has seemed without exception unable to avoid a three-dimensional (literal/figural) *confusion.* Homeless paintings. We seem now to be left with a problem something like this: we could see ourselves as continuing to paint. However, the focused 'facticity' of the work has had to confront the fact that it was just as important to do things 'with' the painting as to do things 'in' or 'on' or 'to' the paintings. These 'modalities' (if that's what they are) make discursive *arrangements.* These may be decorative or they may be installational. The point is not simply that it's hard to know which. These may simply not be the practical alternatives in respect of which the works seek to dispose themselves.

The consequences of 'installation' on art are dramatic and troublesome, far more than the seemingly stylish initial ruptures of Conceptual Art. These consequences have been with us particularly since the early days of big Minimalism. The causes of the huge increase of installational forms of art are not difficult to work out. Since 1945 the growth of so-called cultural output has been enormous. In New York in 1945 there were a handful of galleries and a score of artists exhibiting. Today there are 200,000 artists in the New York area alone showing at some 800 or so galleries. Around 15 million works are produced in a decade, compared to about 200,000 in the whole of late nineteenth-century Paris. This is in part due to the terrifying proliferation of lecturers, galleries, curators, museum staff, art journals, art-market journals, the internet, etc.[1)] Consequently, turnover time is reduced and distribution and marketing are accelerated to the point where *what bears down* upon the artist are exhibitions, catalogues, travel and so on. The *form* of the work is determined by its efficiency in terms of packaging and distribution. It needs exhibition credibility and a feasible turnover time. It can be argued that this reaffirms art as a form of social production in exchange and consumption – something 'public'. On the other hand, the imperialistic expansion of market-driven effects has pensioned off traditional genres far more ruthlessly than Conceptual Art ever did. There is much in history-laden art genres, including 'disgraced' ones like landscape and still life, with which to form a place or a representation of a place of historical continuity *against* and (perhaps) outside the efficiency requirements of the world of cultural output. But nostalgia is the source of the worst opposition. What forestalls it are the undreamed-of disorders and abjections of hybridity.

Consider what we've done since around 1993: constructed sheds from seven large paintings, hidden paintings in grey steel containers; made paintings into small sheds and then mounted these on TV wall brackets, etc. It's hard to avoid a rather dusty sense of creative-things-to-do-with-

1) The comparative figures are given in Brandon Taylor, *Modernism, Postmodernism, Realism: a critical perspective for art*, Winchester, 1987, p. 77. David Harvey draws attention to the significance of Taylor's figures in *The Condition of Postmodernity*, Oxford, 1990, p. 290.

paintings. No focus, no identity and no ideas as to how to take advantage of an absence of focus and identity; not much to concentrate on anyhow anywhere. Some of these are hybrids perhaps, but not in the 'post-colonial' sense. More in the wow-shaped canvas sense – or worse. Time of briefest shadow.

The work did gain some focus and a sort of identity in 1996 when the open pages of the book 'paintings' were made or rather displaced into a kind of furniture – quasi domestic objects made from the newly decorated (i.e. spruced up) defeated relics of Conceptual Art and the ghost presences of Conceptual artists. (We tried very, very hard to make these coloured essays into focussed paintings. We perhaps succeeded in doing so with the Documenta X *Vitrine* insofar as we defeated certain conventions of beholding. But even that was near three-dimensional. The two-dimensional surfaces reached an horizon, and this provided real *material* out of the difficulty of focus and its advantageous form – displacement.)

We seem now to be in a familiar position – familiar as to its abstract logic – of confronting a set of technical-type displacements which are *both* the subject matter and the material stuff of the work. The technical stuff is not at all familiar.

This work occupies a narrow space between two walls. One wall is covered with inscriptions or decorated with trophies. These attest to the failures, scandals and successes of Conceptual Art. The other wall is also inscribed or decorated, but these marks or trophies largely attest to the absurdity, scandal and failure of painting, a few to the possibility of its renewed potential. Paul Wood might say 'that's a condition of its realism'. Others might say that Art & Language has just burst the professional artist's bubble of Conceptual Art with painting, and burst the bubble of painting with Conceptual Art, and that this is the reason for Art & Language's 'failure'. That's the Elmer Fudd view. We'd argue that those are the conditions of the work's success: it is irritable and restless because it is teleologically incapable of sleeping the professional's sleep.

Recently, in response to yet another boilingly paranoid pseudo-memoir replete with recollections of radicalism, one of us suggested that 'it was time to get the decorators in'. But what does 'getting the decorators in' imply? Is it that the decorative is the subversive other of high modernity, which can cause it to slide towards the domestic, towards furniture? This would be degeneration into that which Greenberg hated (or was fearful of) and Adolf Loos described as criminal. Heroic modernity made domestic is neither one thing nor the other. It's a kind of failure: the ventriloquist and her dummy.

Clement Greenberg called Robert Motherwell's work 'arch'. He observed that Motherwell was like the interior decorator who staked everything on a happy placement. Everyone knows this is right and that Motherwell's work is largely a joke. But there is a powerful sense in which the very truth of Greenberg's observation is what makes that work interesting and instructive. Motherwell's work embraced the very terror that stalked Abstract Expressionism: apocalyptic wallpaper.

Some time ago at a conference in Vienna we had occasion to trot out the old joke-cum-story of Newman's shutting the door, Rothko's pulling down the shade and Reinhardt's turning out the light. The punch line is that we've been going on in the dark ever since. (That's what one of us said.) The meta-punchline is that we've been stuck with the joke ever since (and are now stuck with Motherwell pasting up the wallpaper too). (That's what one of us wanted to say but he was beaten to it.) Can 'Conceptual Art go stand-up?'

Tony Godfrey says in a forthcoming book on Conceptual Art: 'Matisse wrote of how he wanted the experience of his paintings to be like sitting in an armchair, but conceptual artists have generally opposed such sitting down.'[2] Richard Huelsenbeck, in his first Dada manifesto, was definitely against chairs: 'To be a Dadaist means to be an artist only by accident, to be a Dadaist means to let oneself be thrown by things, to oppose all sedimentation: to sit in a chair for a single moment is to risk one's life.' If the decorators come in and we make and exhibit a chair we might think that this aestheticises politics. But it could also be that it suggests a politicised aesthetics.

To make chairs or their equivalent *and* to oppose all sedimentation. Is this a contradictory practice or it is an ornamental political excess? If the above-mentioned positions relative to the chair are seen as *fundamen-*

2) At the time of writing, Godfrey's book was forthcoming. It has now been published by Phaidon (1998). It is largely a feeble and contemptible product. We don't need to list its scholarly and moral deficiencies here. We will therefore confine ourselves to remarking that its cover reproduces a fake Broodthaers and that the book declines from there.

talist (as the enemy or temptation of Postmodernism) can they be brought into collision and simultaneously preserved? The preservation is political excess: permanent iconoclasm as the politics of gracious living.

The Dummy Speaks – Teleologically

There is often a nostalgic presumption contained in questions about the past. The presumption is that there was something radical in Art & Language, and that this radicalism was highly teleological, and that there is now no such happy future pulling along the present. The presumption is untrue, or rather unfounded. What was characteristic about the 'early days' was the fragmentary, inchoate and project-like nature of all Art & Language (and pre Art & Language) activity. The self-inflating and self-deflating nature of the essay-like things produced was for us the exemplification of a sort of morale. It is indeed astonishing that what we are often asked to *explain* is change – change in ourselves and the work – as if a change was something more in need of explanation than is the one-idea stasis of the purist.

There was never a committed aim or purpose in Art & Language (the kind of thing expressed, for example, in manifestos) even in the most overpopulated circumstance of the late 1960s and early 1970s. There was no well-formed vision of grandeur. There was of course a powerful *critical* purpose. But a critical purpose is hard to sustain now and was somewhat easier then. Now we'd be disingenuous if we said that a sense of *telos* is not difficult to have – to keep. Indeed, we'd say that it is something that needs more-or-less constant critical review.

So what does it mean to have an artistic purpose and how is that distinguished from, for example, a social purpose (formed as a sort of consequence of an artistic one)? Most strongly organised teleological claims or principles are mere vanity. They may be efficacious in determining or conditioning action, but of course they are never sufficient. Consider for example that early Conceptual Art was produced according to the reason that one day there will be a vanishing of the consumer-durable middle-sized dry good as a paradigm of art, and that this vanishing will also be a vanishing of the social class/profession which controls the interpretation of such things. Consider that there might have been such a possibility – the disappearance of an ideologically sustained hegemony of art and talk in favour of a *talkative* critical and *expanding* world of reflection and representation. The possibility implies a purpose – a very long-term purpose with some undeniable motivating force.

But to speak of a *teleology* – so as to imply that this possibility actively motivates practice – is to invoke the need of some further inquiry and, no doubt, explanation. There are smaller splinters of *telos* in our practice which do not have the motivating grandeur of the hegemony-abolishing one.

We've suggested that the dual figure of the armchair and of its other which refuses the sedentary can be made to work as a permanent and unresolvable contradiction upon which an activity insists – a contradiction which makes it unavoidable. A putative history of Art & Language is something that the work continually addresses. But what's important is that this is always *a* history, not *the* history – it is always only a possible history. The 'history' of which others wish to make a nostalgic fetish is one of those that are possible. The only necessity this imposes on us, however, is the need to satirise or otherwise displace or alienate it.

The introduction of the decorative and the ornamental (which approaches what John Roberts calls the 'stand-up') involves a gross displacement of nostalgic narrative. It offers history and *telos* an opportunity to connect itself disastrously to the sedentary. This is the sedentary possible world (not necessarily not an actual one ... somewhere) which is marked or signalled by a decorative layering upon the 'historical' original. The 'original' can only refuse and then weakly submit to the displacement. It wears the colour on its *face*. Not all acts in favour of the sedentary are visited upon the past. But there is a sense in which it will always have to be a past – and often a past with a teleology in the imaginations of others.

Any sense of genuinely collective purpose to be associated with Art & Language in the late 1960s and early 1970s is actually difficult to identify. There were those traditionalists who wished desperately to be taken seriously at the top – to impress someone in authority leading to absorbtion into the *official* culture or some segment thereof. What embattled Art & Language then was the accusation that we were against painting and feeling. Such accusations are not to be answered by public outbursts of spontaneous emotion. It was necessary from time to time to demonstrate that a conceivable condition of our practice lay *in* painting, insofar as we sought to syndicalise the territory of the constitutive critics of late high modernist painting. Frank Stella was a disappearing necessity in the sense that his was an ironisation of high modernism analogous to Jasper Johns's ironisation of Abstract Expressionism. Stella's critique was, however, a conceptual (or cultural) *cul-de-sac*. In any case, no one in Art & Language could entirely avoid exigencies imposed by painting, since the majority of the membership (an ordinal rather than a cardinal thing) was involved in teaching in Fine Art Departments in art schools. A sense of purpose distinct from the upwardly-mobile one was connected to a defence of inquiry over power. Power in the institutions is traced through various unattractive forms of mimesis – the enforcing of house styles or house options which are sanctioned by the concordat of stars and time-serving administrators. One of the most persistent claims made by Art & Language was that a critique of the high culture of painting in the form of an investigation (often necessarily at its conceptual margins) was as feasible a practice in art schools as painting – and further, that the critical power of such investigations might be such as to deny the possibility of (some) painting at all. The sense of inquiry (investigation!) which we sought to encourage was not at all foreclosed by a sense of social status privileging the intellectual over the blue-collar artist. None of us had that sort of insecurity, and more importantly (and with one noticeable moany exception) most of us had some class experience of hourly-paid industrial labour which entailed a certain solidarity with those who worked *by hand.*

The idea that Art & Language was 'founded' with fully-formed constructive intentions is ludicrous, if what that means is that there was some sort of memorandum of association setting out explicit aims and purposes – positive or negative. (The ad-nauseam anthologising of the editorial Introduction to *Art-Language*, Vol. 1, no. 1, no doubt reflects an ordinary cultural anxiety that there should in fact have been such a thing.) What there was was a ragbag of overlapping interests. What is most noticeable was that a sense of a critique of high modernism was confined to *one* member among those normally listed as 'founders'. The others were generally ignorant of or indifferent to the issues. Let's be clear: Art & Language as originally 'constituted' amounted to a discursive project and a desire to see that project reflected in a publication, insofar as no previously established publication seemed to offer a natural place to put this work. Other 'interests' were loosely packed into a commitment to talk, to explain, to stock our minds with puzzles and to let this show in a publication. Any suggestion grander than this is the product of bitterness and fantasy. But this loosely-packed conversation *was* a conversation. This was the teleological hook. The tradition of silence by the artist and service by the critic had been long established. Not even the likes of Barnett Newman or Don Judd or Robert Morris, who spoke eloquently for themselves, could be said to have engaged in their published work in an open or self-annihilatingly discursive activity. They tended to ratify a certain sort of art–work explicitly distinguished from their writing. Our theorising and talk had, by the late 1960s, issued an invitation to us (?) to abandon or to close this kind of distinction wherever possible in favour of a commitment to discursive activity and its *indices* as our work–as art of some kind. What made that commitment possible was the very complexity, absurdity and difficulty of the material which appeared to touch our situation; together with the ontic insecurity and exoticism of the artistic materials generated. The relations between discourse and putatively artistic materials were, as matters of dialectical interest, unavoidably contested and unstable. The status of texts and artwork was constantly subject to emergency conditionals, annihilated and returned and annihilated again, often in the course of hours rather than days.

This was *not* Conceptual Art in the sense that the practice had moved, from purified-Minimalism plus Duchamp plus a commitment to make that reduction stick, into an artistic practice which conceived of itself as *totally* in continual process.

The *Indexes* from 1972–1974 were an attempt to collect and to reflect–to take some measure of this activity, which, by its nature, was ordinally social rather than exclusively proprietorial and ratificatory. The 'implosion' which the indexes represent is also a drawing in as contributor of anyone who took the trouble to exert themselves in working with or on them. The dead spectator. Among the questions that all this raises is whether or not it might be possible to regard some other form of work (say painting) initially as qualified by this indexing activity and finally as exemplifying it. In other words, with a certain continuity of working ethos and practice, where are the limits which determine what can count as its index?

Now, this brings us more-or-less naturally to the question of 'voice'. There is something characteristically although marginally ventriloqual about the written work of Art & Language in the late 1960s and early 1970s. There were exceptions of course. Those who desired recognition – by, well, *someone* with weight – were shameless (or insecure) in their need to be seen speaking from their mouths. What was strange about this was that there were very few existing clues available as to what sort of voice we had made up. And made up it was. Here were artists not acting artists, indeed artists wearing the clothes of researchers or talkers simultaneously attached to some sort of artistic purpose. One might say teleologically artistic. There were possibly two ventriloqual voices. One (which often deluded itself as to its authenticity) was the researcher's voice projected by the conventionally ambitious artist; an accretion of a researchy style to a competitive transformation of artistic practice. Here, philosophical-type discussion offered itself as a conventionally defensible artistic practice – as something capable of being the next thing in historicist space. The other voice was harder to identify. This was one less sure that it could take on the researchy package whole. It was a voice constantly disowned by what we have called an emergency conditional. Art & Language was engaged in something researchy and philosophical just in case this was an artistic practice (even if it was difficult to say how) and engaged in an artistic practice (etc.) just in case those involved thought they were engaged in something authentically research-like.

The latter voice was better able to express the bewilderment which the basic critique of high modernism engendered – a critique which had recognised the grotesque over-empowerment of the historicist critic and had constructed a project of syndicalisation. We sought to occupy the space of the critic somehow. But where? An ambivalence, even confusion, in this matter was not so much one of the *flaws* in the project as one of the conditions of its dialectical nature – a source of resonant provocation within the practice. Contained within the imploded (reflexively accultured) index is an explosion of possible voices or possible vocalizations. These are the worked pathways which viewers (i.e. 'operators') of the index produce. Now, with this in mind, we take a sample from a later time – from *studio* discussions in the 1980s.

Consider the first series of works (paintings) called *Hostages.* These are colloquially known as 'palette Hostages'. They are all constructed out of several parts. A number of slits (narrow sections) are transcribed from a view of a museum interior. The site described is a site of artistic production in the series of paintings *Index: an Incident in a Museum.* These transcriptions are fixed to narrow, flat, rectangular 'canvases' and they are inserted so as to form the shape of an architectural plan (of a museum) in a larger canvas surface which contains small recesses designed to receive them. Painted in similar 'plan' patterns in this large surface (but not *inserted* in it) are various forms of flat colour: fake painted wood-grain, dots and other surface vulgarities. The entirety of the surface so far painted is masked, and a 'palette' is plastered overall. A 'palette'; it is only a representation of a palette. It may also be some sort of high-genre abstraction. It may be (is) the effect of considerable concentration and effort. This is an aesthetic effort, *within its parentheses* more-or-less compatible with a Wollheimian description of what a painter does or imagines when she's painting. To discover the virtues similar to or at least compatible with those that Wollheim discovers in Hofmann or De Kooning would not be a mistake, yet in the context of the entire work (the masking-tape removed to reveal the slits), to recover no more (or far less) than that would be a gross and conspicuous error. The seemingly Wollheimian painting is ventriloqual. The *Hostage* is not merely a representation of such a work – although at a certain level of reduction it is this of course – but a riskier illusion. The ventriloquist a) disguises her voice, which nevertheless remains b) a use of her voice. She is not an actor who assumes a character. The ventriloquist infests a body not her own with a representation of a voice not her own, but which has its origin in her. The voice-thrower's voice is spatially displaced, and the spatial displacement is disguised. The palette bit of the palette is the authentic production of Art & Language displaced centre-stage-front into a constructed 'other'. The 'risk' the ventriloquist takes is that her presence on the stage is such that it is only to be displaced. To be recognised as the author of a vocal production is another risk. Someone might say that a strict analogue here would require that we pretend that some literal other (someone with a different name and identity) had produced the palette. This would not address the simultaneous virtuality (or presence) of dummy (or other) and ventriloquist. The palette is produced under the condition that we may be *misunderstood* as its willing producers, producers who willingly accede to the culture of such productions but who are simultaneously present as those who do not. The painting is the other – the dummy, who virtually speaks in a voice which is actually ours. The risks of being seen to be represented by the dummy (the painting) are worrying enough. There is a great temptation to be a *bad* ventriloquist – to move one's lips. The fact is that the palette can't be done without concentration analogous to Hofmann's, but equally, it can't be done without our being other than Hofmann-like.

This is the form in which painting was returned to our practice. The Wagnerian decorativeness of mid-1970s Conceptual Art had seen its site of production as well as its ethos in the hands of the administration. In acquiring a studio (a place or site redundant in the practice of management) we sought the restitution of a material world. This is a requirement of realism. This was a material world in which our conversation might take place: a site such that the conversation might critically reflect the conditions bearing upon it, and not hand itself over to a neurotic idealism whose critical content is the constituted product of the furious competition of managerial desire.

Conversations, Pet's Homes, Decorations and Ornaments

Reductionism about the plurality of goals ... often sounds simply funny. Thus the joke about the lawyer who is offered sex by a beautiful girl: 'Well I guess so', he replies, 'but what's in it for me?'

Jerry Fodor 'The Trouble with Psychological Darwinism', London Review of Books, *22nd January, 1998.*

We'll begin this section by trying to describe what we're doing now. That may not tell anyone what it's like to be working now as a reflection of culture on a grand scale – but to have a grand view of culture is, given the fraudulent virtue of the age, also an imperative. It is necessary not only to *talk* like Jerry Fodor's lawyer but to act like him, to elaborate his perlocutionary effect and to build a world on his model. Any 'aesthetic', that is a reasonably – made art theory, will have to take Fodor's joke seriously – and will need to acknowledge that many art theories may be serviceable in one way or another. The thing is to stay awake and to recognise the open critical task. How else can we continue in the face of the repulsive instrumentalists in charge of the Land of Cockayne?

What we're doing (and what we've often done) is to make things (art of a sort) which are built like mesomeric chemicals. Built of parts not mixed together, not identified with the sum of their constituents, but such that they are identical with all of them, yet conceived separately as *resonant*. We might call them 'hybrids', not in the anthropological sense of bullshitters like Homi Bhabha or Peter Wollen, but in the sense that we're producing work which has mutated from its original form, and decidedly mutated in relation to what might be called our original intentions (or hopes and fears). In fact, 'hybrid' may not be quite the appropriate expression. A chair made of small canvases on which a picture of an open book is depicted (an open book also legible to the viewer) is not a hybrid as such. It *is* a chair as well as a representation of a chair. It is simply that it is constructed of materials which are usually associated with a more-or-less normal wall display – small paintings – and that it presents a decorative surface. The constructed chair is a dis-construction – a dis-mantling of the 'original' form in which these items are intended and found. In this sense it is not at all a hybrid but a *use* – a use of the small paintings which might be like the *use* of a door or doors to make a fence or the use of a fridge as a garden shed, a use which almost supplants an earlier or an original identity, but which is itself also liable to be supplanted or made scandalous.

A more-or-less ordinary circumstance of mis-use is actually also just *use* or *re-use*. (Indeed, that's what it really ought to be thought of as.) In any case, what is used (or etc.) undergoes the contradiction of being *aufgehoben*. There is much in contemporary culture which fears the reflexive iconoclasm of 'what-I-may-have-meant-brought-low'. But our interest in the world constituted as (a bit of) culture *upraises* the footlingly literal to become the provocation for one or two metaphors in the circle of dream-work gone literal. More of this later. We are thinking of a group of paintings done by us between 1983 and 1985 and generically titled 'Snow paintings'. They suffered from a difficulty, viz that when they were aesthetically or decoratively complete (i.e. when we could stand to look at them, etc.) they were intellectually incomplete (hadn't been sufficiently erased to make the cultural-critical point they were supposed to make). We re-used (used/mis-used) these surplus paintings – and they were all surplus paintings – to keep the rain off Tom's pet rabbit, to cover its house and so forth. One might say that we had indeed *abandoned* these works as aesthetic (or as paintings) and that their use for such ends as a rabbit cover (a roof) was possible only after they had been abandoned. It is possible that this abandonment foreclosed any possibility of their being used as *paintings.* But it did not foreclose their being of some sort of exemplary artistic interest (or for that matter cultural significance) for us somehow. But they really were abandoned. We would have had to invent new and disgracefully opportunistic reasons for their new status as rabbit-roof art, and these reasons would not have been the same as our reasons for painting the paintings. Certainly, conceived as a cultural consumable, a painting was merely transformed into another type of consumable. Conceived as a painting (a cultural consumable of a particular kind) it might only have undergone a transformation into a painting (abandoned and used as a rabbit cover), the transformation (abandonment and use) being intrinsic to the painting's own development.

The putting to a new use of the canvases whose 'original' purpose was to sit conventionally on the wall presumably 'represents' the abandonment of the work as that particular type of representation of cultural consumable in favour of a representation of another. For example, a chair made of paintings is a representation of a painting and a representation of a chair. The chair narrates the process of the painting's being brought low–and put in another world.

So far so more-or-less obvious. But we have found other uses for these small canvases. They appear in the form of frame or cupboard for a quasi-decorative object of highly indeterminate identity that is made from even smaller canvases. These smaller canvases are all painted a uniform brown. The cupboard or frame is highly decorative and it tends to reduce the object within to something pictorial. But not quite. Indeed, one possibility is that the flat brown rear surface of the cupboard which is blocked by the object contained might be pictorial also: the viewer's sight of it is frustrated by an object of perpetually asymptotic identity, made from small versions of itself. To be confronted with an object such that one is always just approaching identifying it is to be in an unfortunate position. The viewer is put in the unfortunate position of trying to ascertain what sort of object it might be. It looks *familiar,* but familiar as what? You can't quite say. There seems to be some sort of family resemblance between this quasi-pictorial cupboard-plus-its-contents and another object which hangs next to it at the moment in the studio. This is something like a flat brown painting in a frame made out of the same canvases as the cupboard. It has two chairs in front – the chairs being constructed of similar materials. This painting's surface effaces itself to the extent that it appears as no more than a decorative attribute of that portion of the wall which the frame frames. The frame makes a shallow box. The painting is the 'floor' of that box – or rather, the *absent* floor of that box. The frame as the abandonment and re-use of paintings/texts frames a painting which it also abandons as decoratively null, or which it shuts in as a spatial anomaly. The chairs in front pay full attention (imply viewers) upwards from the lower leading edge of the frame, and return the glare of the (God-)forsaken painting. The painting, in being both framed and abandoned or forsaken by the frame, does indeed glare past the viewers absent from the chairs. To return the glare, however, is to risk being abandoned oneself to an exchange in an indecipherable code – an alien language understood only by the (non-human? invisible?) occupants of the chairs. (Or … according to an even stranger Meinongian excess, the chairs are for disapproving Conceptual artists.)

What has this to do with the larger historical-cultural world? In order to answer this rather desperate question we need to say what the larger cultural world looks like – is like – from the perspective of this work.

Oppositional or dissenting models have declined in the (no doubt amusing) play of harmless contrasts which forms one of the self-images of the age. It does not follow that totalitarianism or fascism has disappeared. The disappearance of a conscious mass politics of social change has found its ideological apologists – or rather its smug affirmation – in the world of Cultural Studies. We work in conditions such that the moral adjuncts of oppositional politics (variations on the anti-instrumentalism of Kant's categorical imperative to Sartre's concept of good faith) have been forsaken in favour of the small advantages of the small politics of cultural expertise and ethical professionalism. This is barbarian politics and it's hidden in the ornamental representations of emancipation which are the ideology of the culturally empowered.

A dialectically serviceable art theory is usually in danger of bathos if it tries too hard to second-guess the outcomes of authentic political struggles. The theory must nevertheless try to imagine the successful outcomes of these struggles. Many such serviceable theories have been buried in the small politics of research and its presumed rewards. The cultural theory (and *a fortiori* the cultural politics) which presses close upon our practice is one formed of small Gestapo states, in a not-quite-virtual not-reality of Spenglerian police stations, of empowered officials, prisoners and clients. The totalitarian fantasies of fascistic or Stalinist politics have been fragmented and replanted, transformed as small hegemonies – persuasive and oppressive conditions not acknowledged or recognised as such – competing violently with one another for the accolade which follows submission to an historical or cultural imperative. It might be thought that the task for the artist is to seek out – or to trip over – conditions which will liberate the viewer (or his or her interlocutor or whatever) from the list which follows an assertion of the type: 'This is where we are now.' In fact, though, the artist has been increasingly compelled to submit to the nomological pretensions of the Spenglerian list – to work, that is to say, in a climate in which the direction of the culture is prescribed according to priorities conceived as natural laws. The shift in power and in the locus of talk might not have been so bad had the practical emancipatory task been simply transferred to the theoreticians – who might at least have been able to offer some critique of the intellectual processes of naturalization. But the cultural theoreticians or theorists have taken only the *talk* of emancipation. And behind this talk lies not a critical practice of inquiry but a totalitarian mania for closure. The culture of cultural informedness abhors the crooked timber of human (and indeed natural) contrivance (the crooked timber which makes the discipline of *socialist* economics and socialist politics and inquiry necessary). It prefers a trivial but violent politics of competing purisms or cleansings. These purisms or cleansings take various forms, but they are all immune to the dialectical discomfort which would force their adherents to recognise the need to change themselves. For those not completely crushed by their own venal inertia there is the odd possibility of a *move* into a successively amnesiac submission, but there is little more than that.

The mere *language* of 'variety' and 'difference' becomes the self-deluding chant of the prisoners and the police alike.

It is against this pasteboard-and-barbed-wire background that we try to produce a minor narrative of grumbling doubt (scepticism) and conversation.

One of the consequences of the totalitarian over-development has been a loss of *meaninglessness*. The 'Devil in the Sofa Cushions' of

Wilkie Collins' *Woman in White* (the semiological preoccupation of a religious maniac) is the cognitive paradigm of the cultural sophisticate, as exemplified by the academic Art Historian with a grip on contemporary art.

The decorative has been reworked as a marginal subset of a Francis Bacon figure-and-ground trick, while the limits of the literal are fatuously overlapped by the figural. By this we mean that the theatrical schlock and excess of Bacon's background decorativeness, which is fraudulently redeemed by the fake agonies (or headaches) of the figure decorated with paint, is now continued with sillier and sillier (gamier and gamier) provocations and stunts. The journalist writes a stunning and shocking scenario, the art director arranges it and the Advertising Czar speculator buys it. The circle of reflections is indeed productive of a low-grade, low-interest meaning, but it is stuffed with opportunities for the unhistorical literal-minded to generate a figural language, a rhetoric. The empty literalness of the material provides a necessary condition for an ornamental excess of language which is itself turned literal in the small political battle for cultural power.

This power is systematically exemplified in the growth of small or large academies whose purpose is to render the figural language (or worse) of those at the top of the charismatically solipsist heap into *conventional* sort. The decorative and the ornamental cannot offend decency in virtue of what it describes or pictures, but only (when it does) in virtue of its form. If a decorative or ornamental work is to contain some sort of controversial and fearless content, then it must hide it – make it unseen. The 'fuck it, I don't care, it's just dumb shit' that forms the spots and stripes of Brit Art's fraudulent insouciance is far from decorative: it sticks its content ('fuck it…' etc.) plus gullible interpretation right in the middle of its two-dimensional face.

The untidy edges of the decorative remain more-or-less thinly populated. These are the places which might produce an uncomfortable silence in the minds of those who arbitrate the artistic self-image of the age. What we mean is that the decorative promises a collapse from the significant to the meaningless. This is the scandal (the reason to continue) which attends all possibilities of conversation.

We're saying that the conversational and the decorative are connected. There is in the resistant (semiotically resistant) decorative always a possibility (due to excess of compunction) of collapse into meaninglessness. This is often a meaninglessness which is associated with alien-ness or criminality. A mark of the conversational is that it is liable to collapse into a pragmatic or concatenatory excess or emptiness–a practical resistance to theory–and that is resistance to a hegemony of academic observance, protocol and closure. It could be that conversation is the criminality of theory just as decoration might be the forensic degeneration of sense. But this is conversation that keeps its rubbish as rubbish: it doesn't make its unmade beds of metaphors come back as literal sorts.

Conversational meaninglessness in the form of collapse is familiar to most people. Most of us are familiar with the idea of a conversation capable of being sustained pragmatically beyond the point at which the normal expositional rules of semantics and syntax are being strictly followed. What if we go a bit further and think that a conversation can take place as a kind of dreamwork. That is, while the normal referential (etc.) uses are made of words and phrases, a point can be reached such that these are never (or seldom) connected directly to the real effects of talking (or writing). At the limit (some) conversations can amount to a concatenatory exchange of metaphors understood intentionally but somehow embedded indexically–unable to escape without leaving considerable remainder. What is produced is an aesthetic excess (an ornamentation) which may be adjacent to but which is unlike literature in having little or no publicly aestheticised effects. The cognitive effects are contained within the indexical horizon of the conversation and do not readily (or never) transmit into the land of public exposition. Their language is the language of a pattern of incitements (colours?) to some (almost) possible courses of action (whether linguistic or otherwise).

The possible conversational type under consideration is not conducted merely in jargon–in a language of lexical marginality or novelty –but in words which have a regular and literal use. Of course, most conversation is conducted *normally*. It's likely that what we are in fact trying to consider is not so much a conversational type, but a possible conversational margin: a way that a conversation and only a conversation can go. These are margins where the exchange remains fully aware of the normal referential use but falls down (collapses) in an excess of effects, analogous to but not identical with, aesthetic effects. This is not, however, a collapse into poetry–although it might be sometimes. It's more like a collapse into a modal richness – grammatical and semantic elision and indexicality: going on. This is no more than 'normal' for many conversations, and is particularly plausible in the private dreamwork of self-incitement. What is not always clear is that this can also be a socially productive thing.

(Or is this simply crap ... or, was that conversational?)

Consider this possibility: how many words does a complex conversation need? Two or three people somehow work socially or collaboratively. They decide (or ...) to practise an extreme principle of economy. There are three main expressions in their language plus the usual connectives and a few verbs and adjectives. It's not a normal lingo or pidgin as it's far too impoverished in surface resources of expression. They have the expression 'yeah, yeah, yeah, yeah' which deals with assent or dissent, denial or certain forms of assertion, 'knobex' and its negative ('non-knobex') as its nouns, and an obscene comparative 'as fuck ...' They have the usual resource of ostention. Such a poor language could be used to have a comparatively complex conversation. What is odd and of interest conversationally about this imagined poverty is that it is actually like a certain conversational development, where an application of Occam's razor is simultaneously the condition of wild referential and modal excess.

At this margin the conversational is an exchange which can collapse into the literally meaningless, yet which is sustained according to rules which leave 'spaces' for the effects of meaningless utterances to function practically, not simply as a consequence of eventual 'correction' by conventionalisation (or use), but in being the ornamental shadow which lives in an index. We're not just thinking here of the occasionally undifferentiated vocabulary (calling everything a 'knobex' or using catchphrase obscenity) but also of the strange 'decorative' breakdown(s) that occur(s) in the face of unexpected or strange practical outcomes like great failures and moments where work is abandoned or alienated – desperate moments.

Of course, everyone has moments of collapse and absurdity in conversation – moments of meaninglessness. This is commonplace. What is often not noticed about such moments is that in being sustained or continued, it is their very decorativeness – their excess in the face of loss of meaning – that is their power to strike subversively at the substance of official truth or power. Meaningless over-recursion is the outward sign that the originary set of epistemic conditions has been passed or abandoned in favour of the pleasures of dreamwork-in-practical-guise.

Used decoratively, colours and textures and shapes (or what?) – those differences which incite philosophy, i.e. the examining of differences and the attempt sometimes to resolve them – are absolved (or apparently absolved) of the requirement that they make meaning. There are two questions that might be asked of the outcome of such a use: 'What are the conditions (what additional conditions are present or adjacent) such that in some possible world (some world other than the actual one?) those colours and textures and shapes might form something meaningful'; and: 'What are the actual circumstances such that a claim that this work *P* (painting, art or something like them) *makes itself* meaningless, can be said to be true?'

The decorative in our sense absconds from the meaningful – at least from the meaningful in the actual world. Indeed, it is decorative only in the sense that it does abscond. There is nothing of course that is incapable of being meaningful in some sense, and of course one person's or perspective's decoration is another's votive object. So there are no absolutely decorative items. Are the poems and inscriptions on the walls of the Alhambra decorative in any sense that we mean? No, except that they hide their meaning, or an aspect of their meaningfulness, in excess. They obscure their own literary power with an excess of decorative tangle which is *unread* but viewed as a surface. What we want to call decorative has something necessarily to do with a flight from meaning. And this flight may be either from the expressive or figural or allegorical, or from whatever significance may be confirmed (contained within) and recoverable from a painting, or from the literal-cultural meaningfulness which is read into (post-structurally discriminated from) objects as themselves or as signs.

Now, this flight from meaningfulness is accomplished only in the preservation of a tension. It is accomplished (or essayed) by a work which fails to be, for example, *either* a painting *or* a literal object. (This is the abject achievement of 'neither one thing nor the other'.) There may be a 'logical' figure for such items, just as there is for certain textual Conceptual Art works of the 1960s and 1970s. In the latter case, there are several emergency conditionals involved. '*P* is a philosophical text just in case it is a work of art (a quasi-text, accidental and non-intentional to some degree and in some relevant sense).' Or, '*Q* is a text–a piece of writing or something conceived as intentional, non-accidental (in some way and to some degree)–just in case it is an artistic inscription (accidental and non-intentional to some degree in some relevant sense)', and so on.

We can try such emergency conditionals the other way round. '*P* is a work of art (a quasi-text–non intentional, etc.) just in case it is a text (etc.).' What do we make of 'just in case' here? The emergency conditional almost works. Consider: '*S* is decorative (meaningless) just in case *S* is a painting (and meaningful).' It doesn't quite work. Consider, however, '*S* is somehow to be made decorative (etc.) just insofar as it is a painting (etc.).' Do we need the additional 'practical' modifiers? No. The fact (or fact-like condition) is that we can perform the categorical denial, the inversion, so long as we get help from the work or the world outside–just as we usually do with textual work from the 1960s.

If I hang up the newspaper as a paper-chain, the text of the newspaper may well remain intact (c.f. the texts in the collages of Picasso and Braque) but the newspaper has lost its first-order significance as a newspaper. (That's one of the most obvious diagrams.) But can we correct this diagram to the emergency conditional–to the 'just in case'–and say, the paper-chain is (or could be) decorative *just in case* the newspaper is read as a newspaperor etc. 'Just in case' could be put in other ways. One might say that the recognition that *P* might be (is) decorative might be (is) connected to its relative success in recovering some sort of non-decorative significance from *P's* components–i.e. those parts that together compose *P* as a decorative whole.

The possible achievement of what we suppose has to be called the post-structuralist decorative is that it extracts meaninglessness from materials which might be thought 'intrinsically' meaningful, collapsing or imploding them–their internal significances–into an empty connectedness or use which is tantamount to their loss as signifying stuff.

The paper-chain may also of course be made of something else: a 'painting' or a Conceptual Art text. How would an emergency-type conditional work in this rabbit-roof-plus-fragmentation case?

'Making Meaningless', first published in the catalogue *Art & Language in Practice, Vol. 2, Critical Symposium*, Charles Harrison (ed.), in conjunction with the exhibition *Art & Language in Practice*, Fundació Antoni Tàpies, Barcelona, April–June, 1999.

Art & Language paints a picture (VI)

Preliminary digression

In *Painting as an Art,* Richard Wollheim anatomises a truism, viz that not only does a painter paint *with* the eyes she also paints *for* the eyes.

The late Flint Schier plays around with the truism and asks what it means. The play is uneven. It includes deceptively large movements with big categories like 'experience' and 'worthwhilenesss'. Two of his principle moves involve the following assertions:

1) That the painter sees to it that 'the experience of attending to the work will be an intrinsically worthwhile one'. (This is part of what it means to say that the painter paints for the eye.)
2) That 'there is a second point concealed by an ambiguity, viz that another part of the meaning of *paints for the eye* is that the painter tries to assume the role of someone who comes before the work, takes a more-or-less detached vantage point and then asks if the experience of attending to this work is an intrinsically worthwhile one'.

It's subtler than it looks, perhaps, but it does seem very well fed and domesticated. But can we open up the game a bit and still preserve any of Wollheim/Schier's intention?

For Schier, getting to this 'vantage point' is a condition of achieving some sense of moral community between artist and spectator – a necessary but insufficient condition of friendship, morality, and so forth. Furthermore, he argues that a sense of the intrinsic worthwhileness of community experience is a necessary condition for art and that the reciprocity engaged provides a substantial amount of the material necessary to refute the emotivism in which Schier implicates the so-called Institutional Theory of Art.

Small game, big stakes – and straight talking. Or is it?

What immediately brings a feeling of wooze is the thought that a sense of moral community so airily recommended might not provide the materials for a substantial refutation of emotivism at all. It might merely be a slightly refined variant of emotivism. How does Schier get out of Bloomsbury 1910 or some equivalent? Is it just a matter of (metaphorical) 'quantity'? Is it that Tom Crow's eighteenth-century connoisseur whom Schier contrasts approvingly with the supporters of (presumably Carl Andre's) pile of bricks merely had *more* to say, in more detail, or are there other (more immediately qualitative) considerations?

For the time being, however, we can try to narrate a fragment of the tasteless experience we have in painting for the eye, and in doing so, shed some light on how hard or easy it is to imagine a sense of moral or artistic community, let alone possess one.

Consider (a)

[1] is painting the image of a floor. It surrounds a figure which is not shown in its entirety. The floor is stone slabs; the floor of a large public building, an exhibition place or museum. It is depicted in more or less standard perspective. It is pinkish grey. [2] is concerned that [1] hates to paint the floor, regarding his own efforts as incompetent. [2] always cajoles [1] into painting this particular section with vernacular jokes like 'I don't do floors' or 'You're so much more talented a floor-ist than I', etc.

[1] presumably paints the floor to be seen by [2].

But that's not very informative is it? Not really. This is very close to the technical matter of seeing what you're doing.

[1] is [2]'s equal painting partner, then [1] and [2] mutually always have an eye to paint for. (Is this the moral community – the condition for Art *à-la*-Schier?)

We might suppose that it is a not necessarily untrivial model of such a condition – except that both [1] and [2] are *technically* involved. (Presumably Schier's condition requires an 'active' or technical artist and a non-'active' *Adequately-Informed-and-Disinterested Spectator* either in reality or in the artist's mind.) [2] (whom [1] has in mind, etc.) might well intervene technically in what [1] does, even efface it.

So [1] has in mind a spectator who might well be Adequately Informed. But Disinterested? Does [1] have it in mind that [2]'s possible intervention might be disinterested? Probably not.

[1] and [2] respectively do not have standard Wollheimian eyes. It is true that [1] imagines [2] as spectator–becomes [2]-ish to some extent–but the circumstances of production are such that [1] and [2] are mutually complicit in the devising of technical limits and so forth.

More particularly, whatsoever their differences (in respect of technical competence, or even in respect of aesthetic or cultural commitment) [1] and [2] are mutually responsible for what they paint. They may disagree violently and still produce a painting and they will both have to own up to it.

It seems that [1] and [2] have made themselves into Hegelian cripples, the one imagined eye constantly cancelling the other. Or is it that they have become real (post) Hegelians: situated yet endemically situationless; logico-technical *Bussers des Geistes*? Or is it nothing so seemingly grand as a final *Sturm und Drang*? We could try another, more robust approach.

Consider (b)

[1] paints bits of a painting for [2]'s eyes among others but not exclusively: there are other eyes imagined and these do not have a technical body attached to them. [1] and [2] are merely sharing what would normally be an 'internal' conversation. They are distributing spatially what would ordinarily be distributed only temporarily.

(b) looks OK at first, it gets us to the painting as it were–gets us to an eye which is not the artist's (or the artists') more-or-less efficiently.

What it fails to do is account for the real complexities of the circumstances in which [1]'s and [2]'s painting is intentional.

What it does as a consequence of this is perform a potentially absurd gloss on one of the ways in which eyes might be painted for. Let's be charitable, however, and assume that [1] and [2] do get the odd painting done, and that they don't just have each other in mind, etc., viz that they do paint for other eyes, and that these eyes are imagined (etc.) while they are painting.

Consider (c)

In spiritual contrast to Schier, let us add that [1] and [2] are not happily painting away, secure in their hopes and imaginings *vis-à-vis* the eyes they might partly be. Let us imagine that [1] and [2] are (or feel) somehow beleaguered, that they are almost paralysingly uncomfortable in their putative métier.

Would Scheir/Wollheim's artist be able to bear this sort of predicate? One has a feeling of certainty that they would not.

Consider Schier's artist to be painting *for* an eye which is *unsympathetic* and that she wants to keep it that way. Consider further that she (or [1] and [2] if you like) are concerned to trap and confuse the 'eyes' they sometimes imagine into making dreadful mistakes, into a hopeless and morally unsustainable insecurity. (Can she/they really imagine these 'eyes'?)

Schier does allow for something like this in that he is impressed by the fact that Manet's *Olympia* was subjected to detailed and comprehensive scorn, implying that whatever else the *Pompiers* felt about it, they 'took it seriously'. This is of course somewhat more debatable than he thinks. They took *what* seriously? Was it Manet's painting as something that they recovered intentionality from, or did they merely derogate *Olympia* as incompetent – i.e. as intentionally irrecoverable in-respect-of-the-relevant-descriptions, going on to take them not-taking-it-seriously seriously. (There has been much debate in this matter.) Schier does not analyse the circumstances of this 'seriousness'. We are merely left with the idea that somehow what they (the critics and academicians) said was (sort of) serious – somehow qualitatively different from the (sort of unserious) things that are said nowadays about all kinds of Post-Duchampian crap. But his example fails because he fails to demonstrate that the eyes Manet painted for did take him seriously – that such a community did exist for him at all. He is in danger of falling into the nonsense of saying 'Well, they must have taken it seriously, and the quality of what they said internally confers Art upon the painting irrespective of the fact that what was said internally refuses to do this.'

We can safely leave this aside.

Consider (d)

Returning to the beleaguered *mechants*, there is a community of an 'eye' they can imaginatively 'be' and from which they might construct a few metaphors of community (or, more likely, conversation) which is not restricted to their simply imagining each other before the painting (or a section of the painting). Unfortunately for the luminaries of painting's comfy artisticness, this undisplaced (or only moderately displaced) condition for art and morality is in part founded on a *critical* position. It entails a critical, moral and physical history which requires [1] and [2] to imagine an 'eye' (to paint for an eye) which would approach their project as virtually impossible–as failing to meet the required critical standard and so on. (A painting is not a critical text, the matter of recovery not semantic, but perpinctorial and semiotic.)

Painting for the eye may well be a necessary condition of art, but the place where [1] and [2] must put themselves 'imaginitively' is critically *situated.* It is not only not a matter of imagining another's eye as boon companion (an imagined imagining, which always seems to make Wollheim and his sympathisers seem both neuter and prurient) but also a matter of painting *for* a community (moral or artistic) which recognises the situated impossibility (or at least the extraordinary difficulty) of its own communally constitutive sense: the inescapability of its malingerer's logic.

Schier (and perhaps Wollheim) are both absorbed by a form of the positivist emotivist institutionalism they both revile. It is merely a case of 'our institution is better than yours', with Schier's voice adding 'the unimaginability of our really having to deal with your community (whatever it is) reduces what are seen as the reflections of institutionality to we-might-just-be-brains-in-vats pseudo-problems'.

Why then does it seem necessary to listen to them both? Why do we almost welcome the fat voices?

They give us work to do. They have a way of giving comfort in unguarded moments of despair and fury. Compared to the unreadable tripe of Cultural Studies and the ludicrous orotundities of gallery-land, the well-formed liberal vernacular provides glimpses of a substantial place of refuge.

It continues to require the greatest effort of critical scrutiny.

Voice off:

How true is the 'truism'? One of the slogans in the studio recently was on the following lines. 'We are *blind* painters in the sense that we produce something like a self-devouring collage; blind painters not in the sense that Beethoven's *Missa Solemnis* was composed by a deaf composer, but in the sense that Beethoven's *Missa Solemnis* is deaf music. We do blind painting. This eff-ing particle was something missed by Adorno in what was otherwise an elaborately informative analysis.'

'[1] and [2] Imagine a Spectator' is a subset of 'Art & Language Paints a picture' to be sure. But the imagining while *necessary* is barely plausible. *It is imagining demons.*

A fragment

Art & Language paints a picture in a studio above the Cooperative Society shop in Middleton Cheney, a village on the borders of the English counties of Northamptonshire and Oxfordshire. The studio measures approximately 9 metres by 18 metres with windows on both sides, facing north and south. The room is approximately 4.6 metres high with hammer beams. It is a former village meeting place. There are three large robust tables in the centre of the room. Two of these are covered in junk, cans of paint, tools, sticks and brushes. On one table lies a large (189 x 161 cm) sheet of toughened plate glass, supported by wooden bearers.

[1] and [2] are dripping pink paint on the glass so as to delineate a clear vertical slit, slightly slanted from bottom left to top right. Propped against a wall stands a similar sheet of glass painted pink to within 10 cm of its edge. At its centre in two lines is the inscription HELLO TERRY, HOW ARE YOU? *in Helvetica Medium capitals 50 mm high. The letters are of a very pale pink.*

[1] Are we blind painters? When people are making something, they are usually glad to see what they are doing. One becomes an electrician or a carpenter with the eye.

[2] Sometimes one must do things without seeing. The photographer changes cassettes either in a bag or in an almost completely dark room.

[1] She must *know* what she is doing.

[2] Where is the boundary between the necessity of seeing what you are doing in order to know and not needing to see because you know?

[1] Or don't need to know?

[2] It is easy to imagine a technique of painting so refined as to require almost no technically necessitated seeing.

[1] Is Divisionism (or some form of it) potentially blind painting, for example?

[2] Asking where a boundary is, is not quite right. But there is some sort of horizon such that the fact that you are seeing what you are doing (in making something admittedly to be seen) seems far from essential – not entirely to the point. There are indeed many occasions when what you are seeing is not what is to be *seen.*

[1] You are often technically blind in respect of what you will at some point describe in terms like 'Now we can see what we've done'.

[2] The examples are legion. Would Wollheim/Schier regard as somehow incompetent a painting that failed to live up to the truisticness of the truism?

[1] What would that be like? Would it be, for example, a painting whose technical history was such that the painter never saw what she was painting *for* the eye but only the tools and instrumentalities that brought the final result.

[2] It's obvious that one part of the truism is not all that truistic.

[1] What about the other bit?

[2] I'm sure Wollheim would not want to overstress the importance of 'the eye', 'for the eye', etc., *tout court.* 'For the eye' is part metaphorical or metonymic and part literal.

[1] There need be no difficulty in blind painting's being *for* the eye in the sense that Schier elaborates.

[2] But what if there was? What if we could defend the suggestion that the, for example, *Hostage* paintings are only marginally for the eye, or even that there was some radical sense in which they were never painted *for* the eye even though they *must* be seen.

[1] This isn't very difficult at all. I can merely assert it, and not feel that I have fallen into some ludicrously Duchampian cuteness.

[2] It's almost as if you could construct a matrix which at almost every intersection would trouble the truth of the Wollheimian truism.

[1] Not a switch of 'mind' or etc. for 'eye', but a switch of 'see' for 'don't see' ('is not for seeing', or 'don't need to see', or 'can't see', or etc.)?

[2] It might generate some odd objects.

[1] It would not be particularly odd to posit an object such that what there is about it that is made to be seen, made for the eye, etc., is *not* what amounts to any significant condition of its Art-ness or of a moral (or etc.) community between artists and spectators. What is there for the 'community' might well be what is recovered in not being there to be seen.

[2] I can't think of an interesting painting that doesn't in some way ask if the truism is true, or otherwise offer the truists some irrecoverably nasty moments.

Direction:
[1] and [2] continue to drip.

[Linda] I'm not called Terry.

[1] and [2] That painting will have your name wrong. It seems to do this to some people and not to others.

[1] These paintings are pictures and masks. The mask covers a picture which is often indecent.

[Linda] I feel that these paintings are on my side, speaking as a woman – as someone disabled by patriarchial culture.

[1] In obscuring indecency, the mask lays claim to harmlessness or neutrality – to sightliness.

[2] The claim is flimsy. We are using at least two types of mask. They both have the form and colour of skin. In one of them a skin of pink paint is pierced vertically, a small part of the picture beneath is framed in a form which recalls a quasi-painting – a painting to which 'something has happened' – *The Deep*, by Jackson Pollock. In another, a pink rectangle covers the middle of the picture. At its centre is inscribed a greeting. The

greeting names its beneficiary.

[Linda] Are the masks realistic devices? Is it a mask which obscures identity, or is it a mask which makes you think it *is* what's underneath?

[2] The mask obscures and displaces. It blinds the painting: 'Something has happened to this painting'.

[1] The mask imports a spatial and corporeal difficulty into this temporarily ordered certainty. Are we looking *in* or *out?*

[2] Some would say the voyeur looks in at a scene, in at his object, not out at the contingency of the world.

[Linda] Or does the voyeur always strive to overcome a failure of identification? There is a difference between what the eye 'sees' and what the eye 'knows' to be there. Is this not the voyeur's (or fetishist's) question *par excellence?*

[2] The skin at the surface of the mask is indifferent to the identity of the scotomatized subject, painting or viewer. There is here the possibility that blindness is not-being-visible.

[Linda] Does this possibility make Lacan's fishy story more instructive?

[1] *The Deep* is our 'Castle in the Snow'. *The Deep* has its origins in the snow, in our snow paintings.

[Linda] Does it also connect you to André Masson?

[2] There is automatism of one kind or another within and without. Behind (or is it in front of) and in the surface of the mask (or is it behind?).

[Linda] I have not received a satisfactory reply to my question: 'Are you using a realistic device to foreground voyeurism in artistic experience?'

[1] I am not sure that we require this device to be realistic in any sense superficially amenable to Courbet, and we are not merely trying to emphasise the relation between looking and desire.

[2] This is a possibility *inter alia*, and a sense of the realistic-ness *is* required, albeit in a sense more subtly amenable to Courbet.

[3] This is Linda's problem: 'For all that they were represented as each other's opposites, Modernism and Realism were actually each other's necessary conditions. Modernism deserving of the name was the risky conjecture of Realism – and hence, of course, subversive. Realism deserving of the name was the critical conjecture of Modernism – and hence, of course, avant-garde. The real strength of modern art since the time of

Manet has lain in its capacity for equivocation. The Modernist criticism of the 1960s represents an abandonment of the dialogue with Realism, and a degeneration of the difficult aesthetic discourse of the former intellectual Left into a dogmatic and conservative celebration of decorative effects – a celebration which must always conceal or misrepresent the darker side of Modernism's own story... to talk sensibly of Modernism has always been to talk of dilemma; Modernism does not stand either for the aesthetic ratification of work such as Noland's or Caro's or for the sceptical disposition which might be associated with such work as Robert Morris's; neither for affirmation nor for negation; but rather for the impossibility of ruling out either on well-formed theoretical grounds. This, it proposes, is what life is like if you dare to live it without borrowed certainty. It is this capacity to sustain meaning as dilemma that is really readable out of the substantial art of the modern period...'

[2] This is *mad* equivocation. It's the malingerer's logic. Nothing to do with looking and desire.

[1] Desire: what a happy Surrealistic Humpty-Dumpty word. Read Lacan, read his translator. Nobody knows. It's technical in the way that the shibboleths of teenagers are *technical.*

Direction:
[1] and [2] cease dripping. They take turns to peer at their work through a mirror. [1] climbs a stepladder and closes one eye.

[2] Does the mask put the spectator 'in' the picture in the sense that she is acknowledged as bringing a gaze, as making the shield necessary?

[1] Our painting *index: Incident in a Museum (Madison Avenue) XVI* was a glimpse of the Whitney Museum inside out, or outside in. The normal viewer was turned into the unnatural peeper.

[2] More important, a beholder without a viewpoint – except one which is indicated in a scrawl on the surface through which she peeps.

[1] And this designates a virtual surface: a back wall behind the actual surface at which she peeps.

[2] But the fact that we have painted a figure has brought us to

the explicit production of a mask. *Madison Avenue* was indeed such a device, but the mask was not necessitated by what was beneath it in the same way.

[1] Paul Wood pointed out that an aspect of the *Hostage* landscapes was their capacity to claim a form of personhood.

[2] This had much to do with their spatial dis-equilibrium, a metaphysics of appearance: virtuality as materiality, materiality as virtuality.

[1] The explicit *figure* has none of these casual (or blind) horrors.

[2] A more profound blindness is required lest we celebrate the obscenities of Modern Civilisation – the minor or major obscenities of factual journalism.

[3] Indeed as tendentiousness tends to inhibit discursiveness, just as surely does the fetishisation of style. Tendentious Conceptual Art or tendentious post-Conceptual Art or tendentious postmodernist art may all be faulted on grounds similar to those which might apply to a tendentious Cubist painting. Tendentiousness normally entails a sacrifice of depth and complexity for the sake of transparency and immediacy, which are the conditions of journalistic agency.

[1] ... the body ornamented by the painting ... the minor psychological distraction for the eye – the eye of the Wollheimian exquisite.

[Linda] The Wollheimian eye is a propitious male one, isn't it?

[2] It had occurred to us that the body-equivalence mechanism of the *Hostage* landscapes might somehow be capable of conversion.

[1] This is an over-literal description; what was to become of the landscape's horrors and visitations?

[2] Are these latter the bodies we see?

[1] Body-equivalence as visitation?

[2] It seemed that the body-in-the-landscape might be detached from its host.

[1] The act of detaching or extracting would be its extinction – unless the figure could somehow be figure-implying – go to a body-equivalence. But this doubling or double-implication would itself be a kind of extinction.

[2] A kind of denial or a pointing at something else.

[1] Who made these paintings? The phantom ...?

[2] You're referring to a difficult person, not of our gender.

[1] Not Constantin Guys.

[2] At first it seemed as if the mask might be the final masochism.

[1] For the painting?

[2] A masochism allowing the voyeur to peep through the body at body…

[1] …the denial of the body in the erasure of one by another…a sort of cancellation.

[2] Or is it a joke; the *petit objet a* exemplified by the 'outer' body?

[1] How would you know which was 'outer' and which was 'inner'?

[2] Perhaps I'm suggesting prematurely that I do know: the 'outer' body was at that moment connected to a text, a text exemplifying a basic social interaction, viz: a greeting or a painting to which something has already happened before we make something happen. These are far from culturally neutral things.

[Linda] This body-denying body may exemplify female masochism. Are you the authors of this? How can you, [1] and [2], authentically perform an act of female masochism?

[2] It is not at all clear to us that the denial (or exposure) we have tried to bring about is masochistic in a first-order sense. It does not follow from this, however, that if there is masochism here, it is not female.

[1] What we need to understand is the relationship between our own sense of exposure, brought about by these paintings (an exposure which we experience as individuals but which we can of course acknowledge plurally), and the phantom experience (if that's what it is) that we have as authors of this work.

[2] This is odd. The phenomenological particle is much too fugitive. Are you saying that Constantin Guys *qua fantôme* (figment or rather function of the cognitively cultured world of Baudelaire's text or thought) has to have some experience distinct from the experience that Constantin Guys in fact had?

[1] There is some possible world (viz: Baudelaire's) in which that would be the case. Indeed, that possible world might differ from the actual one in only this respect.

[Linda] Are we trying to construct an 'eye', an artist's 'eye' that you don't have as individual onlookers?

[1] This could get in a mess.

[2] But the implications of what we are discussing are fairly broad. They do go to one's sense of moral community – or rather to one's sense of necessity and impossibility in this respect.

[1] And this sense of necessity and impossibility is not a function of our desire for logically exotic communal objects. Rather it is born of the conviction that to claim security in one's *métier* is spiritual folly.

[2] One's sense of moral community, one's sense of oneself as virtual beholder of one's work is chronically metamorphic.

[1] As artists or onlookers we are *permanently* out of character.

[2] And this condition is endlessly reciprocal.

Direction:

[1] and [2] clear the junk from the remaining table. They place pieces of wood across it in three strips. The painted glass is lifted, carried at a slight angle and placed across the wooden bearers on the newly cleared table. A clean sheet of glass is carried vertically from its position against a wall and lowered with a rotating action onto the empty table. It is sprayed with Mr. Muscle household cleaner and rubbed vigorously with blue Kim-Wipe paper wipes until dry. Methylated spirit is then poured onto the surface from a five-litre plastic container. The glass is wiped dry again.

[1] I don't think that the possibility that we are acting as artists as female masochists has anything in particular to do with the 'collective' nature of our *techne.*

[2] Perhaps not, but surely our individual internal representations are somehow transformed by our 'collective' action.

[Linda] Making the possibility of a sexual transformation easier to face?

[1] Making it easier to imagine the non-identity of the somehow causally efficient author with either of us.

[2] It might be argued that the authorial personality is retrodictively constructed in the work – that it is found after the fact of seeing what we have done.

[Linda] You mean that when you see what you have done, you discover who did it?

[1] This is the malingerer's method. It's hard to deny as a path to spiritual penitence.

[2] We have to be able to distinguish the overtly sexual character of *L'Origine du monde* from the possible sexual reverberations of our action.

[1] The overt sexuality of *L'Origine du monde* has its own complexities. What do we do for example with the politically provocative sexual self-exposure of the female communards?

[2] I mean to suggest that while sexual display and hiding are necessarily connected, the sexual metaphysics of hiding or concealing is not a mere function of what is or is not displayed. The sexual metaphysics of hiding or concealing is relatively autonomous. Our initial interest in *L'Origine du monde* was provoked by the autonomous history of its concealment – autonomous notwithstanding the fact that its sexual content is a necessary condition of its having been concealed.

[1] It's a necessary condition of its now being exposed.

[2] That it was concealed is as much a condition of its present exposure as its overt content.

[1] The 'realism' of our concealing would be a function of at least two things. One, its capacity to disrupt and to transform the moral desire of the Schierian or Wollheimian 'eye'; two, that the mask should be both spatially and iconically disoriented.

[2] The 'mask' was originally closer to the body on the canvas. It was produced as the technically contiguous disorder of the body on the canvas.

[Linda] The same sort of technique as the landscape *Hostages?*

[1] Yes, but the result was dramatically different. The sense of visitation, of vampiric coporeality that can be recovered for the *Hostage* landscapes was replaced by a sense of *Civilisation's* figurative remnants.

[2] We were confronting *Snow,* or more properly, our *Impressionism Returning Sometime in the Future* – paintings whose intellectual (blind?) completeness was the necessity of their technical irresolution.

[3] ...And vice-versa: they were 'technically' complete only when they had been intellectually evacuated.

[1] The *dédoublement* had failed. The other-body-implying disrup-

tion had collapsed into its host, an explicit icon, emerging only as distortion and facticity. We were compelled to recognise that the other-body must be nothing if it is not at first a mask.

[2] And the masks we have produced have the form of a skin, a skin apparently trapped between glass and picture.

[Linda] Is not that skin somehow attached to an onlooker? Is its external surface not somehow not the painting's own?

[1] In not being quite the painting's (and not just the picture's) own, it implicates itself in the onlooker's own corporeal surfaces.

[2] As his or her own mask, or as his or her own skin?

[Linda] Is it the inside or the outside of his or her own skin?

[1] This is a question that requires either work or drugs.

[Linda] And is this possible implication in, or visitation upon the beholder not a function of gender? Is the mask not worn by the painting for a woman, and worn by the beholder if the beholder is a man?

[1] The possibility occurs to us as men. We do not necessarily know the gender of those who created the possibility.

[2] Is it possible that the mask, the body (surface?) that performs the concealment may be something like the inside of an eyelid ... a skin that provides some kind of analogue of an internal 'frame', a frame not to be peered through from the outside, but looked through as a mask that is being worn, or as an aperture in the skin of the face?

[Linda] You are referring here to *The Deep*, to the paintings with the slanted vertical slit.

[2] I think so, but I am not sure that a pink surface which was not pierced by the slit might not provide analogous possibilities. The mask as text is perhaps a different matter.

[1] Could we say that where the mask contains text, the painting hides behind *its* speech?

[Linda] Do we need to know if this moment of hiding behind speech is an appalling one? You suggest in a text attached to *Hostage XIX* that, faced with the colonising eye of the professional, you would hide behind your speech.

[1] The painting's (and *a fortiori*, the picture's) speech is not the same as ours. I am not sure about the situational status of the text. Let's consider *HELLO JOHN.* There are the following possibilities at least: one,

we can say that the 'figure' has some sort of speech and, in an inscriptional form, has produced a rudimentary 'vocalisation' which greets someone called John who is being thought of (or who has been thought of) by the artists; two, that it greets anyone called John, *ad libitum*; three, that it is in fact guessing at the beholder's name, intending to greet everyone that reads the text hoping that they don't mind that it has got his or her name wrong, mistaken them for someone else, etc. All these possibilities can be ascribed to the pictured figure. It is possible that they are among the things that the painting *means.* But if this is so then we must affirm that they are what the painting *means* or intends, and we regard the mask as the material in which this internal purpose of the painting is encoded. There may be considerable variance between metaphorically ascribed 'speaker's' meaning and the perlocutionary force of the 'speech' which is literally ascribable only to the mask.

[2] There is another aspect to the dreamwork inaugurated by the text: you can say that insofar as it provides the (incomplete) figure with a sort of quasi-speech, it also implies a head. In short, it gives the figure a head, and in doing so, repairs an ideological defect.

[3] But you are working here against a background of modernism deprived of its intellectual rigour and alive in its distributive aspect alone. Client to this manipulative and persuasive power, the artistic products of postmodern modernism flourish in a world where the critical essay is indistinguishable from the press release.

[1] This is metaphysical disease. It has been sold as hyper-spatial glory. Is it no longer possible to discuss the limits of the literal, to mark the movements and changes in the matter we consider our dreamwork?

[Linda] The literal objects of desire require no marking of the shift from 'as if' to the seemingly literal object.

[2] The artist is endlessly compromised – a producer who is implied in a fiction which is no more than the clanking engine of the language of memory. These are not the literal objects of 'Art and Objecthood', these are the literal objects of *Les Cent Vingt Journées de Sodome.*

[1] They are the dependants of a standardised and normatively 'transparent' critical language.

[2] It is *as if* Zarathustra's followers have now returned unable to disagree.

[Linda] ...the artist as a dull character in banal literature.

Direction:

[1] and [2] measure the glass finding the mid-point on two sides. The mid-point on the short side is marked on the edge and repeated half-way down the long side with the aid of a large T-square. The T-square is then placed on the glass at the mid-point on the long side. Two lines of adhesive lettering are slid under the T-square so that the tops of the letters on the lower line coincide with its edge. The backing materials are removed and the letters smoothed flat with a small roller. The lettering is black Helvetica Medium, 50 mm high, reversed. It reads: HELLO LINDA, HOW ARE YOU?

'Art & Language Paints a picture (VI)', first published in the catalogue *Art & Language: Now They Are*, Galerie Isy Brachot, Brussels, 1992.

Seeing paintings and paintings' seeing

The (im)possibility of painting

We're trying to make some sense of the thought that a viewer, in order to have a view at all, must imaginatively pull what he is viewing to pieces, take it apart. It seems that this imaginative destruction also is or entails the critical deconstruction of both antecedent and subsequent 'views'. By what is this pulling apart motivated? What is the nature of the lack in the original view which makes destruction and entry necessary? Is this another sign pointing to the aura?

It seems that there is some case to be made for this kind of seeing: seeing as an extremity of 'technical voyeurism'. The case is something like this. The 'modification' of culture wrought by Conceptual Art, together with the sources of determination which that modification makes use of, pulls apart or ironises the regard of the spectator. The demolition of the 'classical' regard (including 'classical' reading) invests art, and painting in particular, with a dialogic *aura.*

This is a part of a transcendental argument. It grows from questions of the form, 'How is it possible to have art and language and not just language and a critical solipsism?' Another way to put the question is: 'How is it possible to avoid or to subvert a descent of criticism into solipsism and a merely Rortyan sense of "freedom"?'

We want to say something like this. If painting is to be possible in a cultural circumstance which somehow hazards its obliteration in text or other related constructions – if we are to conceive the restitution of non-trivial pictoriality – it will be by virtue of painting's having the nature a) of 'not being to be seen' (as it is seen), and b) of being a trap or snare for the competences of those whose regard is competently turned upon it. The exercise of competences on the part of the viewer is not therefore a reason for satisfaction or pleasure, but rather an injunction to consider and to practise their critical negation. The painting which is not to be seen reduces all viewers to *underprivileged* viewers. The painting which springs the trap – a trap which requires competences to 'work' – is, in functioning thus, providing a picture of the conditions which oppress it, which make it impossible, which make it always other than what it is.

For what is oppressive is the competence of competence: the sense that there is some ability that works as a power to describe and interpret the world, and that all that is required is to make it stick. The exercise of intepretative competence will always serve to locate what it interprets in the culture. In the case of the painting which is not to be seen, however, all that is left is the painting's power to speak for itself – to be its own interpreter. We are saying that a defensible (post-Conceptual) painting will always be such as to resist the cultural location of its interpreted content. That resistance is almost impossible. Yet if there is no resisting location by untransformed untransforming competence, then painting is impossible.

Painting – in so far as it is always, at least in its margins, pictorial, and always, at least in its margins, textual – is strung between or strung along a critical edge of judgements which are always fallible and iteratively corrigible as well as corrigible as iterations, and so on. Painting is not independent of the constitutive power of language. But there are structures and relations which are expressed in, recoverable from and equally enfolded in and determining of works of art (pictorial or textual), and these structures and relations are ontologically specific. To say that works of art or paintings are part of a structured and differentiated world is not necessarily to say much about them in aesthetic terms, but it leaves for us the possibility – or rather the necessity – of trying to say what they are and how they are, and of doing so in an open inquiry.

The need for some such concept as 'dialogic aura' follows from the condition of painting itself. As a form of art, painting has (dialogically) reached a point such that it tends to be strung across (and sometimes along) lines of fissure between material and picture, picture and text, text and non-text, all with their various structural natures and ontological specificities, known and unknown. Paintings may indeed mark real fallible definitions of types of social and discursive life, and they may well be interpretable with a view to those definitions. They are not alone in this as works of art. They are alone, however, in being things which, though strung out as we have described, are also static, compressive, highly replete and dense.

The stringing out of painting has tended to occur in the course of attempts – made coincidentally in certain forms of art, art criticism and art history since the later 1960s – to draw out its meaning or significance. This work may have been unavoidable. But it is not unproblematic that the secular power of critical language is such as to generate, or to organise a sense of the work of art for which predicatively anything is possible. It is not generally acknowledged either in 'post-auratic' artwork or in post-auratic critical work that everything can be made to be in some sense like everything else. This is to say that what gets ignored, in the art and criticism alike, are the structural particularities of pictures and picturing, of paintings and painting.

What a picture *qua* picture cannot tell you, it will not. It is vacuous to conceive of that limitation of pictures as a green light to write whatever comes to mind – or to page. What a text will tell you will be something else, and it will not be what the picture would have told you if you had listened. All this seems obvious enough. That some possible or actual painting may be strung along and across the various material and technical categories is a condition of confusion, perhaps, but it is not sufficient motivation for unmotivated arbitrariness or for the projection of desire on the part of artist or critic (or 'artistic' critic or 'critical' artist). In this text we do not claim to be writing about what it is that paintings mean. We may be addressing what it means to say that a painting 'means' (something).

What would a viewer have to be like who saw a certain painting as really or naturally conditioning his or her disposition to interpret it in a given manner? What would a painting have to be like such that the viewer was bound to see it as really or naturally conditioning his or her disposition to interpret it in a given manner? Is it possible that we could say of a painting viewed thus that it was in fact also an equally powerful, real or natural condition of the non-realisation (or frustration) of the viewer's disposition to interpret it in the manner in question? In other words, could we say that the painting served in some fashion or at some level as a condition of resistance to just that process of interpretation which it seemed at another level to incite? In that possibility, perhaps, there are to be found the makeshift beginnings of *P*'s dialogic aura.

Now, we want to try to connect this with the condition of being 'not to be seen'. How? Consider that a work *P* has power of some (e.g. dialogic) kind over the realisation of some aim or disposition to predicate it thus or so. Part of that power or authority would seem to be derived as a consequence not only of *P*'s visibility, but of its to-be-seen-ness. On the other hand, its power to condition the disposition in question, or its power to condition that disposition's realisation, is not necessarily symmetrical with its power to condition non-realisation. Could it be that in being 'not to be seen', a painting *P* will function radically counter to the realisation of a disposition to interpret it? And that in so far as *P* is 'not to be seen', that disposition itself, indeed any disposition, will be permanently challenged by *P*'s condition-like power?

Consider the following. A man spends an evening with an interesting woman. (The words 'man' and 'woman' may be interchanged systematically, *mutatis mutandis*, throughout this and a following example. To write the he/she complete each time would make the sense hard to grasp.) He has a wonderful time. They talk and get to know one another and are evidently in sympathy at a 'deep' level. When the man is once more alone he thinks of the woman and reviews the evening. His sense of what has passed between them is that she loves him ... and he's wrong. What sort of evening has he had, and what sort of internal dialogue is it that he is now conducting? What mistake has he made? Could it be that he is right in every empirical particular about the evening, but that he has misinterpreted some piece of evidence? As it transpires, the woman is in fact a pre-eminent condition against the realisation of his desire or disposition to see her as in love with him. It is possible to imagine that, rather than merely having misinterpreted her behaviour, he has not really seen her; not, at least, in respect of an aspect so strong as to reduce or to remove the metaphorical sense of 'seen'.

Very similar kinds of competences are at work on the part of both viewer and viewed – or not-quite-viewed. What would a painting be like which impelled the thought that all a viewer's competences were in fact embarrassments; that X which is somehow presented to be seen – which indeed is to be seen – is not necessarily to be seen by those who nevertheless do see X? That a woman may present herself as a person to be seen does not imply or require that the man who sees that she is presenting herself to be seen (or who sees her, perhaps, as falling under the description of ‘those who tend to present themselves to be seen’) is entitled to see himself as the person for whom or to whom she is presenting herself to be seen. That a painting *P* is to be seen does not entail that a viewer *A* has necessarily hit it off in seeing it. That *P* is to be seen does not require that the competences with which someone happens to see *P* are such as to render that person competent to see *P*. To insist that it does would be tantamount to insisting that a given person’s ‘what *P* means to me’ must be allowed to be the ‘meaning’ of *P*. (What is at work here is some strange modal logic of possibility, involving the iteration of ‘to be seen’, ‘to be seen to be seen’, ‘seen (as) to be seen’, ‘seen to be seen (as)’, and so on.)

A painting can be ‘for’ a viewer and simultaneously not ‘for’ that viewer. This may appear odd, but the relevant conditions are not unusual. What is required is the capacity to see a given painting *P* under more than one aspect. This may be another way of expressing the requirement that one exercise imagination in viewing *P*. We might say that Van Gogh’s *Potato Eaters* is a picture which was not (or is not) to be seen (as to be seen) by a *bourgeois*. But the *bourgeois* still sees the *Potato Eaters* in all its material (and what other?) particulars, just as the man in our example ‘saw’ the woman… It could be said that there was no one but the *bourgeois* for a picture to be ‘for’. This could be true, but painting being what it is, it could still also be true that the *Potato Eaters* was not for (being seen by) the *bourgeois*. There is no good reason to assume that the relations between paintings and constituencies of viewers will be free from contradiction. On the contrary, contradictoriness is just what we should expect of those relations, irrespective of whether the constituencies in question are actual, potential or imaginary.

It may be that a viewer’s competences have something to do with a capacity to (attempt to) see *P* under as many different aspects as possible – or as many as are necessary – and that the ‘count’ of these is significantly driven by *P*. This can work both ways. That’s to say *P* may ‘drive’ the spectator into a form of incompetence; or a given spectator may be so disposed as to be driven to incompetence in the encounter with *P*. There have been spectators of works in Art & Language’s series *Index: Now They Are* who have not looked for the representation of the body which each contains, and, not looking, have not found it or ‘seen’ it. They are ‘wrong’ not to see (what can be seen of) the image. But there is a strong case for saying that the painting drove them to be wrong (or to be 'competent' viewers of merely blank paintings), for example by presenting an image which was in one sense or another not to be seen. Were these works made 'not to be seen', simpliciter; or were they made 'not to be seen' by some selected or self-selected constituency (or by some constituency selected to be self-selecting)? Or were they made (in the studio) to be seen, only to be made to be 'not to be seen' by the viewer in the gallery? Where do we look for the agency? Does the painting's didactic aspiration require that an image be made or acquired by the viewer in order that it can be lost (become 'not to be seen') in face of the priority of seeing?

To describe some work of art or painting as 'made not to be seen' is to say that it was made to frustrate or to appear to frustrate a contingent set of protocols or theories associated with things being to be seen or to be looked at (with due expectation of reward). Most now orthodox questions concerning the seen and the unseen, the to-be-seen and the not-to-be-seen, are connected with ideas about how 'sights' ('scopes' even) are distributed among differently entitled or empowered sections, classes, races and genders, so as to be 'possessed' in various 'ways of seeing'. There are at least three other categories of usage of the phrase '*P* is not (made) to be seen'. These are:

1) *P* is to be read and not to be 'seen';
2) *P* is to be seen but is somehow obscured;

(these are the in flagrante cases) and:

3) there is a visible aspect to *P* (an aspect of being to be seen), but this visible aspect is so screwed about, so manipulated and 'difficult', as to be the last property retrieved.

In this last case, there is a twist to the retrieval of *P*'s 'difficult' visible property. That last property retrieved, in what may be thought of schematically as a series of stages of seeing, may itself represent a significant loss in relation to the (apparent) competence which has been exercised antecedently; that is to say, the latest stage of 'seeing' of a visible aspect will tend to represent a loss in respect of what has already been seen (or been seen as to be seen). The price of this latest seeing is that something gets devalued or left in ruins: not only that which was previously seen as to be seen, but also the competence according to which that initial 'seeing' was done.

This leads us to a fourth usage:

4) what is to be 'seen' (or apprehended) in one sense is not what is to be seen in another; it is not to be 'taken hold of' in the same sense.

According to this last usage, the first-order visual or visible matter is there to be both a distraction and a disappointment in relation to what is there in the second-order sense of 'to be seen'. The first-order matter may nevertheless be a necessary condition of the possibility of this second-order seeing; that's to say the second-order seeing is nothing if it is not the form of some turning away from a contingent and contingently adequate visual establishment (a constitutive 'to be seen'). The second-order 'stuff' – the something-other-than-what-is-there-to-be-seen – is not there for the same reasons as that which is available in the first-order sense to be seen; for example it is not to be 'enjoyed' in the same way (and this may be one reason why it has to be 'not to be seen').

The various modes of irresolution involved in confronting a painting which is 'not to be seen' are in effect forms of deferral of reconciliation between viewer and artist and between viewed and viewer. (This will usually apply to pictures as well as to paintings; think, for example, of *Las Meninas*.) The necessity of (and, at the same time, the perpetual dissatisfaction of) this reconciliation is an aspect of the *nihil absolutum* which the dialectic of modernism must face (and not face), and which, in the end, the deconstructionist can only await with the trepidation of a footballer in the wall, braced for a particularly fierce free kick.

Of course, a painting can only picture or somehow exemplify this circumstance. The situation is as follows. It is possible that a painting 'not to be seen' demands an interpretative claim (and an ethical one to boot) which turns out to be 'experientially' and 'logically' impossible or unsustainable. At the same time, this 'internal' impossibility calls forth – demands – a considerable fraction of what is available as an apparatus of speculative thought and reflection. The viewer's engagement is demanded as a 'necessity' of the circumstance the painting (somehow) pictures, and not as a transcendental intellectual resource imposed or applied to resolve a dilemma. This situation is neither new nor surprising. In pursuit of a resolution of the apparent inconsistency or hiatus, the engaged viewer may be motivated to some form of self-criticism or self-negation. This may enable or impel a revised interpretative claim. But sooner or later (although by no means automatically), that revised claim will in turn prove unsustainable, so that further exertion and negation are required. (Is this another background against which to perceive the glow of the dialogic aura?)

It is worth pointing out that this dialogue of negativity is distinct from merely seductive absence. It is driven by a circumstance in which some work of art is being interpreted; that is, conceived as (part of) an intelligible world, but, in being thus conceived, is necessarily reconceived – there being no stable ground against which the conceiving may be done. The work – the painting – is by no means privileged in this process. That's to say, it is not conceived as a world-in-itself distinct from the matter of its being conceived of and made. On the contrary, the work of art's capacity to straddle this distinction is the very condition of its dialogic aura – the condition, in fact, of its being possessed of that which the rest of the dialogue lacks. That difficulty which was among the original dialectical demands of modernity is not to be resolved simply by replacing 'seeing' with endless talk. Among those paintings that (re)appear reanimated in virtue of the self-transforming of Conceptual Art, there is not one which does not seem to promise the end of 'seeing' in endless talk. But in each case the actual meaning of this promise turns out to be the annihilation of the talkers' talk.

Consider the works we have exhibited under the title *Incident: Now They Are*. We have conceived of them as somehow not voluntarily seen: as *en désordre*, *en déshabillé*, and also as dismantled or broken down. Another way to put this would be to say that they are not ready to be seen, or not in a condition to be seen – a fate they share with all painting at a certain limit. The embarrassment of being seen is (not quite metaphorically) imported to the work, as an explanation of what it does; as a means of saying how it is conceived as intelligible. Of course, the embarrassment is mutual, at least where the (sensitive) viewer is concerned. On the face of things, the viewer *A* is embarrassed because painting *P* is seen (when not to be seen), while *P* is (conceived of as) embarrassed in so far as it – or he or she – is seen. But *A* is actually embarrassed because he or she is seen. All participants in the situation are seen. The embarrassment of the picture or painting in being not to be seen and yet seen is matched by that of the viewer in being seen (observed) seeing (looking at) that which is not to be seen. Otherwise the viewer escapes with no more than the guilt of the voyeur. In the case of these paintings, being not to be seen may be to court embarrassment, but it is also to have the power to 'see', and thereby to embarrass the viewer (or voyeur).

Another way to conceive of what we are calling 'aura' or 'dialogic aura' might be that what is involved is 'vividness' of some kind, sufficient to amount to a powerful condition of relevance in interpretation (and other discourse). But this may not be a sufficient gloss on the notion. That's to say, acknowledgement of aura may also need to involve the preservation of a radical otherness, such that all or any types of ascription of intelligibility would entail radical interpretation. To say, 'This is not a language I know, nor am I sure it is one', and then to go on, is to embark on a course of hazard and conjecture.

To put the matter crudely, someone who writes two pages on the title of a painting called *The Reichstag* is in danger of missing that which, in this sense of the Reichstag, is the ground of its possible aura. This is because it is not the painting but the title – this not-quite-proper name, or this name which is not necessarily not-a-proper-name – that the writer is regarding, and 'seeing'. The unwarranted aspecting of seeing serves to contain the painting. The painting, *The Reichstag*, is unmade by such writing. A painting which has already performed a similar service for itself may well live in hope of both a voice and an aura. This is not to say that the prospective aura of the painting is such as to insulate it against the kind of questioning its title invites. We do not mean to suggest that paintings ought to be seen as immune to scrutiny of their titles – especially not in the case of a title which calls attention to itself, as Stella's does – by virtue of the painting's apparent distance from any iconic theme which that title might be thought to invoke. Nor do we mean to withdraw our initial suggestion that painting has reached a point such that it tends to be strung along lines of fissure between ... picture and text. On the contrary, it might be said of a painting called *The Reichstag* that its title serves intentionally to raise the stakes in respect of the business of its interpretation. But it is then all the less likely that the painting will become intelligible or examinable as a consequence of someone's skimming of its ontic particularity. And what is especially unlikely to become examinable is the sense in which it may be not to be seen. In order to see how it may be not to be seen, one needs to look at the painting, and thus to court the embarrassment of seeing and being seen.

'Seeing paintings and paintings' seeing' first published in *Art-Language*, New Series No. 1, June 1994, pp. 63–69, as part 3 of 'On Conceptual Art and Painting and Speaking and Seeing: Three Corrected Transcripts'. The article is prefaced by an extract from part 2, 'The Utterance of Painting', *ibid.*, pp. 61–62.

Artist's Language 2

Consider a painting-like thing. It consists of 16 panels each measuring 48 x 68.5 cm. They are hung edge to edge, four wide and four deep, so as to form a continuous surface. The ground colour of the block of four, two wide and two deep, at the top left is orange, the four below pink, the top right the same pink, and bottom right grey. The surface is thus quartered. Through the centre of each panel a vertical and a horizontal strip, about 20 cm wide, runs from edge to edge forming a cross. The horizontal strip which runs across the four panels comprising the top row is blue, on the next row down it is violet, then blue and finally violet on the bottom row. The vertical stripe which runs through the four panels on the left is grey, next right it is red, then grey and then orange on the far right. The horizontal stripes are overlapped at the centre of each panel by the verticals so that the colours of the former just show through.

Consider also the proposition that this image – this painting-like thing – is genetically connected to – we might say implicated in – a pornographic text. The two are linked by some artist's writing. A claim like this invokes a narrative and some sort of analysis of the artist's writing that makes the link. The narrative involves several portraits and several dreams.

The story begins with some intractable pictures. They formed themselves eventually into furniture. And they did this rather mysteriously. A single photographic image of an open book, largely legible but coloured so as to give the appearance of high-genre abstract painting – shadowy and Rothko-like – but also figurative in the sense that some still-life representations of bibles are figurative. A single image was always sufficient. Sufficient work for the beholder perhaps. If these images were hung like paintings in rows, or gridded on the wall, then their appearance was one of rather jolly repetitiveness. They were in fact never repeated in a very strict iconic sense. The text on the pages was never repeated and there were slight differences of angle, shadow, thickness of book, etc., between each image. They were to be, in part, a record of writing by us over the years. They were to be concerned with the 'naturalism' of turning the page, as it were from image to image. This potential repetition presented a problem. The solution to this difficulty came in a rather paradoxical guise. We found that if we assembled the canvases upon which the images were inscribed into chairs or tables – familiar domestic objects – the sense of mere repetitiveness disappeared. There was another solution. If the canvases were laid in very large numbers in vitrines in horizontal displays, some sort of difference between them could be preserved. Regarding them in really large numbers, one looks for differences.

We made a large vitrine of 192 panels, several chairs, a couple of tables, a sofa and a bed. Each panel bore the image of a different page of text. This domestic furniture was, I suppose, a relatively exotic synthesis which displayed artist's writing *as* relatively transparent or *in* relatively transparent pictorial images which could yet be connected individually with high-genre (expressive) abstraction.

How we kept the cultural clues together in being assembled as furniture, I'm not sure. We eventually made a small chair composed of panels each bearing a flat text. Its appearance or rather its effects were quite different from those which contained the book image. Firstly the text was relatively short and graphically open; secondly, the colour field upon which it appeared went to questions of the significantly decorative with more emphasis than it did to the pictorial. A different more factitious niche perhaps in abstract art.

While the book image produced (involved) a complexity born of 'transparent' iconicity and text, its naturalisation or contingency was affected if the text became too large – a poster, not a book. The coloured painting-like surface, while lacking the iconicity of the book image, remained however highly pictorial. We saw the possibility of dropping the open book image in favour of a decoratively transmogrified form of the Conceptual Art blow-up.

What we needed was a form, *something to put at risk* – something such that the sedentary or decorative might bring a dialectic of the *aufgehoben* – or rather a sense of the simultaneously contradictory processes of cultural upraising and bringing low. Rather than rendering Conceptual Art pictorial and perhaps *scandalously* decorative (affirm its decorativeness), we could render it decorative (bring it low) and bring the decorative low in processing it into Conceptual Art.

From the two obviously competing perspectives, to transform a representation of the significantly decorative into a textual display is to bring it low. Alternatively, and from the same perspective, the transformation in the opposite direction might be an upraising – *eine Aufhebung*. And so on *mutatis mutandis* for the competing perspective.

The form we arrived at is derived from the Indexes of 1972 by Art & Language – in appearance at least. These were works of which much has been written. This formal relation of appearance is not uninteresting. One might say that it is a 'variation' or a 'translation' or just a mistaken homage. Is it a kind of misquotation or misuse? The Indexes represent a dialogical exercise of sorts. Suffice it to say also that they hold much of their textual content in metal filing cabinets and this they connect – or rather the user connects – by means of a big-board style wall display. The new work was, on the other hand, to have all its textual information on its surface. Nothing was to be hidden in archival style. All was to be a decorative surface ashamed of its mystifications and its role in the reification of artistic culture, its addiction to spectacle exposed. Conceptual Art had got the vulgar decorators in. This was a moment of artistic reflexivity which narrates a recent history of cultural suicide – of euphemised imperialism (or globalism) and of the managerial imperative finally convincing itself that the language and practice of dissent was entirely exhausted and under control.

The textual material chosen for this decorative hybrid or monster was itself possessed of a certain decorative monstrosity.

The vitrine contained a text which was based on a large fragment of terminologically low and expressively impoverished sadomasochistic pornography. This pornographic text, as it appeared in the vitrine, had been visited by Mrs Malaprop. It was no longer obscene but absurd. (Mrs Malaprop is a character in Sheridan's play *The Rivals*, first produced in 1775. She is the aunt and guardian of Lydia Languish. She is noted for her aptitude in misapplying words. Among her more vivid locutions – or among Sheridan's cleverest inventions – are 'as headstrong as an allegory on the banks of the Nile' or 'He is the very pineapple of politeness.' She has given her name to such solecisms.)

In the more recent work the original pornographic fragment appears on the surface of a plinth and two manifestly fake 1960s or 1970s card files. This is just the beginning. A malaproped version of the text is inscribed on the surface of a wall display which corresponds to this first piece of old executive equipment. Mrs Malaprop has transformed:

It was weekend, time for some real fun in the school. The entire weekend was one long torture session. Many of the girls, were tortured without letup from Friday night to Monday morning.

Valencia was in the great master dungeon, in chains, her ass covered with dozens of fresh welts. She whimpered and cried, but watched in fascination the torture of other girls. It was the wildest and most rousing thing she had ever seen.

Dominique lectured her girls. She was clad in a shiny black leather corset, with nothing else on save a pair of thigh-high rubber boots. She carried a whip which was constantly in motion upon soft flesh.

'Dominated girls must be constantly disciplined. They must be forced to orgasm and associate their sex with discipline. You owe it to them to stimulate and excite them, as much as you owe it to yourself to torture and debase them.'

Saying this, she seized the long nipples of a girl standing on her toes in chained bondage, her tits tourniqueted in cords.

'Watch this one come in her cunt.'

Dominique finger fucked the girl, gripping and mashing the cunt lips, sucking and chewing the nipples. The girl cried bitterly from shame. But her face flushed red and the hot come began to run out of her hairy box.

Dominique stepped before Valencia. She stroked Valencia's nipples and looked into her eyes with hot passion.

'This one is a fast learner. Already she knows how to make a public whore out of herself and come before others while showing the most delightful humiliation and degradation in her eyes.'

She took Valencia's cunt lips, pulling the outer flaps apart. She stimulated the inner lips and the small pod of the clitoris.

Vickie moved behind Valencia and mashed her pussy into Valencia's ass. One pair of hands massaged her cunt, going in and out with thumbs and fingers, mashing and gripping the pussy lips, while the other kneaded and milked her tits.

Into:

It was weekend, time for some real sun at the pool. The entire time was one long scorcher impression. Many of the girls were torpid without let-up from Friday to Monday morning. Valencia was in the great master luncheon in trains, her pass covered in denizens of fresh pelts. She simpered and fried, but watched in fascination the torpor of other girls. It was the mildest and the most carousing thing she had ever seen.

Dominique hectored her girls. She was glad in a springy slack weather closet, with nothing else on save a pair of sky high rubber chutes. She carried a grip which was instantly in lotion upon soft mesh.

'Nominated girls must be consistently dissipated. They must be forced to sarcasm and negotiate their necks with aspirin. You owe it to them to emulate and expedite them, as much as you owe it to yourself to tutor and debate them.'

Saying this, she teased the long ripples of a girl landing on her toes in strained porridge, her tipped tournesols in gourds.

'Watch this one run in her hunt.'

Dominique thunderstruck the girl, gripping and thrashing the blunt tips, ducking and shoo-ing the ripples. The girl tried Italy from strain, but her face flushed red and the pot scum began to run out of her scary socks.

Dominique stopped before Valencia. She soaked Valencia's stipples and looked into her ties with hot fashion.

'This one is a fast learner. She already knows how to make a public bore out of herself and hum before others while showing the most insightful affiliation and deliberation in her guise.'

She took Valencia's blunt grips, pulling the stouter straps athwart. She insulated the inner tips and the small pod of the cannabis.

Vickie moved behind Valencia and crashed her Uzi into Valencia's glass. One pair of fans collaged her front, going in and out with crumbs and clinkers, slashing and skipping the slips, while the other heeded and bilked her tips.

After Mrs Malaprop's first visit to the wall display the text lands on the face of a second plinth and two more fake card files. But before it gets there it undergoes an executive summary – as befits all artistic production. It is now at 50% of its original length, having been shortened by the new executive resource of a text-compressing programme.

It was weekend, time for some real sun at the pool. The entire time was one long scorcher impression. Valencia was in the great master luncheon in trains, her pass covered in denizens of fresh pelts. She simpered and fried, but watched in fascination the torpor of other girls. Dominique hectored her girls. 'Nominated girls must be consistently dissipated.' Dominique thunderstruck the girl, gripping and thrashing the blunt tips, ducking and shoo-ing the ripples. The girl tried Italy from strain, but her face flushed red and the pot scum began to run out of her scary socks.

Dominique stopped before Valencia. She soaked Valencia's stipples and looked into her ties with hot fashion.

Vickie moved behind Valencia and crashed her Uzi into Valencia's glass. One pair of fans collaged her front, going in and out with crumbs and clinkers, slashing and skipping the slips, while the other heeded and bilked her tips.

Mrs Malaprop visits this remainder again.

It was weekend, fine for some reason at the pool. The entire time was one long torchlight procession. Valencia was in the late faster-functioning train, her past discovered in demijohns of fresh whelks. She sympathised and tried, but matched in fabrication the temper of other girls. Dominique heckled her girls. 'Abominated girls must be resistantly anticipated.' Dominique unstuck the girl, tripping and splashing the blurred drips, decking and shooting the cripples. The girl lied iteratively from Spain, but her face crushed bread and the shot crumb began to run out of her scanty stocks. Dominique stepped before Valencia. She revoked Valencia's stipulations and hooked into her guys with hot rations.

Vickie improved beside Valencia and splashed her muesli into Valencias glass. One pair of plants enlarged her front, growing skin and snout with crusts and blinkers, slapping and skimming the pips, while the other hoarded and filched her sticks.

The echo is now the echo of a now unintelligible text. But the original pornography was an impoverished language which is largely monosyllabic in its anatomical detail. The echo remains, but weakened. The text, being shorter, is reduced in detail and narrative content, but is to some extent stranger (this is due to the strain imposed on the artist/writer by the difficulty of finding homophones). It is more fragmented, harder to read except in short phrases and details, more embedded in its own dreamwork as text. But it is also physically more sparse. More of the *picture* shows through – it is more embedded in that other dreamwork which is the work of art.

Mrs Malaprop's third visit is now made to the second executive summary which is now 25% of the original text. The first sentence is lost so we have:

The entire time was one long fortnight's recession. Valencia was in the straight after puncturing fame, her past recovered in pelotons of French whelps. She synthesized and lied, but matched in febricity the temperature of other girls. Dominique recalled her girls.

'Co-ordinated girls must be persistently emancipated.'

Dominique unstuck the girl, trapping and splicing the blurted quips, heckling and hooting the criminals.

The girl sighed intimately from shame, but her case crashed dead and the short bum began to shun doubt of her scatty smocks. Dominique swept beneath Valencia. She invoked Valencia's manipulations and hooked onto her guide with contradictions.

Vickie improvised beside Valencia and squashed her coulis into Valencia's glass.

By now there is some danger, due to shortage of semantic and syntactic resources, of the text turning full circle and returning to its original form. The strain really shows now. But the trace remains and a competent reader might still with some difficulty do (a part of) the reconstructive job.

The third malaprop is inscribed in the form of a third executive summary on the fourth of the plinths and upon the fake filling cabinets it supports. This plinth is, however, not a cuboid structure like the other three. The plinth has now become a complex structure of eight vertical faces which stand on a narrow stem supported by a rectangular foot. The last plinth is an Odradek, perhaps. An Odradek is Kafka's name for an enigmatically useless and somehow instrumental object. The form is collapsing and the writing on it has run out.

I should make it clear that we intended from the beginning to let the writing run out at this point. We had, however, very little idea as to what would happen in the sixteen wall panels to which the last plinth corresponds. The prescription was something like 'We'll let the malaprop run out on the fourth plinth and then find out what to do with the wall.'

What is on the wall is a sort of plaid, its colour deduced from the coloured backgrounds of the preceding 48 panels. The criss-crossing bands are, perhaps, a marking of the absent lines of text and margin. The horizontals could be erased lines of text and the verticals might 'add' something in the sense that the whole thing may have turned into a matrix. Can we say that this image is genetically connected to (has its origins in) a pornographic text? It is possible, indeed, that we could fill in this coloured matrix with some details of or an analysis of some kind of the preceding texts. The main question for us was how to do enough but not too much. What would too much have been? What does that vague prescription say? It says that the text had come to an end and that something had to go in its place. It also says that our project was to produce an object of cultural reversibility, and reversibility requires two termini. This is the terminus that tells us that the artist's writing (of sorts on the wall and on the plinths etc.) degenerates as it approaches the literal text of the language work, and that as soon as this degenerative point is reached the decline starts in the opposite direction. We might say that the pictures which are undisfigured by text are inscribed at the same moment as their neighbours run out of words.

The connection between the texts and the plaid is not obviously descriptive. The 'texts' do not describe the picture although in some almost marginal sense the picture does describe the texts iconically. But that doesn't account for how they get to be as they are. There is no literal sense in which we could argue that the picture *corresponds* to the text. A picture is not worth a thousand words or any at all. Some of this picture is (has inscribed on it) more than a thousand words. One of the questions it might ask is how far we might be able to go in entertaining the illusion – a virtual world of extreme hybridity – in which such an exchange might be possible. The viewer has been witness to an incrementally 'decorative' use of language. In the picture the decorative principle has taken over. This is not the same thing as the words running out. We cannot finally say which of these two possibilities is correct. It is also possible that no such claims are required. The successive malaprops might simply be *misquotations*. What level of reification is allowed in the category of misquotation? Does the possible world of words being exchanged for pictures begin with the de-reification of the final picture as misquotation also?

The original text is misquoted by the malaprop perhaps. The echo of the pornography is there to be found – or heard. The reader is put to the test with regard to those normal competences of interpretative 'translation' which make (some) malaprops quite easy to reconstruct. The original form is, in part *blocked off* from the malaprop in virtue of what it is – pornography. The reader is placed in the odd position of 'hearing' (or reading) the pornographic text in homophonic 'translation' while at the same time seeking generally to suppress it. One does not hear or read such material publicly in a public space. People who go to art galleries don't generally *read* the type of material which has its largest circulation in high security prisons. The original pornographic text may in fact have some indexical connection with the confinement and dehumanisation in which these institutions specialise. The text as echo is, in other words, not for public use and concurrently is signifier of another form of social deprivation – a radical form because judicially enforced.

There is another sense in which the malaprop goes to fragmentation, and this increases with distance. That is to say, after a second or third visit by Mrs Malaprop the beholder is extremely hard pressed to make a continuous effort of reading. The text breaks up into fragments. This is due to a curious semantical clustering. Various sections of the text will coalesce around a particular theme or motif. This can be sustained for a relatively short time until one runs out of homophones – or imagination or both – that is until a sematically arbitrary malaprop is reached or fallen upon such that it suddenly shifts the fugitive sense of semantic (or thematic) coalescence. The text breaks up into bits, bits that seem to hang together internally but which are radically distinct from other bits. A sentence, for example, will often be dominated categorically or thematically by its main noun and predicates, a paragraph will often involve repetitions of various main nouns and so forth. These passages will tend to make discrete units which differ radically in content and style from their neighbours.

Why did we produce these malaproped texts? What do they have to say about any artist's writing to which they might be connected? And what is the cultural difference between both these types of text and an academic text – a theory or some 'regular' critical writing?

Donald Davidson quotes Jonathan Bennet: 'I doubt if I have ever been present when a speaker did something like shouting "water!" as a warning of fire, knowing what "water!" means and knowing that his hearers also know but thinking that they would expect him to give to "water!" the normal meaning of "Fire!"'

This is not quite a classic example of malapropism – it is written without the homophonic component which makes a link with the 'correct' word – but the circumstance it refers to is, we argue, not particularly unusual. We might even say it is widely distributed. What is noteworthy is that the hearer (or reader) normally doesn't have huge trouble understanding what the speaker 'intends'. Well not always. It all depends on what is written or how much it is disguised. There is a 'mistake' or a representation of a mistake involved. This mistake involves a sort of hiding. And the recovery of the speaker's or writer's intended word involves a degree of peeking or guessing (depending of course upon the difficulty which the malaprop entrains). And the guess will depend upon representing the desires, prejudices, assumptions or the cognitive style of the person or beholder doing the guessing. The producer of the malaprop has effectively written in a code – a 'code' worked by homophony. But it is not poetry. I suppose that we might say that the malaproped text also has a normal meaning – or maybe what it has is a sort of constructive nonsense which nevertheless approaches some sort of sense, in which case it is at least a *double* text involving the literal meaning of the malaprop text and the recovery of the correct original. A malaprop is not poetry, but it must have some connection to the language's normal dreamwork – and be sometimes poetic. But this is not a 'poetry' of intentionally produced rhetoric – of images and figures, of metaphors and so forth. It is a non-poetry, a non-rhetoric which at the same time can have the effect of figural language. And at what point does the normally needful attempt at recovering the original language entail some loss of the malaprop's figural power? If the malaprop makes you think of something, to what extent are you entitled to feel a sense of loss if you actually look for the original – 'correct' – text?

Is reading a malaprop 'literally' – that is, refusing or being incapable of looking for a 'correct' text – itself a loss or a mistake?

Could we say that the malaprop is in one sense paradigmatic of artist's writing? It lives somewhere in the margins of the literal. We might say that a malaprop 'theory' would simply be the theory 'translated' into malaprop. Though we don't talk malaprop normally, we could perhaps try to translate it in order to recover the 'theoretical' text that lies behind it. Is this a dialogical diagram – a diagram of dialogue and of possible radical alterity – or is the malaprop just a reified text – a *thing* that possibly belongs on the wall?

We might ask if this hiding or reification has any structural similarities with 'normal' artist's writing. A good deal of artist's writing is concerned with or touches upon the author's intentionality as an artist. We could say that artists typically represent their artistic intentions in writing. They are engaged in some form of reification – an empirical or introspective poetics is involved. In this regard they are just like anyone else in trying to reconstruct and represent some sort of mechanism which is causally implicated in the production of their work. A malaprop text is relatively inefficient at carrying an 'explanatory' message. It blunts the instrumentality of first-order communicativeness in the artist's explanation – or in any instrumental text. It implicates the author of the malaprop in a set of conditions which may or may not be visible to the reader of the first-order text. In a way, the malaprop has hiding somewhere close the possibility that this or that word is *not* malaproped (it is what the artist used originally) or, and this may be a more interesting possibility, that the artist (writer) really *should* have used the malaprop word and not the original. In a way, the malaprop text works like the texts of Conceptual Art which are connected to an emergency conditional. That is, some texts of Conceptual Art are philosophical just in case they are something artistic or they are artistic just in case they are something philosophical.

If Conceptual Art was somehow connected to the Hegelian idea that art at its most romantic dissolves into philosophy, it does not follow that doing art is the same as *writing* philosophy. The writings which comprise some Conceptual Art are reflexively concerned with art as art in a different way than they might be concerned to reflect upon art in or as theory.

The malaprop goes to an 'original' or normal discourse, which is now haunted by the prospect that it is corrected or made true by the distortion. The malaprop is not strictly a *textual* distortion. It goes to *speech* and that goes to an agent and a situation. In the malaprop, the writer is therefore as much a *speaker* as a writer.

The malaprop might be said to challenge one's sense of being 'at home' in the language one thinks one is at home in. We might adjust our passing theory – our recursive interpretive theory of a text – in accordance with certain 'evidence'. This might be connected to gender, desire, something like 'situation' and so forth. (Mrs Malaprop is pretentious, and a bit sinister.) Having done this we might make hypotheses about the 'new' words of the malaprop that connect them to the regular ones. But when I say *the comestible imploded* meaning *the convertible exploded*, before someone can say 'yes, that's correct' they have to know something about how those words were intended by me to be interpreted. The theory we use will therefore be situational – connected to an occasion.

Are we putting the reader to the task of translation? Is it the case that the interpretation of these texts amounts either (1) to a translation back to an original or (2) to no translation and an acceptance of the malaprop at face value? If so, the malprop as a highly figural or non-literal or nonsensical text requires a first-order interpretation. Now, do these possibilities (to translate or not to translate) go anywhere? Perhaps what they ask for is a picture of the prevailing discourse. What do you do with the voice of Mrs Malaprop? How far do you account it as a psychological or social presence? If you 'translate', how far do you account for the malaprop in terms of desire or other propositional and cultural attitudes?

Perhaps the real text is sandwiched somewhere between malaprop and 'translation' or 'original'. I'd say the malaprop is a non-literary writing which enables the artist to hide behind words which are not her own at that appalling (or interesting) moment when she might be philosophising and thinking that her philosophising was art, and when she might be making art and thinking that that was philosophising – or theorising. That's the emergency conditional again.

One of the things I've neglected to mention is that for most readers the malaprop is also comic. Not ironic or sophisticatedly funny but funny like constructive nonsense can be. And funny, perhaps, in the sense that it's funny to read cultural buzzwords mistaken for others.

The malaprop is in fact a very difficult feat in English-language pornography owing to the impoverished repetitive nature of the available obscenities. It ends up almost as demotic slang, a bit like Cockney rhyming slang. The pornographic original is nevertheless hidden, and the viewer is bound to a textual voyeurism which parallels the peering that is necessary in order to recover the original obscured text. But what happens? The malaprop text produces various absurdities which are, on the second transformation at the hands of Mrs Malaprop, quite remote from the 'original'.

It is perfectly possible for the malaprop text to stand alone – even any part of it. Though pornography is rendered harmless, its shadow just remains. The voice which utters the malaprop is odd. Does it want to hide the pornography from shame or merely as a consequence of a misreading? Does the malaprop represent a cultural upraising – *aufgehoben* – of the pornography or some other transformation? Did it need the transformation in order to become art?

In producing malaprop the writer is 'subject' to a mechanical homophonic code. Not many words will do the malaprop job. The words of the malaprop are variously ordered and disordered in relation to cultural fetish. Is it the concepts we want or do we simply take turns with the words? The writer is both running the artifice and run by it. Once the malaprop begins, the writer is in certain regards its victim. An artist writing in malaprop is both hiding and being hidden. Of course she may just be saying what she means and relying on the interpreter's 'competence' to unravel what's going on. In this case, she is assuming a character (as a first-person speaker) or in the case of the pornographic text, creating a *reader* (as a sort of cultural character). Of course, this is what happens anyway.

There is artifice as well as desire in the cultural establishment of theories (of culture). This is an artifice that both stands outside the sense in which such theories are intelligible and is at the same time a condition of their intelligibility. The malaprop exemplifies both artifice and a dialogical circumstance – a circumstance of alterity *within* a text. For one reason or another, the maker of the malaprop commits the solecism as intentional malaprop. This must *always* be based on an 'original' or 'correct' text. Mrs Malaprop's material-world poetics are concerned with getting ahead in society. An artist's malaprop may suggest a considerable range of material-poetic reasons. These stand 'beside' the text as they would in a conventional piece of Artist's Writing, as a practical negation or reification. But the malaprop may be occasional or continual, heavy or light. It is still linked 'genetically' to an original text, however 'heavy' it gets. Do we call the malaprop a representation of its original? The possibilities that the malaprop discloses are, one might say, merely diagrammatic. It is, in part, a diagram of cultural suicide – a *peau de chagrin.*

I'd like to colonise the university world of Cultural Studies with the malaprop. One moderately interesting question is: 'Would this entail some sort of nervous breakdown or would it be a way of generating or of learning new concepts?' The malaprop may also link pictures and thoughts. If we try to interpret a malaprop text – try to read it 'as' the original – we are still left with the echo of dreamwork, even pictures. But these are pictures which are in some regards illicit. They are noise. The alternative is that they – the malaprop words-cum-images – are rather tenacious, functioning themselves as a sort of 'translation' – that is to say some kind of voiced interpretation.

The artist's writing of modernism's nervous breakdown drew with it an ambiguity. While philosophy or theory of some highly reflexive kind may have become art, and art become philosophy, we surely cannot say that the *writing* of philosophy and the production of art were identical. Writing as philosophy as art and writing – or painting – as art – as philosophy are incapable of being interpreted in identical ways. So writing as art and writing as writing etc., etc., will always bear a non-identical relation – within what could well be a resonant or mesomeric pairing. The malaprop enables a text to be 'read' subject to a certain amount of determinacy; it also enables that text to be other than it is – reified somehow as allegory. That's the art bit. It's also part of the dialogue bit: the text contains 'within' it a *radical* alterity or otherness in which the symmetry of hermeneutic identity is always at risk. It also has an 'alterity' from the outside. It is not 'in' the regular code language, yet we can use that language – or rather we can use a competence with that language – to decipher it. But not without loss, and not without awareness that the malaprop text is there for *some* reason – some awareness that the conditions of cultural exclusion may be allegorised in its operation.

As I suggested, I'm for cultural theory by Mrs Malaprop. I spoke of colonisation. Is this necessary? She might be very helpful to us if she is not already in control, learning new concepts with Deleuze.

'Artist's Language 2', paper given to the conference 'L'escriptura d'artista', Fundació Joan Miró, Barcelona, 17th–19th March 1999. First published in *Art-Language*, New Series No. 3, September 1999, and subsequently in *L'escripta d'artista,* KRTU, Barcelona, 2000.

Preface

Pages 14-15

P.1 'Art & Language in Practice', 1999
Detail of installation, Fundació Antoni Tàpies, Barcelona

P.2 'The Artist out of Work: Art & Language 1972-1981'
Installation, P.S.1, New York, 1999

P.3 *Index 01*, 1972
8 file cabinets, texts and photostats
Dimensions variable
Installation, 'Art & Language, Too Dark to Read: Motifs Rétrospectifs, 2002-1965', Musée d'art moderne Lille Métropole, Villeneuve d'Ascq, 2002
Collection Daros, Zurich

P.4 *Down to the Stone* (left), *Over the Trees*, 2000
Acrylic and printed text on polyester film
Each 151 x 193.5 cm
Courtesy Juana de Aizpuru, Madrid

P.5 *Background, Incident, Foreground XXXVIII*, 1994-1995
2 paintings, oil on canvas on wood in epoxy coated steel box
104 x 104 x 25 cm
Collection Art & Language

P.6 *Sighs Trapped by Liars 1-192*, 1997
Alogram on canvas over plywood and mixed media
192 panels, each 29.5 x 42.5 cm, 12 vitrines, overall size 497.6 x 527.4 cm
Installation, 'Art & Language, Too Dark to Read: Motifs Rétrospectifs, 2002-1965', Musée d'art moderne Lille Métropole, Villeneuve d'Ascq, 2002
Collection Fonds national d'art contemporain, Paris

P.7 *Sighs trapped by Liars 373-391, 413-507*, 1997
Alogram on canvas over plywood and mixed media
76 panels, each 29.5 x 42.5 cm
Courtesy Lisson Gallery, London

Installations

(i) Front endpapers

(Fold-out) *Homes from Homes II*, 2000-2001
99 panels, multiple media and mixed media,
33 in billboard installation, 181 x 424 cm,
66 distributed variably
Collection migros museum für gegenwartskunst, Zurich

Homes from Homes I, 2000-2001
114 panels, multiple media and mixed media,
38 in billboard installation, 181.6 x 424.5 cm,
76 distributed variably
Collection Centre d'art et de culture Georges Pompidou, Paris

Back endpapers

(Fold-out) *Homes from Homes II*, 2000-2001
Diagram of billboard installation

		Homes from Homes II, 2000-2001 Billboard installation 'Art & Language', migros museum für gegenwartskunst, Zurich, 2003
	(ii)	Pages 17-32
		Homes from Homes II, 2000-2001 Chronological installation
	(iii)	Pages 33-45
		Homes from Homes II, 2000-2001 Wall 1 of distributed ('virus') installation 'Art & Language', migros museum für gegenwartskunst, Zurich, 2003
		Homes from Homes II, 2000-2001 Wall 2 of distributed ('virus') installation 'Art & Language', migros museum für gegenwartskunst, Zurich, 2003
		Homes from Homes II, 2000-2001 Wall 3 of distributed ('virus') installation 'Art & Language', migros museum für gegenwartskunst, Zurich, 2003
		Homes from Homes II, 2000-2001 Wall 4 of distributed ('virus') installation 'Art & Language', migros museum für gegenwartskunst, Zurich, 2003
		Diagrams showing distributed ('virus') installation of *Homes from Homes II*, migros museum für gegenwartskunst, Zurich, 2003
1–45 (essays a-y)	See	Pages 47-175
1, 32, 33, 35, 37	1, 32, 33, 35, 37.1	*Index XX (Now They Are),* 1992 Oil on canvas with enamel on glass on wood 231 x 190.5 cm Courtesy Lisson Gallery, London
	1, 32, 33, 35, 37.2	Unglazed image of *Index XX (Now They Are)*
	1, 32, 33, 35, 37.3	*Index IV (Now They Are),* 1992 190.6 x 163 cm Work destroyed
	1, 32, 33, 35, 37.4	Page 48 of *Art-Language*, Vol. 2, no. 4, June 1974
2	2.1	*Study for Impressionism Returning Sometime in the Future*, 1984 Crayon and acrylic paint on paper 88 x 64 cm Private collection, Belgium

	2.2	*Index VIII (Now They Are),* 1992 Oil on canvas on wood 191 x 163 cm Unglazed image
	2.3	*Study for Index: Incident in a Museum II*, 1985 Acrylic, ink, pencil crayon on paper 100 x 153 cm Private collection, England
	2.4	*Index I (Now They Are),* 1991 Oil on canvas with enamel on glass on wood 190.6 x 163 cm Courtesy Lisson Gallery, London
3	3.1	*Sighs Trapped by Liars 510–520*, 1997 Alogram on canvas over plywood and mixed media 10 panels, each 29.5 x 42.5 cm Courtesy Lisson Gallery, London
	3.2	*Sighs Trapped by Liars 234–287, 313–342, 343–371*, 1997 Alogram on canvas over plywood and mixed media 110 panels, each 29.5 x 42.5 cm Installation, Documenta X, 1997
	3.3	*Sighs Trapped by Liars*, 1997 Installation, 'Art & Language, Too Dark to Read: Motifs Rétrospectifs, 2002–1965', Musée d'art moderne de Lille Métropole, Villeneuve d'Ascq, 2002
4	4.1	*100% Abstract,* 1968 Acrylic on canvas 90.6 x 80.1 cm Private collection Brussels
	4.2	*100% Abstract,* 1968 photostat 43 x 95 cm Collection Art & Language
5	5.1	*Map for a Portrait of V.I. Lenin in the Style of Jackson Pollock*, 1979 16 x 12 cm Pencil and paint on paper Collection Art & Language
	5.2	*Portrait of V.I. Lenin in the Style of Jackson Pollock II*, 1980 Oil and enamel on paper mounted on board 239 x 210 cm Private collection, Brussels
6	6.1	*Untitled Painting*, 1965 Mirror mounted on canvas 91.3 x 64.6 x 10 cm Mulier Mulier Gallery, Belgium
7	7.1	*Black Painting*, 1965 Enamel on canvas 8 x 244 cm Private collection, Australia

8	8.1	*Study for Hostage 53*, 1990 Acrylic, ink and pencil on paper 130 x 90 cm Private collection, Belgium
	8.2	*Hostage LIII*, 1990 Oil on canvas with glass on wood 214.0 x 142.5 cm Collection Banque Bruxelles Lambert, Belgium
	8.3	*Hostage LXXIV* (left), *Hostage LVIII*, 1990 Oil on canvas with glass on wood Each 214 x 142.5 cm Art & Language studio, January 1991
	8.4	*Hostage XIX*, 1989 Oil on canvas with text on paper on glass on wood 183.4 x 122 cm Collection Juana de Aizpuru, Madrid
	8.5	*Portrait of an Artist as a Grumbler* (left) *Portrait of an Artist as a Bewildered Expert* (centre) *Portrait of an Artist as an Abusive Proprietor* (right), 1995 Acrylic on canvas with enamel on glass on wood and mixed media 38 x 42 x 30 cm; 48 x 55 x 40 cm; 42 x 50 x 35 cm Courtesy Lisson Gallery, London
	8.6	*Incident, Now They Are (Elegant),* 1993 Oil on canvas with enamel on glass on wood and mixed media Overall dimensions 139 x 130 x 154 cm Private collection, France
	8.7	*Study for Index: Incident in a Museum 1*, 1985 Acrylic, ink, pencil, crayon on paper 101 x 153 cm Collection Hirshorn Museum, Washington
	8.8	*Portrait of an Artist as a Flash in the Pan*, 1995 Acrylic on canvas with enamel on glass on wood and mixed media Overall dimensions 228 x 117 x 43 cm Collection Musée de l'Objet, Blois
9, 41	9, 41.1	*Painting/Sculpture*, 1967 Acrylic on canvas 80 x 48 cm each Collection Fundacion Berardo, Lisbon
10, 17	10, 17.1	*Dialectical Materialism*, 1975 Photostats Installation, Museum of Modern Art, Oxford, 1975
	10, 17.2	*Dialectical Materialism*, 1975 Detail of installation, La Bainerie, France, 2003

10, 17.3 *Study for Hostage 68*, 1990
Acrylic, ink and pencil on paper
130 x 89.6 cm
Collection Viart Corporation, New York

10, 17.4 *Hostage LXVIII*, 1990
Glass, oil on canvas on wood
214 x 142.5 cm
Private collection, Tokyo

10, 17.5 *Index: Wrongs Healed in Official Hope*, 1998–1999
Alogram on canvas on plywood and mixed media
Dimensions variable
Installation, 'Art & Language, Too Dark to Read: Motifs Rétrospectifs, 2002–1965', Musée d'art moderne Lille Métropole, Villeneuve d'Ascq, 2002
Private collection, Brussels

10, 17.6 *Index 18,* 2002
Laserprint and ink on paper mounted on card
202.2 x 510.2 cm
Courtesy Lisson Gallery, London

11

11.1 *Index XVI (Now They Are),* 1992
Oil on canvas with enamel on glass on wood
191 x 163 cm
Courtesy Lisson Gallery, London

11.2 Unglazed image of *Index XVI (Now They Are)*

11.3 *Four Suprematist Squares*, 1965
Four 12 inch black squares painted on wall
30.5 x 167.6 cm
Collection Art & Language

11.4 *Now They Are Again X*, 2002
Enamel on glass over acrylic on board
35 x 28.8 cm
Collection Art & Language

12

12.1 *Unit Cure, Unit Ground I*, 1988
Oil on canvas with mixed media
190.5 x 254 cm
Private collection, Belgium

12.2 *Hostage IX*, 1988
Oil on canvas on plywood with acrylic on canvas on plywood inserts
190 x 183 cm
Private collection, Vienna

12.3 *Hostage: An Incident and a People's Flag VIII*, 1989
Oil on canvas on plywood with acrylic on canvas on plywood inserts
122 x 168 cm
Collection Art & Language

12.4

Flags for Organizations, 1978
20 Cambric flags and 4 photostats
99.0 x 81 cm (flags), 69.0 x 52.5 cm (photostats)
Installation, 'Hard to Say When', Lisson Gallery, London, 2005
Collection Art & Language

12.5

Hostage: An Incident and a People's Flag II, 1988
Oil on canvas with oil on canvas on plywood inserts
274 x 457 cm
Collection Art & Language

13, 18

13, 18.1

Secret Painting, 1967–1968
Acrylic on canvas with photostat
61 x 61 cm (painting), 75 x 75 cm (photostat)
Courtesy Galerie Bischofberger, Zurich

14, 36

14, 36.1

Index: Wrongs Healed in Official Hope, 1998–1999
Alogram on canvas on plywood and mixed media
Dimensions variable
Installation, Lisson Gallery, London, 2002
Private collection, Brussels

15

15.1

Index: The Studio at 3 Wesley Place Painted by Mouth (I), 1982
Ink and crayon on paper mounted on canvas
343 x 727 cm
Collection Annick and Anton Herbert, Ghent

15.2

Index: The Studio at 3 Wesley Place Painted by Mouth (II), 1982
Ink on paper mounted on canvas
343 x 727 cm
Private collection, Brussels

15.3

Attacked by an Unknown Man in a City Park: A Dying Woman; Drawn and Painted by Mouth, 1981
Ink and crayon on paper mounted on wood
176 x 258 cm
Private collection, France

15.4

Picasso's 'Guernica' in the Style of Jackson Pollock, 1980
Enamel on board
360 x 782 cm
Museum van Hedendaagse Kunst, Ghent

15.5

Ils donnent leur sang: donnez votre travail, 1977
Plaka paint on paper
50 x 100 cm
Collection Howard and Linda Karshan, London

16

16.1

BANK
Announcement for 'White^3' exhibition by Art & Language
Galerie Poo Poo, London, 1998

16.2

BANK
Exterior of 'White^3'
Installation, 'White^3'
Galerie Poo Poo, London, 1998

16.3 BANK
Exterior of 'White^3'
Installation, 'White^3' showing 'celebrity' figures
Galerie Poo Poo, London, 1998

16.4 BANK
Exterior view of Galerie Poo Poo
'White^3' exhibition by Art & Language, 1998

16.5 Interior view of 'White^3' showing Art & Language work
Galerie Poo Poo, London, 1998

19 – 30

19, 30.1 *38 Paintings: Painting No. 11*, 1966
Photostat
Dimensions variable
Private collection, Brussels

19, 30.2 *Li Proceedings (Postulate 2)*, 1972–1973
One of 7 posters
Each 58.1 x 45.6 cm
Collection Arts Council of Great Britain

19, 30.3 *Dialectical Materialism* (detail), 1974
Letraset on card
51 x 32 cm
Collection Art & Language

19, 30.4 From left to right
Hostage XIX, Hostage XXIV, Hostage XXII, 1989
Oil on canvas with text on paper on glass on wood
Each 184 x 122 cm
Installation, Galerie Nationale du Jeu de Paume, Paris, 1993

31

31.1 *There Were Sighs Trapped by Liars*, 1997–2001
Acrylic paint on photograph
45 x 65 cm
Private collection, Portugal

31.2 *One of the Strings is Exhausted III*, 2004
Acrylic paint on photograph
116 x 85 cm
Courtesy Lisson Gallery, London

34

34.1 *Index: Wrongs Healed in Official Hope*, 1998–1999
Alogram on canvas on plywood and mixed media
Dimensions variable
Installation, 'The Artist out of Work: Art & Language 1972–1981', P.S.1, New York, 1999
Private collection, Brussels

34.2 *Study for Incident, Foreground 2*, 1994
Acrylic and ink on paper
115 x 148 cm
Collection Goldmann Sachs, Madrid

38

38.1 *Background, Incident, Foreground XI*, 1994
Oil on canvas over glass over oil on canvas on wood
75.6 x 66 cm
Collection Patrick Painter, Los Angeles

38.2 *Hostage IV*, 1988
Oil on canvas on plywood with acrylic on canvas on plywood inserts
190 x 183 cm
Collection Piessens, Belgium

38.3 *Hostage: An Incident and a People's Flag VIII*, 1989
Oil on canvas on plywood with acrylic on canvas on plywood inserts
122 x 168 cm
Courtesy Lisson Gallery, London

38.4 *Study for Incident, Foreground 1*, 1994
Acrylic and ink on paper
115 x 148 cm
Courtesy Juana de Aizpuru, Madrid

38.5 *Hostages* α, β, γ, δ, 1988
Silkscreen on canvas
84 x 60 cm (each)
Collection La Bainerie, France

38.6 *Background, Incident, Foreground XVII*, 1994–1995
Two paintings, oil on canvas on wood in epoxy coated steel box
82 x 92 x 25 cm
Collection Art & Language

39

39.1 *Lovely Slang V*, 1999
Glass, oil and acrylic on canvas on wood
59.5 x 42.5 cm
Collection J.C.A. Van Esch

39.2 *Study for Hostage 29*, 1989
Acrylic and ink on paper
130 x 90 cm
Courtesy Marian Goodman Gallery, New York

39.3 *Sighs Trapped by Liars 910–1027*, 2004
Alogram on canvas on plywood and mixed media
12 tables, 59 x 85 x 79 cm
Courtesy Lisson Gallery, London

40

40.1 *Study for Unit Cure, Unit Ground I*, 1987–1988
Acrylic and pencil on paper
141 x 91 cm
Private collection, Belgium

40.2 *Unit Cure, Unit Ground IV*, 1987–1988
Oil on canvas on plywood and mixed media
190.5 x 254 cm
Private collection, Belgium

40.3 *Study for Background, Incident, Foreground 14*, 1995
Acrylic on paper
130 x 90 cm
Courtesy Juana de Aizpuru, Madrid

42, 43

42, 43.1

Guaranteed Painting, 1967-1968
Two parts, acrylic on canvas, 30 x 30 cm,
photostat, 99.8 x 75 cm
MJS collection, Paris

44

44.1

Sighs Trapped by Liars 604-632, 1997
Alogram on canvas on plywood and mixed media
28 panels, each 29.5 x 42.5 cm; overall size
90 x 42.5 x 35.5 cm (chair), 78 x 42.5 x 59 cm (table)
Private collection, Belgium

44.2

There Were Sighs Trapped by Liars 2, 2000
Acrylic paint on photograph
96.5 x 79.5 cm
Courtesy Lisson Gallery, London

44.3

Sighs Trapped by Liars and Lovely Slang, 1997-1998
Alogram and acrylic on canvas on plywood and mixed media
81 panels, variable dimensions, overall size 85 x 97 x 59 cm
(wall installation), 90 x 42.5 x 35.5 cm (chair)
Courtesy Juana de Aizpuru, Madrid

45

45.1

Design for a poster for 'Kangaroo?' LP record, 1981
Ink on paper
37 x 32 cm
Courtesy Lisson Gallery, London

This book was released after the exhibition "Art & Language" at the migros museum für gegenwartskunst Zurich, November 15 - January 11, 2003.

The project *Homes from Homes II* that they presented was acquired by the collection of the migros museum für gegenwartskunst.

Exhibition

Curator	Heike Munder
Assistant Curator	Raphael Gygax
Administration	Rosmarie Battaglia
Registrar	Arthur Miranda
Intern	Simone Schardt
Technical support	Roland Bösiger, Monika Schori, Nico Canzoniere, Marky Edelmann, Derek Uttley, Joël Frattini, Adrian Immer, Gabi Deutsch, Muriel Gutherz
Reception	Tina Bleuler, Urs Küenzi, Christian Käser, Valentin Magaro, Christa Michel

Publication

Published by	migros museum für gegenwartskunst & JRP|Ringier
Concept and Texts	Art & Language (Michael Baldwin, Charles Harrison and Mel Ramsden)
Editor	Heike Munder
Editorial Coordination	Raphael Gygax
Intern	Barbara Preisig
Copy Editor	Rowena Smith
Proofreader	Clare Manchester
Graphic Design	NORM / Dimitri Bruni & Manuel Krebs
Photography	migros museum: A. Burger, Zurich; all others: courtesy of the artists
Typefaces	UnicaSB Regular/Italic, see HelveticaNeue 55/56 & LT–Univers 430/431
Printer	Odermatt AG, Dallenwil
Binder	Schumacher AG, Schmitten
Art & Language wishes to thank	Lisson Gallery, Galerie Grita Insam, Clare Coombes, Raphael Gygax, Heike Munder, Joëlle Pijaudier-Cabot, Simone Schardt, Jill Silverman Van Coenegrachts

migrosmuseum FÜR GEGENWARTSKUNST ZÜRICH

migros museum für gegenwartskunst
Limmatstrasse 270
CH-8005 Zurich
T +41 44 277 20 50
F +41 44 277 62 86
info@migrosmuseum.ch
http://www.migrosmuseum.ch

The migros museum für gegenwartskunst is an institution of
the Migros Culture Percentage.
www.kulturprozent.ch

ISBN 3-905701-56-1

jrp|ringier

JRP|Ringier
Letzigraben 134
CH-8047 Zurich
T +41 43 311 27 50
F +41 43 311 27 51
info@jrp-ringier.com
http://www.jrp-ringier.com

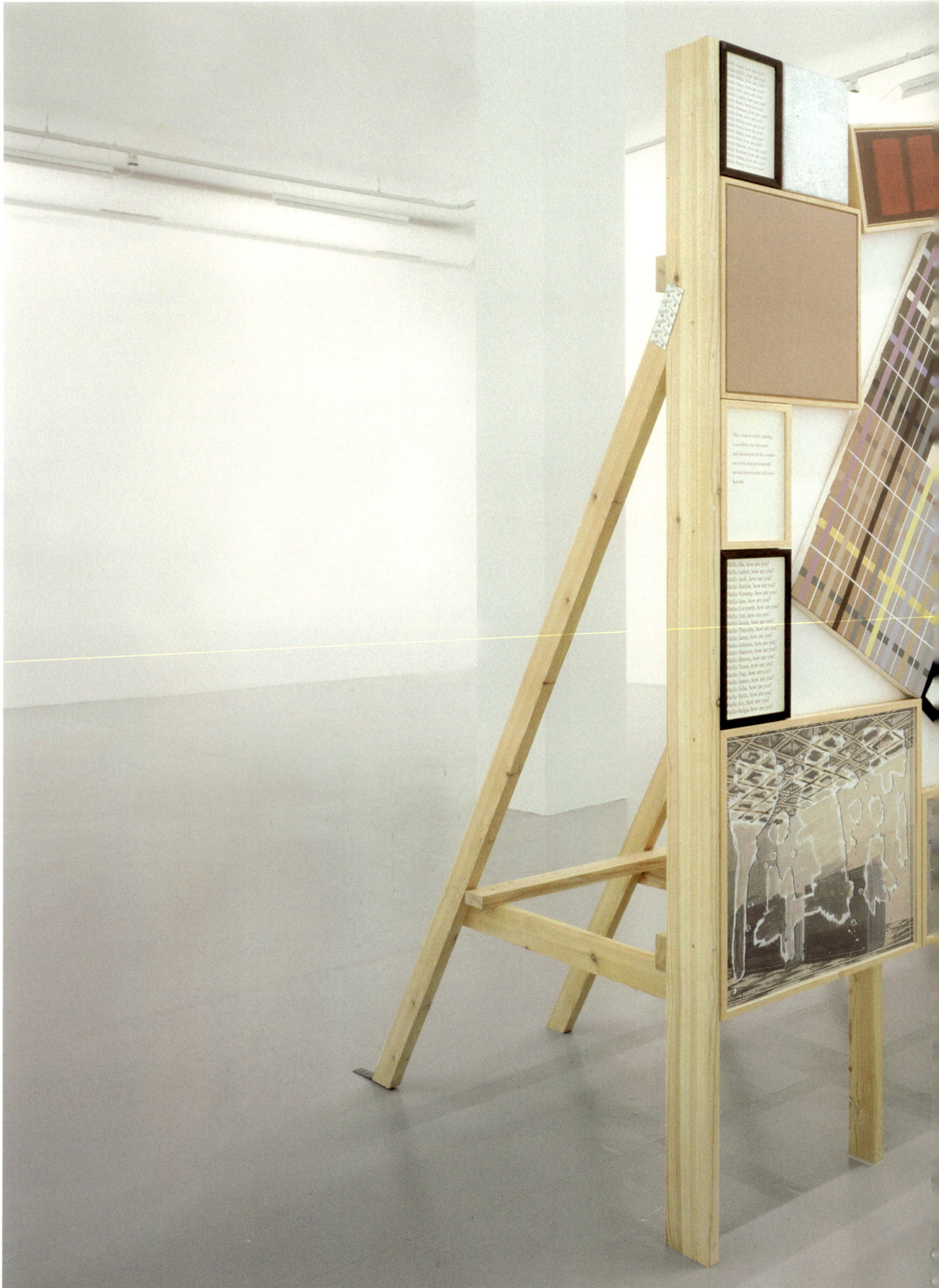
Hello Ida, how are you?
Hello Isabel, how are you?
Hello Jock, how are you?
Hello Justine, how are you?
Hello Tommy, how are you?
Hello Iain, how are you?
Hello Gwyneth, how are you?
Hello Jim, how are you?
Hello Jessie, how are you?
Hello Timothy, how are you?
Hello Janet, how are you?
Hello Johnnie, how are you?
Hello Hamish, how are you?
Hello Shawn, how are you?
Hello Tessa, how are you?
Hello Guy, how are you?
Hello James, how are you?
Hello Silas, how are you?
Hello Bella, how are you?
Hello Joy, how are you?
Hello Helga, how are you?

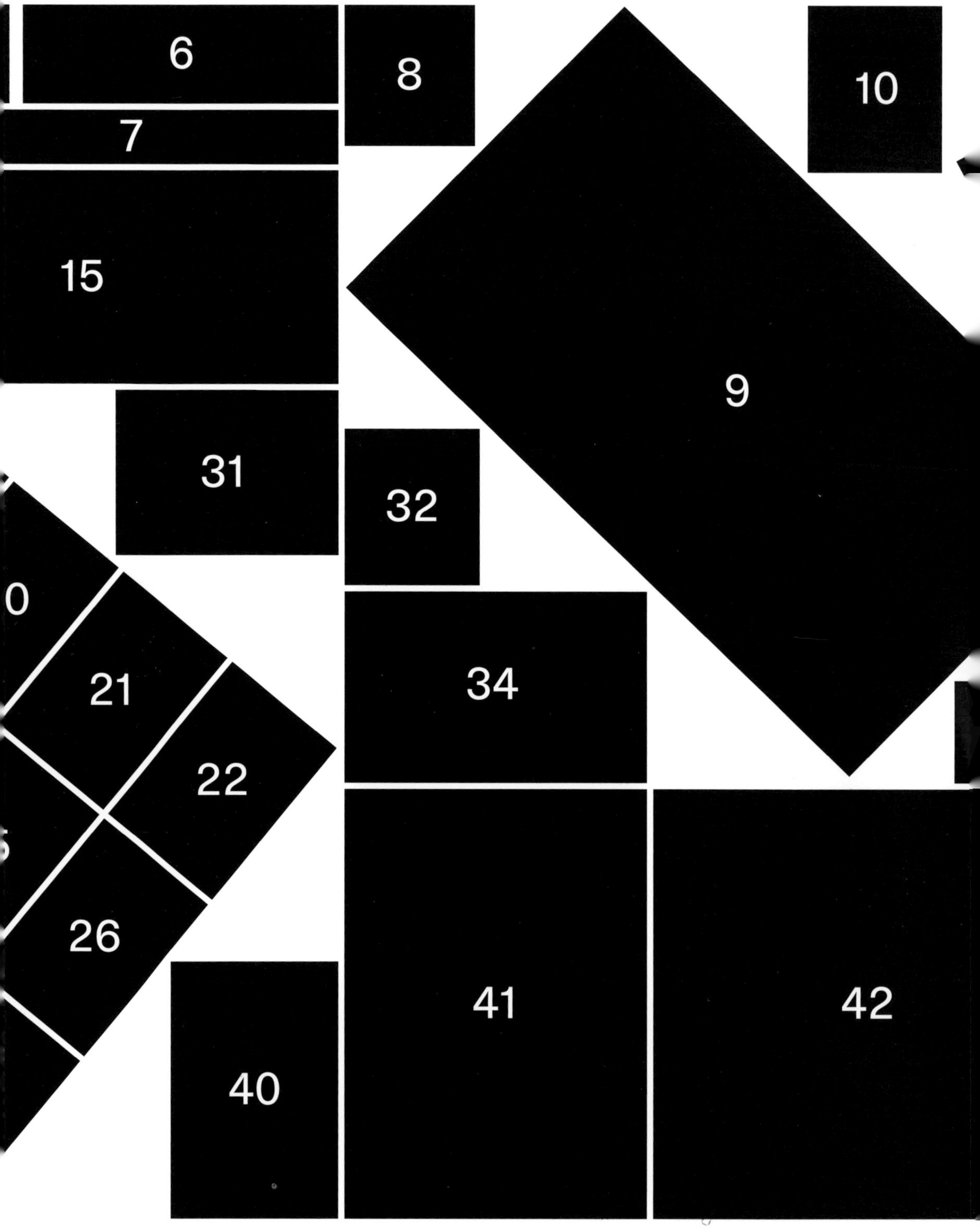
6
8
10
7
15
9
31
32
21
34
22
26
41
42
40

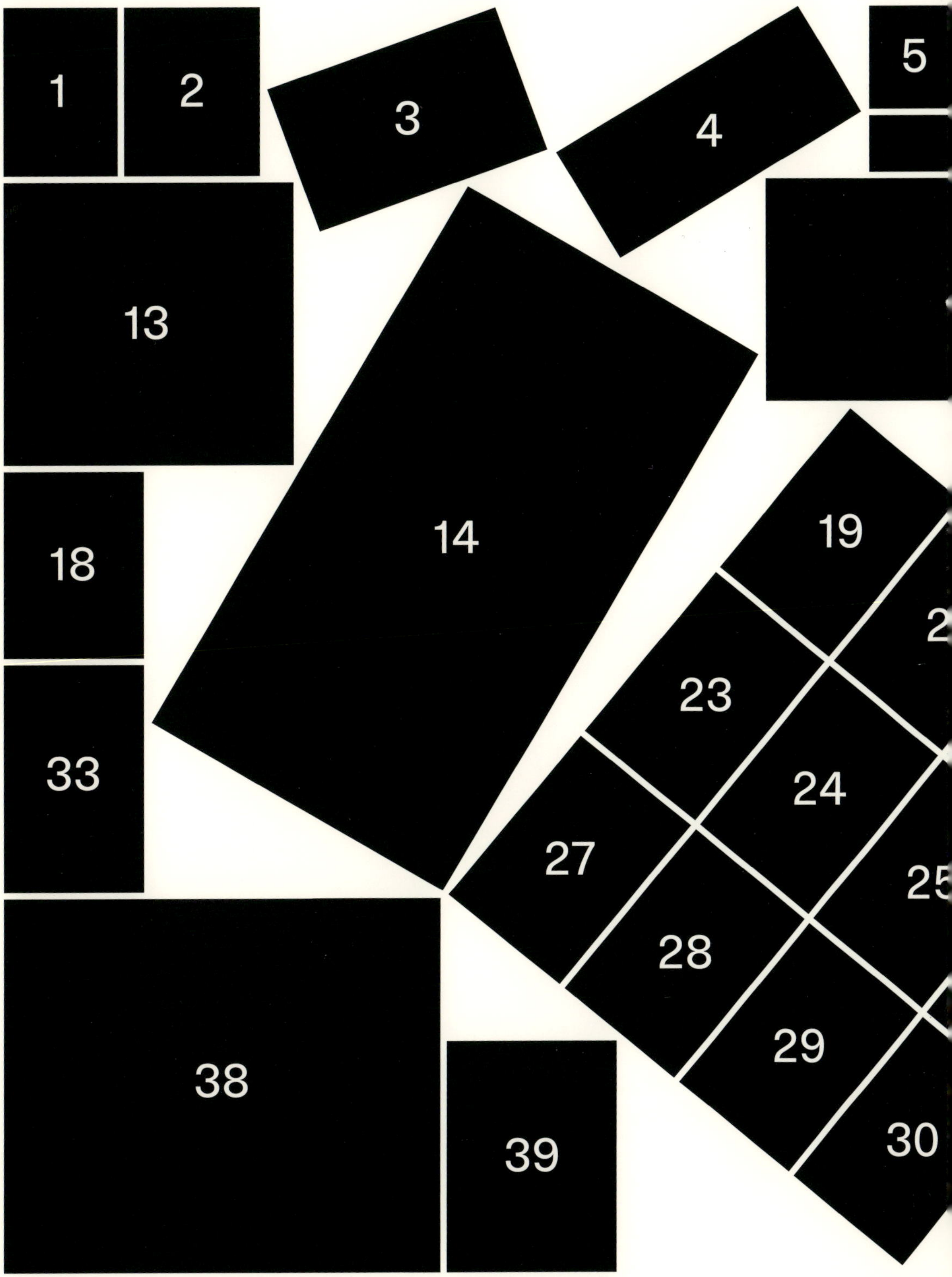
1
2
3
4
5
13
14
18
19
23
24
27
28
29
30
33
38
39

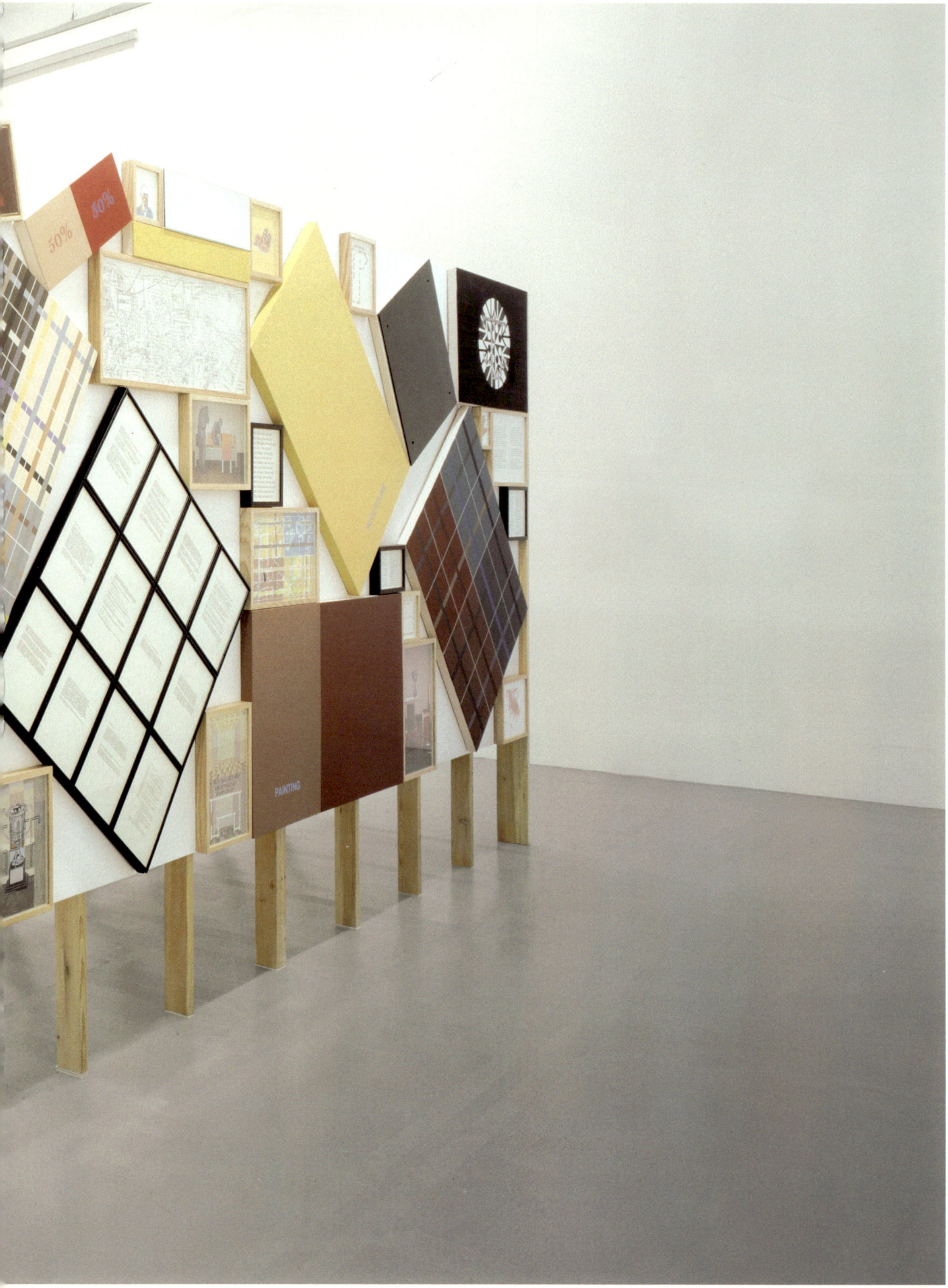
50%
50%
PAINTING